Lecture Notes in Computer Sci

Edited by G. Goos, J. Hartmanis and J. van]

Springer

Berlin
Heidelberg
New York
Barcelona
Hong Kong
London
Milan
Paris
Singapore
Tokyo

Kevin Hammond   Tony Davie
Chris Clack (Eds.)

Implementation of Functional Languages

10th International Workshop, IFL'98
London, UK, September 9-11, 1998
Selected Papers

Springer

Series Editors

Gerhard Goos, Karlsruhe University, Germany
Juris Hartmanis, Cornell University, NY, USA
Jan van Leeuwen, Utrecht University, The Netherlands

Volume Editors

Kevin Hammond
Tony Davie
University of St Andrews, Division of Computer Science
North Haugh, St Andrews KY16 9SS, UK
E-mail: {kh,ad}@dcs.st-and.ac.uk

Chris Clack
University College London, Department of Computer Science
Gower Street, London WC1E 6BT, UK
E-mail: clack@cs.ucl.ac.uk

Cataloging-in-Publication data applied for

Die Deutsche Bibliothek - CIP-Einheitsaufnahme

Implementation of functional languages : 10th international
workshop ; selected papers / IFL '98, London, UK, September 9 - 11,
1998. Kevin Hammond ... (ed.). - Berlin ; Heidelberg ; New York ;
Barcelona ; Hong Kong ; London ; Milan ; Paris ; Singapore ; Tokyo
: Springer, 1999
    (Lecture notes in computer science ; Vol. 1595)
    ISBN 3-540-66229-4

CR Subject Classification (1998): D.3, D.1.1, F.3

ISSN 0302-9743
ISBN 3-540-66229-4 Springer-Verlag Berlin Heidelberg New York

© Springer-Verlag Berlin Heidelberg 1999
Printed in Germany

Typesetting: Camera-ready by author
SPIN: 10704703   06/3142 – 5 4 3 2 1 0   Printed on acid-free paper

Preface and Overview of Papers

This volume contains a refereed selection of papers presented at the 1998 International Workshop on the Implementation of Functional Languages (IFL'98), held at University College, London, September 9–11, 1998. This was the tenth in a series of international workshops that have been held at locations in The Netherlands, Germany, Sweden, and the UK, and the third to be published in the Springer-Verlag series of Lecture Notes in Computer Science (selected papers from IFL'96 and IFL'97 are published in LNCS volumes 1268 and 1467 respectively).

The workshop has grown over the years, and the 1998 meeting attracted 64 researchers from the international functional language community, many of whom presented papers at the workshop. We are pleased that, after due revision and rigorous peer review, we are able to publish 15 of those papers in this volume.

The papers selected from the workshop cover a wide range of topics including work on parallel process co-ordination (Aßmann; Klusik, Ortega, and Peña), parallel profiling (Charles and Runciman; King, Hall, and Trinder), compilation (Grelck) and semantics of parallel systems (Hall, Baker-Finch, Trinder, and King), programming methodology (Koopman and Plasmeijer; Scholz), interrupt handling (Reid), type systems (McAdam; Pil), strictness analysis (Pape), concurrency and message passing (Holyer and Spiliopoulou; Serrarens and Plasmeijer) and inter-language working (Reinke).

Some of the work developed out of research reported at previous IFL workshops. In *Implementing Eden, or: Dreams Become Reality, pp 103–119*, Klusik, Ortega, and Peña show how expressions in the parallel functional language, EDEN, are compiled, work arising from their previous operational specification of the distributed abstract machine, DREAM (IFL'97). Grelck (*Shared Memory Multiprocessor Support for SAC, pp 38–53*) continues work on Single Assignment C (IFL'96), describing the compilation of SAC programs for multithreaded execution on multiprocessor systems. Scholz also describes work on SAC (*A Case Study: Effects of WITH-Loop-Folding on the NAS MG Benchmark in SAC, pp 216–228*) showing how the WITH-Loop-Folding optimization supports high-level array operations efficiently. Much work has been done in recent years on optimization of functional programming compilers. This paper shows that code generated from the SAC program not only reaches the execution time of code generated from FORTRAN, but even outperforms it by a significant amount. Aßmann (*Preliminary Performance Results for an Implementation of the Process Coordination Language K2, pp 1–19*) builds on earlier work on K2 (IFL'97), analysing the efficiency of a number of benchmarks. Pil (*Dynamic Types and Type Dependent Functions, pp 169–185*) describes work on type dependent functions which will be added to the Clean language using overloading. These will facilitate communication between independent (possibly persistent) functional programs using a minimum of dynamic typing. Two papers continue work on profiling parallel functional programs. King, Hall, and Trinder (*A Strategic Profiler for Glasgow Parallel Haskell, pp 88–102*) show how the GRANSIM-SP profiler attributes costs to the abstract evaluation strategies that created various threads. Charles and Runciman (*An Interactive Approach to Profiling Parallel Functional Programs, pp 20–37*) concentrate on the user interface to profiling tools, describing a system that interactively combines graphical information with a query interface. Finally, Koopman, and Plasmeijer (*Efficient Combinator Parsers, pp 120–136*) describe how elegant combinators for constructing parsers, which, however, have exponential time complexity, can be made more efficient using continuations.

Other papers represent work on new lines of research. Reinke (*Towards a Haskell/Java Connection, pp 200–215*) describes preliminary work on a system to support inter-language working between functional and object-oriented languages, a timely coverage of a vitally important issue. Reid (*Putting the Spine Back in the Spineless Tagless G-Machine: An Implementation of Resumable Black-Holes, pp 186–199*) shows how to tackle interrupts in lazy languages, an issue that has been problematic for some years. Serrarens and Plasmeijer (*Explicit Message Passing for Concurrent Clean, pp 229–245*) describe a language extension providing efficient flexible communication in a concurrent system. Holyer and Spiliopoulou also present concurrency research (*Concurrent Monadic Interfacing, pp 72–87*) in which the monadic style of interfacing is adapted to accommodate deterministic concurrency. Three papers describe more theoretical work, albeit for use in practical implementations. Pape (*Higher Order Demand Propagation, pp 153–168*) gives a new denotational semantics mapping function definitions into demand propagators, allowing the definition of a backward strictness analysis of the functions even when they are higher order and/or transmit across module boundaries. McAdam (*On the Unification of Substitutions in Type Inference, pp 137–152*) describes a polymorphic type inference algorithm which reduces the confusion which often arises when type errors are reported to users. Finally, Hall, Baker-Finch, Trinder, and King (*Towards an Operational Semantics for a Parallel Non-strict Functional Language, pp 54–71*) present a semantics for a simple parallel graph reduction system based on Launchbury's natural semantics for lazy evaluation.

The 15 papers published in this volume were selected using a rigorous *a-posteriori* refereeing process from the 39 papers that were presented at the workshop. The reviewing process was shared among the program committee, which comprised:

Chris Clack	University College London	UK
Tony Davie	University of St. Andrews	UK
John Glauert	University of East Anglia	UK
Kevin Hammond	University of St. Andrews	UK
Werner Kluge	University of Kiel	Germany
Pieter Koopman	University of Nijmegen	The Netherlands
Rita Loogen	University of Marburg	Germany
Greg Michaelson	Heriot-Watt University	UK
Markus Mohnen	RWTH Aachen	Germany
Marko van Eekelen	University of Nijmegen	The Netherlands

We would like to thank the many additional anonymous referees who provided us with timely, high-quality reports on which our decisions were based.

The overall balance of the papers is representative, both in scope and technical substance, of the contributions made to the London workshop as well as to those that preceded it. Publication in the LNCS series is not only intended to make these contributions more widely known in the computer science community but also to encourage researchers in the field to participate in future workshops, of which the next one will be held in Nijmegen, The Netherlands, September 7-10, 1999 (see `http://www.cs.kun.nl/~pieter/ifl99/index.htm`).

Significantly, this year the workshop attracted industrial sponsorship from both Andersen Consulting and Ericsson. This indicates the growing importance of functional programming languages and their implementation within two key commercial spheres (IT Consultancy and Telecommunications, respectively). We thank our sponsors for their generous contributions.

March 1999   Kevin Hammond, Tony Davie, and Chris Clack

Table Of Contents

Performance Results for an Implementation of the Process Coordination Language *K2*

Claus Aßmann

Department of Computer Science, University of Kiel, 24105 Kiel, Germany
ca@informatik.uni-kiel.de

Abstract. This paper is on process coordination language *K2* which is based on a variant of high-level Petri nets. It strictly separates the specification of processes and their communication structures from (functional) specifications of the computations to be performed by the processes. The purpose of this separation is to facilitate both correct program construction and formal reasoning about essential safety and liveness properties. More specifically, the paper presents and analyzes performance measurements obtained from a *K2* implementation based on the message passing system PVM. Two simple *K2* benchmark programs are to determine the overhead inflicted by the *K2* runtime system relative to a direct PVM implementation of the same programs. A third benchmark program, the implementation of a relaxation algorithm for the solution of PDEs, is to investigate the efficiency of distributing some given workload on a multiprocessor system by recursively expanding process (sub-)structures. The measurements show that coarse-grain *K2* programs are only marginally slower than their PVM counterparts, and that good scalability of recursive programs can be achieved on multiple computing sites.
Keywords: coordination language, concurrent computing, Petri nets, performance results

1 Introduction

Functional programs, due to the absence of side effects, are considered perfect candidates for non-sequential execution. They specify in the form of function equations and function applications just desired problem solutions but (ideally) leave it completely to compilation or interpretation, and to some extent to the runtime system, to figure out how these solutions are to be computed. If this is to be done non-sequentially, it involves partitioning a program (recursively) into concurrently executable pieces, creating tasks for them, scheduling these tasks on available processing sites, handling communication and synchronization among tasks, and (recursively) assembling problem solutions from partial results produced by terminating tasks. Crucial with respect to attainable performance gains are a fairly high ratio of useful computations within the tasks versus the overhead inflicted by the task management on the one hand and a fairly balanced workload distribution over the processing sites on the other hand.

It has been recognized fairly early in the game that this cannot be had without at least some program annotations which identify terms that may be

H. Hammond, T. Davie, and C. Clack (Eds.): IFL'98, LNCS 1595, pp. 1–19, 1999.

executed concurrently, control job granularities and the degree to which terms must be evaluated (which primarily relates to lazy languages), put upper bounds on (or throttle) the number of tasks that participate in a computation, and even allocate terms to specific (virtual) processing sites for execution [16, 15]. Concurrently executable program parts may also be made explicit by means of so-called skeletons [8]. They define a few standardized control and communication structures, e.g., for divide-and-conquer or pipelined computations, which are complemented by compilation schemes that produce efficient code.

Another approach that makes concurrency explicit uses language constructs for the specification of processes (tasks) and for the communication structures that must be established among them. These constructs may either be integrated into a functional language [5] or provided by a separate so-called process coordination language [6]. Cleanly separating the specification of the process system from the computations to be performed by the individual processes, as is the underlying idea in the latter case, considerably facilitates both correct program construction and formal analysis of the process system wrt the existence of essential safety and liveness properties. It also has the pragmatic advantage that, proper interfacing with the process level provided, different languages, functional or procedural, may be used to specify what the individual processes are supposed to compute. This does not only considerably enhances the re-usability of existing (sequential) code but to some extent also portability to different, possibly heterogeneous machinery.

To be a useful tool for the design of non-trivial systems of communicating processes, a coordination language should

- be compositional to allow for the systematic construction of complex process systems from simpler subsystems;
- provide only a small set of fairly simple, well-understood process interaction schemes, including controlled forms of nondeterminism (to realize, say, client/server interactions), which ensure an orderly system behavior largely by construction;
- support some concept of recursively expandable process structures which, at runtime, may be dynamically adapted to actual problem sizes (workload) or available resources (processing sites);
- be based on some process calculus which provides computationally tractable formal methods for analyzing and reasoning about the existence of basic safety and liveness properties;
- lend itself to some easily comprehensible form of high-level debugging, e.g., by step-wise execution of selected process instances and inspection of intermediate system states, and also facilitate performance analysis.

Two approaches to concurrent computing in the area of functional languages which in one form or another use process specifications are Eden [5] and Caliban [7], both being extensions of Haskell.

Eden provides explicit process abstractions which may be called from within Haskell code to create processes and communication channels at runtime. Neither communication structures nor the number of processes are fixed at compile time, but may rather freely be changed during execution. Higher-order functions can be used to construct complex systems from simpler subsystems. Nondeterminism may be introduced into programs only by primitive MERGE processes.

However, as complete freedom of building and modifying process structures at runtime tends to invite chaos, it appears to be extremely difficult to ensure basic safety and liveness properties for non-trivial programs. Other difficulties may arise from intertwining communications with computations as the effects of flaws in the former may be hard to isolate from flaws in the latter, particularly if nondeterministic phenomena are involved.

Mixing computations and communication also runs somewhat counter to the concept of modular programming. As programmers are not forced to cleanly separate one from the other, it may be difficult to migrate existing code written either in Haskell or any other language, or to re-use Eden code in other contexts.

Caliban is a flexible annotation language for Haskell that describes which expressions should be evaluated on the same computing sites. They are transformed into specifications of static process networks, i.e., their structures are fixed at compile-time. Neither dynamically changing process structures nor nondeterminism are supported. Conceptually, Caliban programs from which the annotations are being removed are semantically fully equivalent to their Haskell counterparts. Caliban can therefore not really be considered a process coordination language that is in the same league as Eden or *K2*.

Beyond these conceptual shortcomings, there are also some problems with the Caliban implementation. For instance, as streams are evaluated in order, stream elements whose values are not needed but are getting trapped in a non-terminating loop, cause the entire program to loop without end, if a later element in the stream is needed. Similarly, the Caliban compiler itself may not terminate since it may have to evaluate expressions that are not needed.

The functional coordination language *K2* [2] has been developed with the requirements listed above as design goals in mind. It derives from a variant of colored Petri nets [12, 13] in which programs are composed of processes and streams corresponding to transitions inscribed with functions and to places that carry tokens inscribed with argument objects, respectively. The choice of colored Petri nets as a conceptual basis for *K2* was motivated by the fact that they are a perfect match for the operational semantics of functional computations: both the rewrite rules for function applications and the firing rules for transitions in Petri nets follow the concept of context–free substitutions, i.e., both are characterized by the orderly consumption and (re)production of computational objects, and thus are completely free of side–effects. A deterministic (functional) behavior of entire *K2* process systems is ensured by restricting the communication structures among processes to so-called synchronization graphs, in which each stream connects to at most one producing and one consuming process. However, good-natured forms of nondeterminism which essentially relate to to the splitting and merging of streams are supported by special primitive process types, When properly applied, these primitives produce only locally contained nondeterminism, e.g., within client-server subsystems, but have no global effects. *K2* also provides abstraction mechanisms for subsystems of cooperating processes which are similar to code abstractions as they are available in conventional programming languages, including recursively expandable process specifications.

Processes in *K2* may, in a first step, simply be specified as empty containers which just provide interfaces to incoming and outgoing streams. These containers may, in a second step, be inscribed with function specifications, written in some functional or even in a procedural language, which must be made compatible with the respective interfaces. Existing program modules may thus be readily migrated from sequential processing.

The strict separation of the process from the program specification level, in conjunction with the restrictions imposed on the communication structures, facilitates the application of analysis methods that are well-known from Petri net theory to verify the existence of structural invariance properties which are essential pre-requisites for safety and liveness of the process system (see [10, 11, 1]). The correctness of the process inscriptions may be independently verified or validated by other means. Other than that the computations carried out by the processes must terminate eventually, they have no impact on the dynamic behavior of the process system.

K2 is implemented on widely available (de-facto) standard message passing software (PVM [9]) for easy portability to different platforms. *K2* specifications are compiled to C code for efficient execution.

The remainder of the paper is organized as follows: it first gives a brief introduction into *K2*, followed by an overview of its PVM implementation. The main part presents and analyzes performance results obtained from three benchmark programs which are to determine the overhead inflicted by the *K2* runtime system relative to direct PVM implementations of the same programs, and to investigate the efficiency of recursive process structures wrt to scaling workload distribution to available processing sites. The last section summarizes the current system status and discusses further work.

2   The Coordination Language *K2*

This section briefly introduces *K2* to the extent necessary to follow the remainder of the paper, a detailed description may be found in [2].

K2 process systems are composed of processes and of streams which communicate objects of the underlying computation language(s). Streams are realized as FIFO-queues of finite capacities which establish finite synchronic distances[1] within which producing and consuming processes may operate concurrently.

Conceptually, processes conform exactly to the firing semantics of transitions in ordinary Petri-nets. A process instance consumes at least one object (or token)

---

[1] A synchronic distance generally defines the number of occurrences by which one of two transactions can get ahead of the other before the latter must catch up.

from every input stream, performs some operation on them, and produces at least one result token in each of its output streams. It is therefore enabled to take place iff it finds sufficiently many tokens in its input streams and sufficient free capacities in its output streams. Each stream connects just one producing and one consuming process, thus excluding conflict situations (which may cause unintended nondeterminism) as enabled processes can never be de-activated by the firing of other processes.

The basic building blocks of *K2* programs are atomic processes whose computations need to be specified by inscriptions with functional or procedural pieces of code. The current implementation only requires that the code of the inscriptions can be called from C because *K2* has been implemented in that language; no other requirements exist. C has been chosen for the implementation because it is very portable and PVM routines can be called directly from it.

Controlled forms of (local) nondeterminism which are, for instance, necessary to realize client- server (sub-)systems are supported by the primitive process types SPLIT and SPREAD which pass tokens from one input stream to one of several output streams, and by SELECT and MERGE which route tokens from one of several input streams to one output stream. In the case of SPLIT and SELECT primitives the selection depends on the value of a control token supplied via a designated control stream, while SPREAD and MERGE primitives perform a nondeterministic, fair selection.

K2 also provides a general abstraction mechanism for the construction of process hierarchies and of recursive processes. Hierarchical processes may be recursively assembled from subsystems composed of atomic, primitive and hierarchical processes which, for reasons of compositionality, interface with other processes in exactly the same way as atomic processes, i.e., they consume sets of tokens from input streams, perform computations on them, and produce sets of result tokens to be placed in output streams. Hierarchical processes may also be operated as pipelines of some pre-specified depths (or finite synchronic distances) between input and output. They specify the maximum number of token sets which, in their order of arrival, can be processed simultaneously.

The programming environment of *K2* currently consists of a graphical editor, a compiler, and a runtime library. The user may specify process systems with the help of the editor, whose graphical interface is shown in Fig. 1. It depicts a simple master/slave program. The equivalent textual representation, which is used as input for the *K2* compiler, looks like this[2]:

```
extern C int mastergen(int i,int *o);
extern C int slavecomp(int i,int *o);
atomic master(IN int r<>, OUT int t<>) { mastergen(r,t); }
atomic slave(IN int i<>, OUT int o<>) { slavecomp(i,o); }
void main() { int r<:2:>,t<:2:>,t1<>,t2<>,r1<>,r2<>;
 master(r,t); spread(t,t1,t2);
 slave(t1,r1); slave(t2,r2); merge(r,r1,r2); }
```

---

[2] This is one of the benchmark programs used in Sect. 4

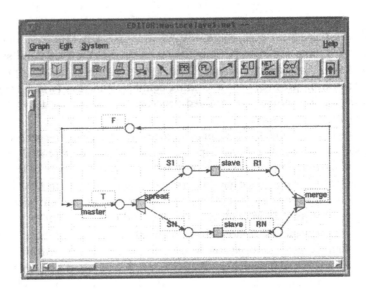

Fig. 1. The graphical interface of the K2 system, showing a simple master/slave process system

The first two lines define the signatures of the C interfaces of the functions that are used as process inscriptions. Next are two atomic process definition which have parameter lists that define the types of input and output streams. The **main** process declaration is similar to **main()** in a C program. It defines a hierarchical process that (indirectly) contains all process applications. Stream declarations are denoted as **stream_name** **<:n:>**, where **n** specifies the stream capacity (with **<>** used as abbreviation for a capacity of one).

To illustrate what a simple program inscription for an atomic process looks like, here is a C wrapper for a function called **hitc_slave_()** which does the actual computing of the **slave** process:

```
int slavecomp(int t,int *o) {
  if (t <= 0) return TERMINATION;
  hitc_slave_(&t); *o = t*t;
  return COMPUTATION; }
```

Note that neither the C wrapper nor the function contain any calls to communication constructs as communications are implicitly handled by K2. The function is called with the actual parameters taken from the input stream, and its results are passed along via C pointers to the output stream.

3   Implementation

The implementation of the *K2* runtime system is based on PVM [9], primarily for reasons of portability, since it is available on almost all UNIX based platforms, and even on many multiprocessor systems with proprietary operating systems. Moreover, PVM allows to dynamically spawn and terminate tasks, which is essential for the concept of recursively expanding process structures.

The following gives a brief overview of the *K2* implementation which highlights just those parts which are relevant for the performance measurements to be discussed in the next section. More details about the implementation can be found in [2].

Each user-specified *K2* process is translated into a so-called wrapper, which constitutes a PVM task. Since the communication structure of *K2* is restricted to synchronization graphs, it is convenient to include into the wrappers the input streams of processes. A wrapper has thus direct access to the input parameters of the user-specified process, which is essential for fast process invocation. Moreover, it can be locally (within a wrapper) decided whether the respective *K2* process is activated, which is crucial for the efficiency of *K2* implementations on distributed platforms. The output streams of a process are part of the wrappers of the respective consuming processes, to which they are input streams. A wrapper manages the input and output streams connected to it, ensures that the finite capacities of the streams are never exceeded, checks whether the user-specified process is activated, in which case it calls it with the input values supplied, and passes the result values on to the output streams.

Since it is generally too expensive to keep a producing process up-to-date on the number of tokens in its output streams (which would require sending control messages each time tokens are taken out by the consuming processes whose wrappers own the output streams), the *K2* implementation uses a more tolerant so-called flow control mechanism. It sends from consumer to producer just as many control messages as are necessary to ensure that the stream capacities are never exceeded. These messages simply inform the producers to deliver new object (if at all possible) before the consuming wrappers run out of tokens in their input streams (for more details see [3]).

Since the external behavior of hierarchical processes must be exactly the same as that of atomic processes, the runtime system must provide additional synchronization barriers for token sets entering and exiting. These barriers also serve to enforce the synchronic distances, i.e., the upper bounds on the number of token sets (or instantiations of the hierarchical processes) that can be processed simultaneously.

A *K2* process system is translated into a single C program which contains all wrappers. It is compiled and linked against the *K2* runtime library, yielding a single executable. To illustrate what this program is doing, consider the following piece of pseudo-code which realizes a simple *K2* system of two processes named p1 and p2.

```
p1() { ... }
p2() { ... }
main() {
if (IamParent()) {
  t1 = pvm_exec(t);           t2 = pvm_exec(t);
  pvm_send(t1,"p1");          pvm_send(t2,"p2");
  wait_for_children_to_terminate(); }
else {                  pvm_recv(m);
  if (m == "p1") { p1(); }    if (m == "p2") { p2(); }
}
```

The first two lines abbreviate the definitions of the wrappers for the two processes. The function call IamParent() in the first line of the main() function decides whether the PVM task that executes it is the parent of the entire task system. This being case, the task starts two children with task identifiers t1 and t2 and subsequently sends to each of them a message specifying which of the two wrappers it ought to execute. If the task is not the parent, it receives such a message and thereupon executes the wrapper function as specified by its contents.

Thus the main task starts the wrappers for all top-level K2 processes. Essentially the same start-up procedure applies recursively to hierarchical processes and to recursively expanding process structures as well, the only difference being that the main() function of the parent task also has to take care of some housekeeping (cleanup) functions after all child tasks have terminated.

A K2 process system terminates after all its processes have terminated. To do this in an orderly way, the function inscription of an atomic process returns a status code which informs the runtime system whether the process terminates or can continue. This code is used to start the termination of the entire process system. Termination of a process takes two steps. First, termination messages are sent out to all directly connected processes and to the parent process. The process itself terminates upon receiving acknowledge signals from all processes to which it sent out termination messages. Other atomic processes start this termination procedure upon receiving termination messages. This can happen in two different situations: if the message is received from a consumer, then the process terminates immediately since the tokens it produces can not anymore be consumed; if it is received from a producer, then the process enters the termination procedure as soon as there are no tokens left in the input stream connected to it.

4 Performance

There are basically two problem areas that need to be investigated with respect to the performance of K2 programs.

On the one hand, the K2 runtime system involves some additional overhead compared to programs that use the PVM message passing library directly. This overhead may roughly be attributed to

- the time required to spawn new tasks, which could be expected to differ noticeably since *K2*, as indicated by the pseudo-code given in the preceding section, does it sequentially, whereas PVM programs may use a parameter for the spawn function which specifies the number of tasks to be created in one conceptual step;
- the *K2* implementation using a flow control mechanism for the communication of object tokens between wrappers, whereas a PVM implementation transmits these objects without additional control messages;
- the stream management within the wrappers of a *K2* implementation, specifically repeated tests for the activation of the respective processes upon the arrival of object tokens from producing processes;
- process termination, which in a *K2* implementation requires many control message to be exchanged between atomic processes until, starting from some first terminating process, the entire process system comes to a halt, whereas a PVM implementation can terminate processes directly as soon as they have completed their jobs.

On the other hand, there is the more important question of just how much faster can *K2* programs be executed on multiprocessor systems relative to programs written for sequential execution, i.e., without overhead for coordination or communication.

These performance issues have been thoroughly investigated by means of three different benchmark programs:

- `circle` is a simple program which has been designed to determine the worst-case overhead inflicted by the *K2* runtime system compared to equivalent direct PVM implementations. It creates eight tasks connected as a cyclic structure about which a single token is circulated several times (or completes several laps).
- `hitc` is a more realistic program to compare the performance of *K2* and PVM programs. It creates a master/slave process system with a simple dynamic load balancing scheme.
- `relax` is used to investigate how well *K2* programs scale with increasing numbers of processes and processing sites. It implements a relaxation algorithm which approximates solutions of discrete Poisson problems in the context of more sophisticated multigrid methods. The program is designed to recursively partition, by means of recursive process structures, a given grid into equally sized smaller pieces which can be relaxed concurrently, and to establish direct communication links between processes operating on adjacent grid partitions, along which border line columns of grid points can be exchanged.

Since until recently there was no functional language available which uses PVM, for the time being the comparisons between PVM and *K2* implementations of process systems had to be done with C and Fortran programs. Program execution times have been measured on three different platforms, these being a Sun SPARCstation 10, an nCUBE/2E (a distributed memory machine with

32 processors), and a Sun Enterprise E4000 (a shared memory machine with 4 UltraSPARC processors).

Figs. 2 and 3 respectively depict the XPVM [4] traces for the PVM and the K2 implementations of `circle`, the time scales being identical in both cases. The tracing has been done on the SPARCstation 10. The horizontal bars represent the tasks involved in the program execution. The black sections of the bars denote useful computations, the white sections denote idle times, and the lines running across the bars depict communications. The PVM version requires only eight tasks since the main task at the top also participates in the circle, whereas the main task in the K2 version assumes the role of a parent which starts the eight circular tasks and then retires until termination of the entire system.

The K2 processes are started one after the other (as reflected by the skewing of the bars in Fig. 3), whereas the PVM processes are being created in one step at about the same time. Nevertheless, the total start-up times do not differ much in both cases since the work to be done (by one processor) obviously is about the same. However, the token circulation phase (annotated as *Comm* in both diagrams) shows significant differences between both implementations. Under PVM, there are just forward communications among the tasks for the passage of the circulating token, whereas the K2 version also involves backward communication of flow control messages, which consumes considerably more time. Essentially the same applies to the termination phase (shown on the right of both figures and annotated as *Term*). It is significantly longer for the K2 version since many control messages must be exchanged among the task (visible as the lines criss-crossing the task bars), whereas the PVM tasks simply terminate after having performed a pre-specified number of laps.

The actual execution times of `circle` on the SPARCstation 10 are shown in Table 1, where the K2 version has been run with stream capacities of 1, 10, 100, and 1000. Due to significantly more communications of control messages, the K2 implementation is always slower than the PVM implementation. However, larger stream capacities reduce the overhead inflicted by the control flow mechanism per token passage, resulting in faster execution[3]. On average, the control mechanism requires about one control message per $\lceil 3 * c/4 \rceil$ tokens sent from producer to consumer, where c is the capacity of the stream involved.

The K2 version of the `circle` program has also been executed on the nCUBE with varying parameters. Table 2 shows the execution times for eight processes, with the columns *Laps* specifying the number of times the single token was circulated about the task cycle, *Capacity* denoting the stream capacities, *Flow control* specifying whether or not the flow control was activated, *Time* giving absolute execution times, and *Speedup* specifying relative performance gains (in percent) with the flow control turned off. As can be expected, a noticeable speedup can only be attained if the stream capacity is one and the number of token circulations is at least 100. For fewer iterations, the effect is marginal. If the stream

---

[3] Stream capacity approaching 1000 increase the memory demands of the tasks to the extent that cache problems cause the performance gains to deteriorate again.

Laps	PVM	*K2* Cap: 1	Overhead %	*K2* 10	Overhead %	*K2* 100	Overhead %	*K2* 1000	Overhead %
1	0.9	1.0	11	1.0	11	1.0	11	1.0	11
10	1.0	1.2	19	1.1	10	1.1	10	1.1	10
100	1.6	2.8	74	2.0	24	1.9	18	1.9	18
1000	8.6	18.9	119	10.6	23	9.4	9	9.8	13
10000	76.4	184.7	141	97.8	28	85.9	12	87.3	14

Table 1. Execution times of `circle` on a SPARCstation10

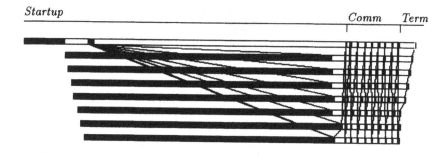

Fig. 2. XPVM trace of `circle` (PVM version)

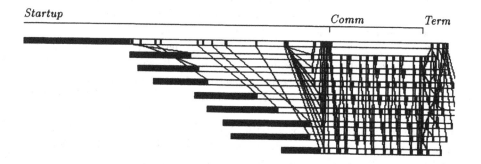

Fig. 3. XPVM trace of `circle` (*K2* version)

capacity is ten (or even larger), the speedup is less dramatic as the overhead inflicted by the flow control becomes negligible.

Laps	Capacity	Flow Control	Time	Speedup (%)
1	1	Yes	6.90	
1	1	No	6.90	0.0
10	1	Yes	7.30	
10	1	No	7.10	2.7
10	10	Yes	7.10	
10	10	No	7.10	0.0
100	1	Yes	10.10	
100	1	No	8.60	14.9
100	10	Yes	8.60	
100	10	No	8.50	1.2
1000	1	Yes	37.50	
1000	1	No	22.40	40.3
1000	10	Yes	23.40	
1000	10	No	22.50	3.8
10000	1	Yes	311.10	
10000	1	No	160.10	48.5
10000	10	Yes	169.70	
10000	10	No	161.10	5.1

Table 2. Execution times of `circle` on an nCUBE/2E ($K2$ version, 8 processes)

The program `hitc`, which is one of the example programs that comes with the PVM distribution, creates a simple master/slave process system. The master process spawns as many slaves (N) as virtual machines are available and sends jobs to each of them, and then waits for the completion of the slaves. The master holds $10 * N$ jobs to be computed. After having distributed the first N jobs, the remaining $9 * N$ jobs are on a first come / first serve basis submitted to slaves which have their jobs completed, until all jobs are done.

The $K2$ version of `hitc` (which for two slaves[4] is depicted in Fig. 1) uses the primitive processes SPREAD and MERGE to distribute the jobs and to collect the results, respectively. By restricting the capacities of the streams connecting the SPREAD process and the slaves to one, load balancing is done implicitly by the SPREAD process.

The $K2$ version turns out to be only about three per cent slower than the PVM version. For instance, execution times on the E4000 are 19.08s for $K2$ versus 18.44s for PVM. This difference is related to several factors; as already mentioned before, the termination of the $K2$ process system being the most significant one. Another, very small part comes from the distribution of the first

---

[4] it can be easily expanded for any number of slaves, the benchmark has been executed with two to eight slaves.

jobs, which is done via broadcast in the PVM version but via single messages in the $K2$ version.

The third benchmark concerns three versions of the **relax** program; a graphical specification of the recursive version **relaxd** is given in Fig. 4. This program consists of the processes **input**, which generates an argument array (the grid to be relaxed), **in_depth**, which defines the depth N of the recursive unfolding, **build_grid**, which is a hierarchical process that recursively unfolds the process system, and **output**, which writes the resulting array to a file. **build_grid** itself contains the processes **D** to partition an array into two subarrays, **C** to combine two relaxed array partitions into one, and **IT** which actually performs relaxation steps on an array partition. **build_grid** creates 2^N processes **IT**, which are connected as a bidirectional pipeline. The processes **IT** initially are supplied with array partitions generated by **input** and split up by the **D** processes, and perform some pre-specified number of relaxation steps on it. After each step, they exchange the border line rows of their array partitions with their left and right neighbors. Once the relaxations in each **IT** process are done, the **C** processes recursively assemble the resulting array from the partitions and send it to **output**.

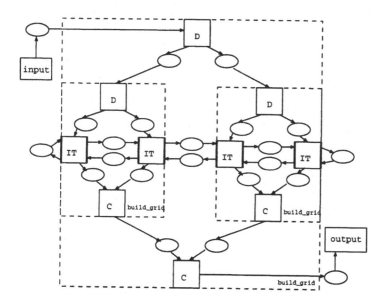

Fig. 4. Relaxation process system

Another version of this program called **relaxs** defines the complete process structure statically, thus eliminating the overhead of expanding the structure at runtime and of the additional barrier synchronizations that get involved when exchanging grid columns between IT processes embedded in adjacent build_grid hierarchical processes.

For reasons of uniformity, both the relaxd and the relaxs programs have their bidirectional pipelines terminated with IT processes that feed their border line columns back to themselves. This superfluous data exchange has been eliminated in an optimized version relaxo of relaxs which has the IT processes at both ends replaced by specialized versions which exchange data only to the right (on the left end) or only to the left (on the right end).

Performance measurements were carried out for all three programs on the nCUBE/2E and on the SPARC E4000, where only four processors were available. The number of IT processes has been stepped up on the nCUBE/2E from two to four to eight (i.e., with $N = 1, 2$, and 3) and on the SPARC E4000 only from two to four. On both systems, the programs where run with 0, 100, 1000, and 10000 relaxation steps. As points of reference, the performance measurements also included a sequential version called relax.

The performance figures for the nCUBE/2E are shown in Table 3, and those for the SPARC E4000 are given in Table 4. They list numbers of processes against absolute program runtimes for varying numbers of relaxation steps. The tables also list in the columns T/S the times it takes to perform one relaxation step in order to show how well, with increasing numbers of processing sites, the programs scale relative to themselves, i.e., relative to executing them with just two IT processes. To eliminate the overhead unrelated to relaxation, these values are obtained by subtracting from the total execution time the time required for zero relaxation steps (which roughly includes the start-up time for the process system, for generating and partitioning the array, and for assembling the result), and by dividing this time by the actual number of relaxation steps.

For the nCUBE/2E, the values show that the static version relaxs and the optimized version relaxo scale quite linearly, e.g., for 1000 relaxation steps to be performed by the relaxs program from 0.292 to 0.150 to 0.080 seconds/step when going from 2 to 4 to 8 IT processes, whereas the program relaxd, which dynamically unfolds the process system from the hierarchical process build_grid does not do quite as well. This is clearly a consequence of the overhead required for the barrier synchronizations between adjacent IT processes belonging to different build_grid hierarchies.

Another observation relates to Amdahl's law: since the startup time is relatively large compared to the computation time for 100 relaxation steps, the program is getting slower if eight instead of four IT processes are used (e.g., for relaxs, the execution time increases from 48.1 to 50.5 seconds). This indicates that it does not pay to create relatively large process systems if little computational work is left to be done by each process.

Essentially the same observations apply to program execution on the E4000 system, except that the recursive program relaxd does very badly with four IT processes; both absolute runtimes and times per iteration are even poorer than for two IT processes. This phenomenon must largely be attributed to the fact that there are only four processors available to run the four IT processes. Thus,

N	Steps	Time	Steps	Time	T/S	Steps	Time	T/S	Steps	Time	T/S
1	0	31.1	100	59.4	0.283	1000	324.6	0.293	10000	3178.1	0.315
2	0	39.6	100	56.1	0.165	1000	191.8	0.152	10000	1786.6	0.175
3	0	57.9	100	72.2	0.143	1000	144.9	0.087	10000	1142.6	0.108

relaxd (recursive version)

N	Steps	Time	Steps	Time	T/S	Steps	Time	T/S	Steps	Time	T/S
1	0	30.2	100	60.8	0.306	1000	322.1	0.292	10000	3049.9	0.302
2	0	35.5	100	50.8	0.153	1000	185.3	0.150	10000	1599.6	0.156
3	0	45.9	100	53.9	0.080	1000	125.4	0.080	10000	882.3	0.084

relaxs (static version)

N	Steps	Time	Steps	Time	T/S	Steps	Time	T/S	Steps	Time	T/S
1	0	7.3	100	27.3	0.200	1000	214.1	0.207	10000	2088.2	0.208
2	0	11.9	100	22.6	0.107	1000	123.4	0.112	10000	1126.3	0.111
3	0	21.8	100	28.0	0.062	1000	78.3	0.057	10000	585.3	0.056

relax (optimized version)

Steps	Time	Steps	Time	T/S	Steps	Time	T/S	Steps	Time	T/S
1	1.50	100	36.90	0.354	1000	365.10	0.364	10000	3667.20	0.367

relax (sequential version)

Table 3. Execution times of the various **relax** versions on the nCUBE/2E

N	Steps	Time	Steps	Time	T/S	Steps	Time	T/S	Steps	Time	T/S
1	0	3.8	100	15.2	0.115	1000	103.0	0.099	10000	1376.7	0.137
2	0	7.4	100	44.0	0.366	1000	104.3	0.097	10000	1981.6	0.197

relaxd (recursive version)

N	Steps	Time	Steps	Time	T/S	Steps	Time	T/S	Steps	Time	T/S
1	0	2.7	100	3.1	0.004	1000	8.9	0.006	10000	68.6	0.007
2	0	3.9	100	4.2	0.004	1000	7.3	0.003	10000	39.5	0.004

relaxs (static version)

N	Steps	Time	Steps	Time	T/S	Steps	Time	T/S	Steps	Time	T/S
1	0	2.5	100	3.0	0.005	1000	8.8	0.006	10000	66.7	0.006
2	0	3.8	100	4.0	0.002	1000	7.3	0.004	10000	39.2	0.004

relaxo (optimized version)

Steps	Time	Steps	Time	T/S	Steps	Time	T/S	Steps	Time	T/S
1	0.07	100	1.33	0.013	1000	12.77	0.013	10000	127.17	0.013

relax (sequential version)

Table 4. Execution times of the **relax** versions on the E4000

whenever data need to be exchanged between IT processes, expensive context switches have to be made to the respective hierarchical build_grid processes which actually pass the data along. In contrast to this, both the relaxs and relaxo programs scale reasonably well for 1000 and more relaxation steps, at least with respect to execution times per step, when going from two to four IT processes.

Another set of interesting performance figures can be extracted when comparing execution times of the concurrent program versions against those of the sequential version and introspectively the runtimes for two against four (and eight) IT processes, based on 10000 relaxation steps in each case. These comparisons also allow to determine which percentages of the total execution times are taken up by the process coordination overhead and how this overhead scales with the number of processes.

These data are compiled in Tables 5 for the nCUBE/2E system and 6 for the E4000 system. They list execution times of the sequential version (relax), and of the three $K2$ programs relaxd, relaxs, relaxo[5] with $N = 1, 2, 3$. The overheads of the concurrent versions relative to the sequential version are listed in the columns O_s (in percent), and the overheads of the concurrent versions with $N = 2$ and $N = 3$ relative to $N = 1$ are listed under O_p (again in percent).

Program	Seq	N=1	O_s %	N=2	O_s %	O_p %	N=3	O_s %	O_p %
relax	3667.20								
relaxd		3178.10	73	1786.60	95	12	1142.60	149	44
relaxs		3049.90	66	1599.60	74	5	882.30	92	16
relaxo		2088.20	14	1126.30	23	8	585.30	28	12

Table 5. Comparison of execution times on the nCUBE/2E

Program	Seq	N=1	O_s %	N=2	O_s %	O_p %
relax	127.17					
relaxs		68.58	8	39.55	24	15
relaxo		66.68	5	39.17	23	17

Table 6. Comparison of execution times on the E4000

The process coordination overhead relative to the sequential version relax is quite substantial in the nCUBE/2E system, specifically for the relaxd program, owing largely to the fact that almost all data and control messages are communicated between processing sites, which due to the implementation of the low-level message passing mechanism involved is inherently slow. In the E4000 system, this overhead is significantly lower since all communication is handled through fast shared memory.

---

[5] The relaxd program is not included in the table for the E4000 system due to the poor performance caused by the context switching problems.

5   Conclusions

The development of the *K2* system so far has primarily concentrated on the efficient PVM implementation of the process coordination language, without much concern for a specific underlying computation language. With sophisticated compiler technology for procedural and functional languages readily available, the efficiency of process interactions clearly is the dominating factor in attaining good overall performance for application programs which at runtime spawn fairly complex process networks. There would be no justification to continue with this project unless this problem can be satisfactorily solved.

The current *K2* system therefore consists of little more than the components that are necessary to demonstrate the credibility of the *K2* concept in the performance department. These components include a graphical editor for the specification of *K2* programs, a compiler that translates textual representations of *K2* programs into C, and a runtime library.

It turns out that for applications which are not too fine-grained, *K2* adds a fairly small overhead to the execution of concurrent process systems compared to equivalent programs implemented directly on PVM, as indicated by the programs `circle` and `hitc`. Relative to equivalent sequential programs the overhead of process coordination also remains within tolerable limits on shared memory machinery (the E4000 system) but becomes quite heavy on distributed memory platforms (the nCUBE/2E system), particularly if data have to be exchanged quite frequently among hierarchical processes (as is the case with the `relaxd` program). This is mainly due to the passage of data and of control messages, through which producing and consuming processes need to be synchronized with each other, across processing sites, which is always a rather costly (time-consuming) undertaking.

Otherwise, the performance data are encouraging enough to continue with the *K2* project, particularly since there is considerable room for optimizations both in the *K2* compiler and in the runtime system. For instance, it is possible for some process systems (or subsystems) to prove that the capacities of the streams, if chosen large enough, will never be exceeded due to tighter synchronic distances enforced by other means between producing and consumer processes, The flow control mechanism can in these cases be disabled, eliminating one possible cause for considerable overhead.

Another source of substantial overhead is the barrier synchronization that controls entry and exit of tokens into (from) hierarchical processes. This synchronization may be eliminated if there is, apart from processes that handle initialization and termination, just one internal process each that repeatedly receives tokens directly from the input barrier or delivers tokens directly to the output barrier. In such cases, synchronization can be directly handled by the respective internal processes. Removing this superfluous barrier synchronization constitutes the single most important optimization for recursively expandable process structures. As in the case of the `relaxd` program, they all feature a single input process and a single output process (with more or less complex process networks in between) through which they interface with the incoming and outgoing streams of the hierarchically higher process (of which they are the recursive refinements) along which tokens are repeatedly communicated as the computation proceeds.

These and some other compiler optimizations will be included in an upgraded version of the *K2* implementation. This version will also support, as a means for high-level debugging, stepwise execution of process systems under user control and inspection of intermediate system states in intelligible form. To this end, the compiler is already equipped to generate code whose execution can be halted (and resumed later on) at well-chosen break points corresponding to completed executions of process instances. What remains to be done is to integrate into the editor the means to re-translate intermediate system states reached at these break points into graphical net representations as shown in Fig. 1, with tokens appropriately distributed over the streams.

Another important system extension will be an analysis tool to verify that the process systems to be designed satisfy certain structural invariance properties which are essential for a stable and orderly dynamic behavior. The idea is to do this verification in incremental steps as the system design grows: very much like a syntax-oriented editor, the tool checks for every process or subsystem added whether or not one of these invariance properties is violated and, if so, rejects the add-on immediately and identifies the cause of the problem. This analysis tool, in conjunction with high-level debugging by stepwise execution, is expected to enhance the design of correct concurrent programs considerably.

Though *K2* currently interfaces just with C as the computation language, the upgraded version will also support $\mathcal{K}i\mathcal{R}$, a syntactically sugared version of a full-fledged applied λ-calculus [14] as the primary choice for a functional language.

References

1. C. Aßmann. A Language for Concurrent Processing based on Petri Nets. In D. Tavangarian, editor, *Architektur von Rechensystemen*, pages 221–230, 1997. 14. GI/ITG Fachtagung (ARCS'97).
2. C. Aßmann. Coordinating Functional Processes Using Petri Nets. In W. Kluge, editor, *Proc. 8th. International Workshop on the Implementation of Functional Languages*, Bad Godesberg, Germany, September 1996, volume 1268 of *LNCS*, pages 162–183. Springer-Verlag, 1997.
3. C. Aßmann and J. Lukoschus. Implementation of a Coordination Language. In H.R. Arabnia, editor, *Proc. 1998 International Conference on Parallel and Distributed Processing Techniques and Applications (PDPTA'98)*, volume I, pages 175–182, 1998.
4. A. Beguelin and V. Sunderam. Tools for Monitoring, Debugging, and Programming in PVM. In Arndt Bode, editor, *Parallel virtual machine, EuroPVM '96, Munich, Germany, October 7–9*, volume 1156 of *LNCS*, pages 7–13. Springer-Verlag, 1996.
5. S. Breitinger, R. Loogen, Y. Ortega-Mallén, and R. Peña. Eden — Language Definition and Operational Semantics. Technical report, Universität Marburg, FB Mathematik, 1998. Bericht 96-10, Reihe Informatik, revised version, April 7.
6. N. Carriero and D. Gelernter. *How to Write Parallel Programs: A First Course.* MIT Press, Cambridge, MA, 1990.

7. S. Cox, S.-Y. Huang, P.H.J. Kelly, J. Liu, and F. Taylor. Program Transformations for Static Process Networks. *ACM SIGPLAN Notices*, January 1993.

8. J. Darlington, A.J. Field, P.G. Harrison, et al. Parallel Programming using Skeleton Functions. In A. Bode, M. Reeve, and G. Wolf, editors, *Proc. PARLE '93 — Parallel Architectures and Languages Europe*, volume 694 of *LNCS*, pages 146–160, Eindhoven, The Netherlands, Spinger-Verlag, June 1991.

9. A. Geist, A. Beguelin, J. Dongarra, W. Jiang, R. Manchek, and V. S. Sunderam. *PVM: Parallel Virtual Machine A Users' Guide and Tutorial for Network Parallel Computing*. Scientific and Engineering Computation Series. MIT Press, Cambridge, MA, 1994.

10. H.J. Genrich, K. Lautenbach, and P.S. Thiagarjan. Elements of General Net Theory. In *Net Theory and Applications*, volume 84 of *LNCS*, pages 21–163. Springer-Verlag, 1980.

11. K. Jensen. How to Find Invariants for Coloured Petri Nets. In 10th. Symposium on Mathematical Foundations of Computer Science, volume 118 of *LNCS*, pages 327–338, Springer-Verlag, 1981.

12. K. Jensen. Coloured Petri Nets: A High Level Language for System Design and Analysis. In G. Rozenberg, editor, *Advances in Petri Nets 1990*, volume 483 of *LNCS*, pages 342–416, Springer-Verlag, 1991.

13. K. Jensen. *Coloured Petri Nets: Basic Concepts, Analysis Methods and Practical Use*, volume 1 of *Monographs on Theoretical Computer Science*. Springer-Verlag, 1992.

14. W.E. Kluge. A User's Guide for the Reduction System π-RED. Technical Report 9409, Institut für Informatik und praktische Mathematik, Universität Kiel, 1994.

15. M.C.J.D. van Eekelen and M.J. Plasmeijer. *Functional Programming and Parallel Graph Rewriting*, Addison-Wesley, 1993.

16. P.W. Trinder, K. Hammond, H.-W. Loidl, and S.L. Peyton Jones. Algorithm + Strategy = Parallelism. *Journal of Functional Programming*, 8(1):23–60, January 1998.

An Interactive Approach to
Profiling Parallel Functional Programs

Nathan Charles and Colin Runciman

Department of Computer Science, University of York
Heslington, York, YO10 5DD, UK
{Nathan.Charles,Colin.Runciman}@cs.york.ac.uk

Abstract. The full details of a parallel computation can be very complex. To understand and improve performance one useful resource is a log-file recording all the computational events that change the number or status of parallel tasks. Raw log-files are not easy reading for the programmer, so profiling tools present only graphical summary charts. These charts sometimes show just what the programmer needs to know, but they often become too crowded, or fail to show enough, or both. Moreover, the charts are static so the programmer has little control over what is displayed. In this paper we discuss a tool that combines the advantages of graphical representation of computations with a query interface. The programmer interactively extracts specific information about the computation. Results of queries can be displayed in a graphical form; and parameters of subsequent queries can be specified by pointing within a past display.

1 Introduction

It is often claimed that as functional languages are referentially transparent they are suitable for programming parallel computers. However, writing a parallel functional program is not straightforward. Modern compilation and run-time systems [25] handle many of the complex issues, such as task scheduling, automatically. But the programmer still has to annotate their program to specify *what* to evaluate in parallel. Effective placement of these annotations is not a simple task. Addition or removal of an annotation can significantly affect the performance of a program.

Profiling tools are available to help detect bad parallel programs [10, 11, 13, 23]. The aim of these tools is to provide a bridge between the high-level view held by the programmer and the low-level details of the parallel computation. Tools typically produce two forms of output which can help to understand the computation: a *log-file* from which are derived *static graphs* depicting the computation. The log-file can be thousands of lines long, much too large for the programmer to trace through. The static charts often display too little information for the programmer to understand their program. Yet even so, for large computations the graphs are too crowded. If the information needed to confirm some hypothesis is not displayed on any of the graphs, the programmer may have to resort to tedious analysis of the log-file.

H. Hammond, T. Davie, and C. Clack (Eds.): IFL'98, LNCS 1595, pp. 20–37, 1999.

In response to the current situation we have implemented a prototype tool that allows the user to analyse the events of a parallel functional computation in a structured way, using a query language linked to a graphical display. Sect. 2 introduces the current prototype tool by analysing a simple example. Section 3 summarises the implementation of the tool. Sect. 4 discusses the problems we have met, and possible solutions to them.

2   Interactive Parallel Profiling

2.1   An Example

Fig. 1 shows a parallel Haskell program based on an example from [1]. The program calculates the sum of the results of applying a naïvely defined Euler totient function to the numbers from one to a hundred. The program introduces parallelism using the **par** and **seq** combinators [22]. The **par** combinator evaluates its first argument in parallel with its second argument and returns the result of the second argument. The **seq** combinator, used to control the order expressions are evaluated, evaluates its first argument, and then its second argument, returning the evaluation of the second argument as its result. We have introduced parallelism in two places within the program:

1. the **sumEuler** function applies **parList**, a function that evaluates all the members of a list in parallel, to the list [**euler 1, ..., euler n**];
2. the **euler** function evaluates the spine of the list of relative primes in parallel with the calculation of the result.

2.2   GranSim Graphs

Our tool works with log-files generated by GranSim [10, 15], a highly configurable parallel simulator built on top of the Glasgow Haskell compiler. A program, when compiled for GranSim, generates a log-file during its execution. This log-file records various events in each task's life-time, such as when it is running, runnable, blocked and fetching. We chose GranSim as it is the most developed parallel profiling system for the standard lazy functional language Haskell [19].

When the **sumEuler** example is run, on a simulated 32 processor distributed memory machine with fairly low latency, GranSim generates a log-file and reports a run-time of 281954 cycles. This figure alone is fairly meaningless. Traditionally the log-file is processed using the tools that accompany GranSim to produce two PostScript charts; an *activity graph* and a *per-thread graph*.

Our tool can display similar graphs but in an X-Window as illustrated in Fig. 2 and 3. The activity graph is a useful summary of the overall level of parallel activity throughout the computation. The per-thread graph provides extra information such as how long threads last and how often they block. Unfortunately, when there are many threads things become crowded. Our tool provides a partial solution to this problem by allowing the user to scale the width and height so that the threads can be seen in more detail. Sect. 2.6 describes a better solution.

```
main = (print . show . sumEuler) 100

sumEuler :: Int -> Int
sumEuler n
  = let eulerList = map euler [1..n]
    in seq (parList eulerList) (sum eulerList)

euler :: Int -> Int
euler n
  = let relPrimes = filter (relprime n) [1..(n-1)]
    in par (spine relPrimes) (length relPrimes)

parList :: [a] -> ()
parList = foldr par ()

spine :: [a] -> ()
spine []     = ()
spine (_:xs) = spine xs

hcf :: Int -> Int -> Int
hcf x 0 = x
hcf x y = hcf y (rem x y)

relprime :: Int -> Int -> Bool
relprime x y = (hcf x y==1)
```

Fig. 1. The sumEuler program

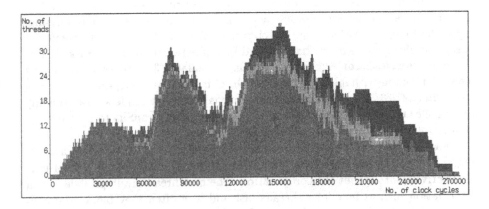

Fig. 2. Activity graph for Version 1 of the program. The bands from bottom to top represent the number of running, runnable, fetching, and blocked threads.

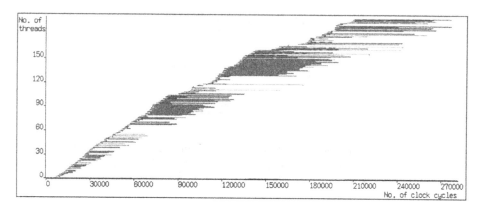

Fig. 3. Per-thread graph for Version 1 of the program. The lifetime of each thread is represented by a horizontal line, shaded grey when the thread is running, light-grey when it is runnable and black when it is blocked.

2.3   Using Queries to Extract Information

The activity graph for **sumEuler** shows that not all the processors are being used during the whole computation. To find out why we begin our investigation by asking how much parallelism each **par**-site generated. This simple question is hard to answer using current tools: the programmer has to search through the log-file, which in this case is 2876 lines long! Our tool provides a structured way to ask such questions using SQL[1] [18] queries. The relational tables and underlying model on which the queries are based are briefly described in Sect. 3. To ask one interpretation of the question *How much parallelism did each **par**-site generate?* the programmer enters the following query:

```
SELECT   Spark.Par_Site, AVG(Activity.End_Time-Activity.Start_Time)
FROM     Activity, Spark, Thread, Run
WHERE    Spark.Spark_Id = Thread.Was_Spark
         AND Thread.Thread_Id = Activity.Undertake_for
         AND Activity.Activity_No = Run.Activity_No

GROUP BY Spark.Par_Site
ORDER BY
```

In plain English: *What is the average length of time of all the running periods, for threads created by each **par**-site?* The answer is shown in Fig. 4.

The **par**-site inside the **euler** function generates smaller threads than the other **par**-site and main thread. The cost of creating a thread, and controlling communication can be high. Where a thread does not perform much evaluation, the costs can outweigh the benefit of parallelism. To test whether this is the case in this example we remove the **par**-site within the **euler** function.

---

[1] We do not impose a restriction on the SQL queries that can be expressed apart from those inherited from the database system we use.

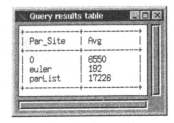

Fig. 4. Average run-time for each **par**-site. The left column contains the **par**-site names: 0 is the main thread; **euler** refers to the **par**-site inside the **euler** function, and similarly for **parList**. The right column shows average length of running periods for each **par**-site.

```
euler :: Int -> Int
euler n = length (filter (relprime n) [1..(n-1)])
```

Call this Version 2 of the program. Using GranSim with the same set up as the previous run, the run-time drops by more than 30% to 182791 cycles; so the **par** inside the **euler** function was a wasteful.

2.4 Using Graphs to Extract Information

Fig. 5 shows the Per-Thread graph for Version 2 of the program. The dominant solid grey shading re-assures us that the threads spend most of their time running. Life-times of the threads increase over time. This means at the beginning of the execution all the processors were *hungry* for tasks, most of which resulted in little computation. Might it be better if some of the larger tasks were created at the beginning of the execution, so that the processors' idleness is distributed across the computation? One way to do this is to reverse the order of the list of **euler** function applications. In Version 3 of the program **sumEuler** is defined accordingly:

```
sumEuler :: Int -> Int
sumEuler n = let eulerList = map euler [n,n-1..1]
             in seq (parList eulerList) (sum eulerList)
```

The reader may wonder *why* creating larger tasks at the beginning and small tasks at the end could be an improvement. The simplest way to understand this is to look at a mini per-thread graph. If we assume that a program creates four tasks, lasting 1, 1.5, 2, and 2.5 ticks respectively, and the main thread takes 0.5 ticks to evaluate the expressions that create the parallelism, then we would get per-thread graphs (omitting the main thread) resembling those in Fig. 6.

Running Version 3 of the program results in a run-time of 158497: 15% faster than Version 2, and 45% faster than Version 1. This part of the analysis has not used any novel feature of our tool. But it serves to illustrate the usefulness of supporting the traditional graphs in connection with the query interface.

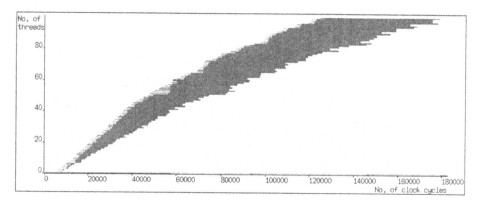

Fig. 5. Per-thread graph for Version 2 of the program.

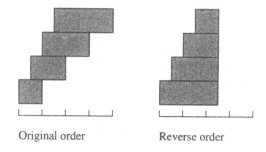

Original order   Reverse order

Fig. 6. Mini per-thread graphs showing short euler applications evaluated first (left) and longer euler applications evaluated first (right).

2.5   Using Graphs to Compose Queries

Fig. 7 shows the Activity graph for Version 3 of the program. During the first quarter of the computation the level of parallelism rises steadily. However, in the period after this there is a drop in parallelism, followed by a pick up in parallelism, and another peak and trough.

So, why do we get the two drops in the level of parallelism? The graph in Fig. 8 is the per-thread graph for the same run. To work out why we get the tidal effect we use an important feature of our tool: the ability to *click on regions of the graph help fill in a query*. The user can click on any part of any bar in a per-thread graph to generate an *activity reference* that is sent to the query editor (see Sect. 3 for details of the data model).

Fig. 8 shows us that there are no *runnable threads* during the drop in parallelism, but we do not know whether there are any *unevaluated sparks*[2] waiting to be evaluated, and if so, on what processors these sparks lie. To answer this question we *click* on the end of one of the threads on the graph at a point where

---

[2] When a **par** application is evaluated a *spark* is created to evaluate an expression in parallel. When this evaluation begins, the spark is turned into a *thread*.

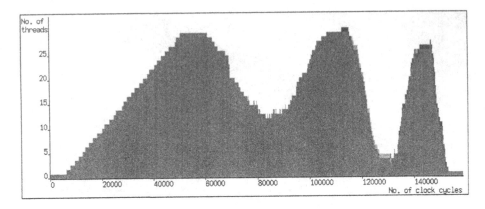

Fig. 7. Activity graph for Version 3 of the program.

the level of parallelism is low. This sends a reference of this point to the Query editor (shown in Fig. 8 as the highlighted 72). We fill in the rest of the query to ask how many sparks lie on the different processors, at the point we clicked. Submitting this query returns the table:

```
+--------------+--------------+
| Processor    | Count        |
+--------------+--------------+
| 0            | 25           |
+--------------+--------------+
```

There are 25 sparks but they all lie on processor 0. Clicking on other areas with low parallelism results in much the same table being produced. This information holds the key to understanding what is happening: one reason for the drop in parallelism is because all the threads terminate at approximately the same time. This would cause no problems if each of the idle processors had some *sparks* waiting to be evaluated, but because all the parallelism is *sparked* by the main thread, all the sparks lie on the processor evaluating the main thread. It takes time for each of the processors to obtain more work. As soon as each of the processors import a spark the level of parallelism picks up again.

Had there been no limit on the number of processors, the peak and trough effect would not have emerged. The activity graph for an unlimited processor machine would be approximately the same as the activity graph for a 32 processor machine with the peaks stacked on top of each other. This would make the per-thread graph look similar to the right-hand mini per-thread graph in Fig. 6.

We have shown that the lack of parallelism in some regions of the graph is due to the lack of distribution of sparks across the processors. We leave as an exercise to the reader to work out how to distribute the sparks more effectively.

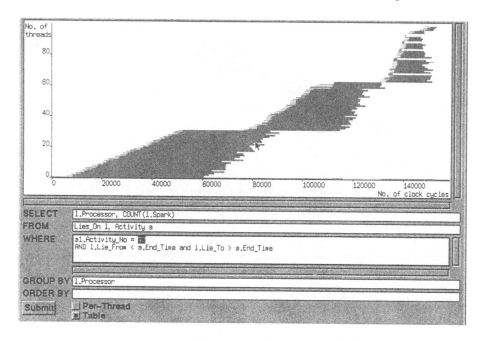

Fig. 8. A query about Version 3: how many sparks lie on each processor at the point where the user clicks?

2.6   Using Queries to Generate Graphs

The final, and probably most important, feature of the current prototype of our tool is the ability to select what information is displayed in a graph using a query. Selective display is useful, because a display of the full graph is too crowded. As a simple example consider the very first question we asked at the beginning of this paper: *How much parallelism does each **par**-site generate?*. In Sect. 2.3 we answered this question using a query, and the result was displayed in a table. An alternative way to answer this question is to filter the information so that only the data for selected **par**-sites is displayed. Fig. 9 shows the per-thread graph for only threads created by **par**-site **parList**. A simple query (shown in the query editing box) was used to filter the information displayed. A similar query can be used to display only the threads created by **par**-site **euler**, for which the threads are considerably shorter.

Of course it is not reasonable to enter *any* query and expect a graphical result, so we limit the type of queries that can be displayed. Currently we do this by *locking* the **SELECT**, **GROUP BY**, and **ORDER BY** fields so that the user only has control over the filtering **WHERE** clause. Even with such a restricted class of queries, it is possible to create a highly complex filter. For example, we could choose to display only those threads that were created by processor 0 by **parList**, lasted longer than the average thread, and never blocked.

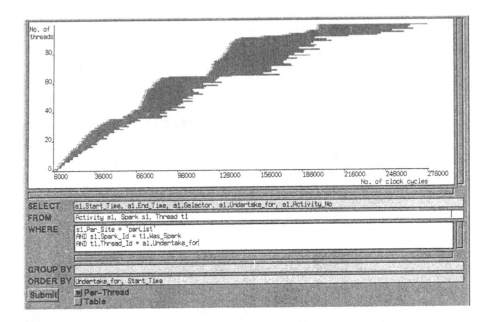

Fig. 9. Per-Thread graph for Version 1 of the program, filtered to display only threads created by **par**-site **parList**.

If we combine the ability to click on graphs to help compose queries with the ability to generate graphs from queries, we are able to *dynamically* change a graph, circumventing one of the major weaknesses of current tools that use *static* graphs.

3   Implementation

Fig. 10 shows the five main components of our tool.

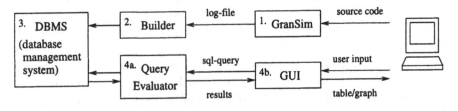

Fig. 10. Structure of the tool.

GranSim As we said in the previous section, GranSim [10, 15, 16] is a parallel simulator. We use GranSim to compile and run our parallel programs to produce a log-file.

Builder The Builder takes a GranSim-generated log-file and processes it to produce relational tables. These relational tables are derived from the entity-relationship [5] diagram in Fig. 11. A brief description of the entity-relationship diagram follows, with an example query. We describe the development of this data model and the importance of data modelling for profiling tools elsewhere [4].

In Fig. 11 the boxes represent entities, the connecting arcs relationships, and the bullets attributes of entities. The diagram can be summarised: a *thread* has many activities which take place on different *processors*; during a single *activity* period a thread may *run* and create sparks, *block* on a piece of graph being evaluated by another thread, *queue* in a runnable state, *migrate* to another processor, or *fetch* a section of graph from another processor; and before a *spark* is turned into a thread it may *lie-on* different processors.

The diagram can be used as a template to compose queries. For example, to ask *Which thread* t1 *created thread* t2? we use the following path through the entity-relationship diagram:

$$
\begin{array}{l}
\text{t2 = THREAD(thread\_id)} \xrightarrow{\text{was\_spark}} \text{SPARK(spark\_id)} \xrightarrow{\text{sparked\_by}} \\[2mm]
\text{RUN(activity\_no)} \xrightarrow{\text{activity}} \text{ACTIVITY(activity\_no)} \xrightarrow{\text{undertake\_for}} \\[2mm]
\text{THREAD(thread\_id) = t1}
\end{array}
$$

We apply standard transformations [26] to the entity relationship diagram to generate the format for the relational tables. In general, each of the entities becomes a table, and its attributes, and connecting arcs become fields. For example, the Thread table has the following fields: *Thread_Id*, *Created_At*, *Ends_At*, and *Was_Spark*. There are five main tables (Spark, Thread, Activity, Lie-On and Processor) and five tables for the entities that are subtypes of ACTIVITY (Run, Migrate, Queue, Fetch, and Block)[3]. The TIME entity is replaced by attributes of each of the other entities to which it is related. It is easy to translate a query written using the entity relationship diagram into a query over the relational tables. For example, using SQL as the relational query language the above query *Which thread* t1 *created thread* t2? is written as:

```
SELECT t1.Thread_Id
FROM Thread t1, Thread t2, Spark, Run, Activity
WHERE t2.Was_Spark = Spark.Spark_Id
  AND Spark.Sparked_By = Run.Activity_No
  AND Run.Activity_No = Activity.Activity_No
  AND Activity.Undertake_for = t1.Thread_Id
```

---

[3] It is also necessary to have an extra table Pruned, as there is no simpler way to translate an either-or relationship into relation tables.

In Sect. 2.6 we said that when the user clicks on a graph an activity reference is sent to the query editor. Such a reference is an *Activity_No* (an attribute of the Activity table). It can be used to form queries about individual activities (say, their start and end times), and also about other entities (such as threads and processors) that are associated with the activity.

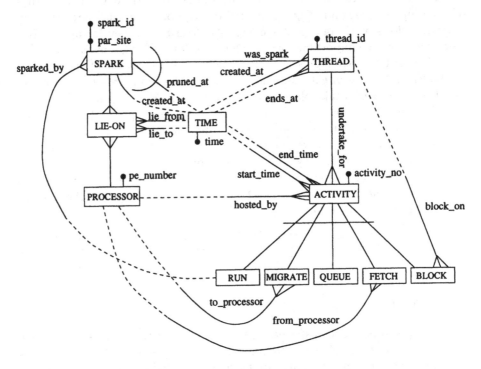

Fig. 11. The data model used by our tool.

Building the relational tables: To build the relational tables there are four phases. All but the first are implemented in Haskell.

1. *Remove redundant data and sort* – GranSim log-files are quite verbose and contain a lot of redundant data. We use the UNIX utilities **awk** and **sort** to provide quick removal of redundant data and to sort the file.
2. *Parse the log-file.*
3. *Create relational tables* from the parse tree.
4. *Submit tables to the database engine* using the GreenCard pre-processor [20] to generate the routines that communicate with the database server.

DBMS We could have written our own query retrieval system. However, to save on production time we decided to use a popular database server and client.

This has the advantage that file storage and implementing clever algorithms to retrieve the data efficiently, is left to the database server.

The builder and query evaluator (both Haskell applications) communicate with the database server using a C API and GreenCard 2 [20] – a foreign language interface pre-processor. We use PostgreSQL [28], a freely distributable relational database system supporting a fairly large subset of SQL, as the database server. Originally we used the Mini-SQL database engine but bugs effectively prevented any use of indexes. One thing that surprised us was the ease of converting from one database server to another. Despite our tool being designed around the C API that accompanies Mini-SQL it took no more than a couple of hours to change it over to use PostgreSQL. One reason for this was because of the similarities in the C API's between both database servers. However, the main reason we managed to convert with relative ease was because of how well the GreenCard functions integrate into Haskell. Changes to the C API meant little or no changes to the Haskell code, and only moderate changes to the GreenCard sources.

Query Evaluator The query evaluator exchanges messages between the GUI and the database server[4]. It communicates with the GUI using socket streams, implemented using GreenCard [20], and with the database server using PostgreSQL's C API and GreenCard.

In general we have found GreenCard to be very suitable for interfacing with the database server. It was useful to get Haskell to garbage collect C data structures automatically, and convenient that side-effect free C functions could be treated as pure functions in Haskell. For example, consider the function getValue:

```
%fun getValue :: PG_Result_Ptr -> Int -> Int -> String
%call (pg_Result_Ptr x) (int col) (int row)
%code res = PQgetvalue(x,col,row);
%result (string res)
```

This function takes a pointer to a database result table, a column and row number, and returns the value at that position by calling the C function PQgetvalue. To return the whole table we can use the function getTable:

```
getTable :: PG_Result_Ptr -> [[String]]
getTable ptr = map fetchRow [1..(numRows ptr)]
    where
    fetchRow n = map (getValue ptr n) [1..(numFields ptr)]
```

As getValue is a pure function (because PQgetvalue is side-effect free) the result of getValue is only translated in Haskell on demand. So given an expression such as (getTable ptr !! 3), that returns the fourth row of the table, only

---

[4] If HBC (the compiler used for the GUI) had a GreenCard pre-processor, then this part of the system would not have been required as the GUI could have communicated directly with the C API.

the entries in the fourth row are translated into Haskell. As some tables returned from SQL queries are very large, this can save a lot of time and space.

One problem we found with GreenCard (and as far as we know it is present in other foreign language interfaces to Haskell [6]) is that there is no standard way to access Haskell file handles within C across different Haskell implementations. So there is no portable way to read/write a file opened in C using the standard Haskell `readFile` and `writeFile` routines.

GUI We shall first give an overview of how the GUI is implemented. Then, for the reader with experience using the Fudget library, we outline a problem we found writing our program using Fudgets and a possible solution to this problem.

Implementation overview: We wanted to implement as much of our tool in Haskell as possible, including the GUI. We chose to use the Fudget Library [7] because it was both a purely functional solution and had previously been used to write substantial applications, such as a web browser [3].

Fudgets are stream processors with a high-level and low-level stream. The low-level stream is connected to the I/O system and is usually transparent to the programmer. Fudgets communicate by sending and receiving messages along high-level streams connected by the programmer.

The GUI is implemented as a parallel composition of fudgets wrapped in a loop (so that the fudgets can communicate with each other):

```
mainF = loopRightThroughF handler $
              graphOutputF >+<    -- Display graphs
              graphInputF  >+<    -- Handle input from query evaluator
              sqlEditorF   >+<    -- SQL editing box
              statusF      >+<    -- Status bar
              buttonsF     >+<    -- Request buttons
              ...
```

When the user clicks on a button to evaluate a query `buttonsF` handles the request, passing an appropriate message to `graphInputF` that sends a request to the query evaluator. When the query evaluator returns the result it is passed to `graphOutputF` for display as a graph/table.

Communication between fudgets: In a parallel composition of two fudgets (e.g. `fud1F >+< fud2F`) an incoming message is sent to the appropriate Fudget by tagging the message with `Left` or `Right`. As anyone who has written a program using Fudgets will know, when there are several fudgets in a parallel composition the tags become long and can be confusing to program. For example, to send a message to `sqlEditorF` above, the tag `Right . Right . Left` is used. As our program increased in size, arranging communication between fudgets became tricky. After we discussed this problem with Thomas Hallgren, he wrote a new fudget to arrange communication between n fudgets using n one-level tags.

Fudgets are composed in parallel with a new combinator >&<. This combinator extends the standard parallel combinator >+<: in addition to the composite fudget itself it returns a dictionary of one-level tags that can be used to communicate with the component fudgets directly. For example:

```
TagF combF insideH
  (toGraphOutputF  :&: toGraphInputF  :&: toSqlEditorF  :&: ...)
  = tagGraphOutputF >&< tagGraphInputF >&< tagSqlEditorF >&< ...
```

In this definition the `TagF` structure has three components: the composed fudget `combF`; `insideH`, which is required but whose role is not of concern to us; and a dictionary of message tags (`toGraphOutputF :&: toGraphInputF :&: ...`) whose structure matches the parallel composition on the right-hand side. Now to send a message to `sqlEditorF` the one-level tag `toSqlEditorF` is used. Using this new fudget increased the speed of development and made our code much more understandable.

4 Current Problems and Bottlenecks

Speed: One of the first questions potential users may ask is *How fast is it?*, especially as the tool is written in Haskell. One of the aims of the tool is to speed up the development of parallel programs. If the tool was considerably slower than current tools then we might not achieve this objective. Table 1 gives the time in seconds taken to compile, run, process, and display both the activity graph and the per-thread graph for the example in this paper (1) using the tools that accompany GranSim[5] and (2) using our tool. Each time is a minimum over three runs[6]. Each experiment was performed on a 270 MHz Sun Ultra 5 Server, 192MB of RAM, GUI running with 25MB heap, Query evaluator with 500KB heap.

The table shows that the main increase in time using our tool is the time taken to process the data to build the database. It turns out that most of this time is spent creating the indexes. In the current version of the database indexes are created on *every* primary key for every table. Some of these tables are used rarely. We plan to look carefully at what indexes are useful. However, even with the indexes as they are, the time taken to process the data is not necessarily longer using our new tool. Table 1 only shows the times taken to process the data for two graphs. Our tool processes the data *only once*. Other tools need to process the data *every time* a new graph or view of a graph is required. So, a more realistic estimate of the time taken to process the data for this example is $(q \times 12.3)/2$ seconds, where q is the number of queries. The time taken to process the data using our tool is constant, 31.0 seconds. If more than five queries are required then for this example our tool will be faster.

---

[5] David King has written faster versions of these tools in C rather than Perl and Bash, but our measurements are against the standard tools.

[6] It was necessary to measure the *real* times rather than the *user* and *system* times because otherwise any work performed by the database server would not have been accounted.

Method	Compile	Run	Process data	Run browser	Display graphs	Total
Current	21.8	1.0	12.3 (Create PostScript graphs)	1.0 (Ghostview)	6.0	41.8
New Tool	21.8	1.0	31.0 (Build database)	7.0 (GUI)	7.1	67.9

Table 1. Time (in seconds) taken to compile, run, and display both the Activity graph and Per-Thread graph using GranSim's tools and our tool.

Space usage: One problem we have found with the GUI part of the tool is that it is sometimes necessary to allocate a very large heap. The main reason is that some of our code is too strict. We aim to make future versions more lazy.

Composing queries: Writing SQL queries can be laborious. One solution to this problem is to extend the query editor so that common queries are quicker to write. Another is to use a more concise functional query language (e.g. [17]), translated automatically into SQL.

Recording information: The current version of GranSim does not record information such as the relation between threads blocking on a closure, and the thread that evaluates that closure. This restricts the class of data models that can be used as a basis for the relational tables. In [4] we highlight some inconsistencies with the implicit data models used by current tools.

5   Summary and Conclusions

We have described a prototype tool for profiling parallel programs. It has the advantage over current tools that it is possible *both* to view high-level graphical views of a computation *and* to pose queries over lower-level information in a structured way. With current tools the only link between the log-file and the graphs is a hidden translation. Our tool allows the programmer to click on the graphs to fill in parts of query, and to use queries to control and filter the information that is displayed.

An initial version of our tool was purely text-based and only allowed the user to enter SQL queries and view the answers in a table. This was almost unusable: one did not know where to start. Even with the PostScript graphs at hand we still found it difficult to use. It was not until we linked together both the query evaluator and the graphical charts that we were able to use the tool effectively.

Although we have had little experience using our tool, the small examples we have worked with so far have been encouraging. We have had success in understanding them and making them run faster. Clearly, having a query language to retrieve information is going to be a lot more productive than searching through the log-file manually. However, with the examples we have analysed, the main strength identified is the ability to *interact* with the graphs both to compose queries and to filter the information displayed in graphs.

The main disadvantage of our tool over current tools is that it takes longer to process the log-file and view the charts. However, when the programmer needs more information than standard charts provide the query interface is significantly faster than searching through the log-file. In the end the time taken to write a good parallel program should be less than using conventional tools.

We have also found that it is possible to implement profiling tools largely *within* a lazy functional language. Most other profiling tools written *for* functional languages are implemented *in* other languages. Development in Haskell had its disadvantages, such as the extra demand on resources. However, it would have taken a lot longer to develop the tool in a conventional procedural language.

5.1   Related Work

The most similar work to ours is that of Lei et al. [14]. They have implemented a performance tuning tool for message-passing parallel programs. As with our tool they use a database query system. The data model they use is at a lower-level than ours, and is designed mainly to extract communication and synchronisation costs. The results of a query can be displayed in either tables or graphical visualisations. However, one of the most important features of our tool, the ability to interact with the graphs to help fill in the queries, is not implemented in their tool. One interesting feature of their tool is the incorporation of a 3-D spreadsheet to analyse data between program runs. For example, it is possible use the 3-D spreadsheet package to compare the run-times for different program runs and display them in a bar chart.

Halstead's Vista system [8] (based on an earlier system called Pablo [21]) provides a generic browser that can be used to analyse different types of performance data. In particular, Halstead has used Vista to analyse parallel symbolic programs [9]. Vista presents the programmer with different views of the parallel execution which resemble the activity and per-thread graphs generated by our tool. The programmer can interact with the graphs, to choose what information to display, and how to display it. Vista provides a wide range of options to filter the information displayed but does not allow the complex filtering of data that our query interface provides.

Our tool currently uses the **par**-site as a reference to the source-code. Two independent projects are working on extending GranSim to record alternative source-code references. Hammond et al. [11] have extended GranSim with the *cost-centre* mechanism. King et al. [13] have developed a profiler for programs that introduce parallelism using *evaluation strategies* [24]. It should not take much work to adapt our tool to handle the alternative source-code references and display the adapted graphical views used by these two tools.

5.2 Future Work

The current prototype of our tool only allows the programmer to click on the per-thread graph to help compose queries. We plan to extend this so that other graphs can also be used.

We have tried to make the tool as generic as possible. It should not be too difficult to extend the tool to handle data from heap profiling and time profiling. The advent of standard log-files [12] would promote this development.

Writing SQL queries can be a chore. We plan to implement a more functional query language on top of SQL. One way to do this would be to use something similar to list comprehensions [2].

Acknowledgements

Our thanks go to Thomas Hallgren for his help with the more tricky aspects of Fudget programming, and quick response to the occasional bug report. We also thank Malcolm Wallace for guidance on GreenCard and nhc.

References

1. L. Augustsson and T. Johnsson. Parallel Graph Reduction with the $\langle \nu, G \rangle$-machine. In *Proc. 1989 ACM Conference on Functional Programming Languages and Computer Architecture (FPLCA '89)*, pages 202–212, 1989.
2. P. Buneman, L. Libkin, V. Tannen, and L. Wong. Comprehension Syntax. *SIGMOD Record*, 23(1), 1994.
3. M. Carlsson and T. Hallgren. *Fudgets – Purely Functional Processes with Applications to Graphical User Interfaces*. PhD thesis, Department of Computer Science, Chalmers University of Technology, Sweden, 1998.
4. N. Charles and C. Runciman. Performance Monitoring. In *Research Directions in Parallel Functional Programming*. Springer-Verlag, 1999. In preparation.
5. P. P. Chen. The Entity-Relationship Model: Towards a Unified View of Data. *IEEE Transactions on Data Base Systems*, 1(1), 1976.
6. S. Finne, D. Leigen, E. Meijer, and S Peyton Jones. H/Direct: A Binary Foreign Language Interface for Haskell. In *Proc. 3rd. International Conference on Functional Programming (ICFP '98)*, pages 153–162. ACM Press, 1998.
7. T. Hallgren and M. Carlsson. Programming with Fudgets. In *Advanced Functional Programming, 1st. International School on Functional Programming Techniques, Båstad, Sweden*, volume 925 of *LNCS*, pages 137–182. Springer-Verlag, 1995.
8. R. Halstead. Self-Describing Files + Smart Modules = Parallel Program Visualization. In *Theory and Practice of Parallel Programming*, volume 907 of *LNCS*. Springer-Verlag, 1994.
9. R. Halstead. Understanding the Performance of Parallel Symbolic Programs. In *Parallel Symbolic Languages and Systems (Workshop Proceedings)*, volume 1068 of *LNCS*. Springer-Verlag, 1996.
10. K. Hammond, H-W. Loidl, and A. Partridge. Visualising Granularity in Parallel Programs: A Graphical Winnowing System for Haskell. In A.P.W. Bohm and J.T. Feo, editors, *Proc. HPFC'95 – High Performance Functional Computing*, pages 208–221, 1995.

11. K. Hammond, H-W. Loidl, and P. Trinder. Parallel Cost Centre Profiling. In *Proc. 1997 Glasgow Workshop on Functional Programming*, 1997.
12. S. Jarvis, S. Marlow, S Peyton Jones, and E. Wilcox.   Standardising Compiler/Profiler Log Files. In K. Hammond, A.J.T. Davie, and C. Clack, editors, *Draft Proc. 10th International Workshop on the Implementation of Functional Languages (IFL '98)*, London, England, pages 429–446, September 1998.
13. D. King, J. Hall, and P. Trinder. A Strategic Profiler for Glasgow Parallel Haskell. In *This Proceedings*, 1998.
14. S. Lei, K. Zang, and K.-C. Li. Experience with the Design of a Performance Tuning Tool for Parallel Programs. *Journal of Systems Software*, 39(1):27–37, 1997.
15. H-W. Loidl. *GranSim User's Guide*, 1996.
    http://www.dcs.glasgow.ac.uk/fp/software/gransim/.
16. H-W. Loidl. *Granularity in Large Scale Parallel Functional Programs*. PhD thesis, Department of Computer Science, University of Glasgow, 1998.
17. R. Nikhil. *An Incremental, Strongly-Typed, Database Query Language*. PhD thesis, University of Pennsylvania, 1984.
18. Oracle Corporation, Belmont, California, USA. *SQL Language, Reference Manual, Version 6.0*, 1990.
19. J. C. Peterson, K. Hammond, L. Augustsson, B. Boutel, F. W. Burton, J. Fasel, A. D. Gordon, R. J. M. Hughes, P. Hudak, T. Johnsson, M. P. Jones, E. Meijer, S. L. Peyton Jones, A. Reid, and P. L. Wadler. *Report on the Non-Strict Functional Language, Haskell, Version 1.4*, Yale University, 1997. Available at http://haskell.org.
20. S. L. Peyton Jones, T. Nordin, and A. Reid.   Green Card: a Foreign-Language Interface for Haskell. In *Proc. of 2nd. Haskell Workshop, Amsterdam, 1997*. Oregon Graduate Institute, 1997.
    http://www.dcs.gla.ac.uk/fp/software/green-card/.
21. D. Reed, R. Aydt, T. Madhyastha, R. Noe, K. Shields, and B. Schwartz. Scalable Performance Environments for Parallel Systems. In *6th. Distributed Memory Computing Conference (IEEE)*, 1991.
22. P. Roe. *Parallel Programming using Functional Languages*. PhD thesis, Glasgow University, UK, 1991.
23. C. Runciman and D. Wakeling. Profiling Parallel Functional Computations (Without Parallel Machines). In *Proc. 1993 Glasgow Workshop on Functional Programming*, pages 236–251. Springer-Verlag, 1993.
24. P. Trinder, K. Hammond, H.-W. Loidl, and S. L. Peyton Jones.   Algorithm + Strategy = Parallelism. *Journal of Functional Programming*, 8(1):23–60, 1998.
25. P. W. Trinder, K. Hammond, J. S. Mattson, A. S. Partridge, and S. L. Peyton Jones. GUM: a Portable Parallel Implementation of Haskell. In *Proc. PLDI '96, Philadelphia, Penn.*, pages 79–88, 1996.
26. R. P. Whittington. Logical Design. In *[27]*, chapter 10. 1988.
27. R. P. Whittington. *Database Systems Engineeering*.   Clarendon Press, Oxford, 1998.
28. A. Yu and J. Chen. *The POSTGRES95 User Manual, Version 1.0*, 1995.

Shared Memory Multiprocessor Support for SAC

Clemens Grelck

University of Kiel
Dept. of Computer Science and Applied Mathematics
D-24105 Kiel, Germany
cg@informatik.uni-kiel.de

Abstract. SAC (Single Assignment C) is a strict, purely functional programming language primarily designed with numerical applications in mind. Particular emphasis is on efficient support for arrays both in terms of language expressiveness and in terms of runtime performance. Array operations in SAC are based on elementwise specifications using so-called WITH-loops. These language constructs are also well-suited for concurrent execution on multiprocessor systems.

This paper outlines an implicit approach to compile SAC programs for multi-threaded execution on shared memory architectures. Besides the basic compilation scheme, a brief overview of the runtime system is given. Finally, preliminary performance figures demonstrate that this approach is well-suited to achieve almost linear speedups.

1 Introduction

SAC (Single Assignment C) is a strict, first-order, purely functional programming language primarily designed with numerical applications in mind. Particular emphasis is on efficient support for array processing. Efficiency concerns are essentially twofold. On the one hand, SAC offers the opportunity of defining array operations on a high level of abstraction, including dimension-invariant program specifications which generally improves productivity in program development. On the other hand, sophisticated compilation schemes ensure efficiency in program execution. Extensive performance evaluations on a single though important kernel application (3-dimensional multigrid relaxation from the NAS benchmark [5]) show that SAC clearly outperforms its functional rival SISAL[17] both in terms of memory consumption and in terms of wallclock execution times[23]. Even the FORTRAN reference implementation of this benchmark is outperformed by about 10% with respect to execution times.

Although numerical computations represent just one application domain, certainly, this is a very important one with many applications in computational sciences. In these fields, the runtime performance of programs is the most crucial issue. However, numerical applications are often well-suited for non-sequential program execution. On the one hand, underlying algorithms expose a considerable amount of concurrency; on the other hand, the computational complexity

H. Hammond, T. Davie, and C. Clack (Eds.): IFL'98, LNCS 1595, pp. 38–53, 1999.

can be scaled easily with the computational power available. So, multiprocessor systems allow substantial reductions of application runtimes, and, consequently, computational sciences represent a major field of application for parallel processing. Therefore, sufficient support for concurrent program execution is particularly important for a language like SAC.

Due to the Church-Rosser-Property, purely functional languages are often considered well-suited for implicit non-sequential program execution, i.e., the language implementation is solely responsible for exploiting concurrency in multiprocessor environments. However, it turns out that determining where concurrent execution actually outweighs the administrative overhead inflicted by communication and synchronization is nearly as difficult as detecting where concurrent program execution is possible in imperative languages [25]. Many high-level features found in popular functional languages like HASKELL or CLEAN, e.g. higher-order functions, polymorphism, or lazy evaluation, make the necessary program analysis even harder.

As a consequence, recent developments are often in favour of explicit solutions for exploiting concurrency. Special language constructs allow application programmers to specify explicitly how programs are to be executed on multiple processors. Many different approaches have been proposed that reach from simple parallel map operations to full process management capabilities and even pure coordination languages [26, 19, 4, 9, 12, 16]. Although the actual degree of control varies significantly, explicit solutions have in common that, in the end, application programmers themselves are responsible for the efficient utilization of multiprocessor facilities. Programs have to be designed specifically for the execution in multiprocessor environments and, depending on the level of abstraction, possibly even for particular architectures or concrete machine configurations.

However, typical SAC applications spend most of their execution time in array operations. In contrast to load distribution on the level of function applications, elementwise defined array operations are a source of concurrency that is rather well-suited for implicit exploitation, as an array's size and structure can usually be determined in advance, often even at compile time. This allows for effective load distribution and balancing schemes. Implicit solutions for parallel program execution offer well-known advantages: being not polluted with explicit specifications, a program's source code is usually shorter, more concise, and easier to read and understand. Also, programming productivity is generally higher since no characteristics of potential target machines have to be taken into account which also improves program portability. Functional languages like SISAL[17], NESL[6], or ID[3], have already demonstrated that, following the so-called data parallel approach, good speedups may well be achieved without explicit specifications [11, 7, 13].

Successfully reducing application runtimes through non-sequential program execution makes it necessary to consider at least basic design characteristics of intended target hardware architectures. Having a look at recent developments in this area, two trends can be identified. Up to a modest number of processing facilities (usually ≤ 32) symmetric shared memory multiprocessors dominate. If a decidedly larger number of processing sites is to be used, the trend is towards networks of entire workstations or even personal computers. Both approaches are characterized by reusing standard components for high performance computing which is not only more cost-effective than traditional supercomputers but also benefits from an apparently higher annual performance increase.

In our current approach for SAC, we focus on shared memory multiprocessors. Machines like the Sun Ultra Enterprise Series, the HP 3000/9000 series, or the SGI Origin have become wide-spread as workgroup or enterprise servers and already dominate the lower part of the Top500 list of the most powerful computing facilities worldwide [10]. Although their scalability is conceptually limited by the memory bottleneck, processor private hierarchies of fast and sufficiently large caches help to minimize contention on the main memory. Theoretical considerations like Amdahl's law [2], however, show that an application itself may be limited with respect to scalability anyway. Our current approach may also serve as a first step to be integrated into a more comprehensive solution covering networks of shared memory multiprocessors in the future.

As a low-level programming model, multi-threading just seems to be tailor-made for shared memory architectures. It allows for different (sequential) threads of control within the single address space of a process. Each thread has its private execution stack, but all threads share access to the same global data. This programming model exactly coincides with the hardware architecture of shared memory multiprocessors which is characterized by multiple execution facilities but uniform storage. To ensure portability between different concrete machines within the basic architectural model, the current implementation is based on POSIX-THREADS[18] as the major standard.

The rest of the paper is organized as follows: after a short introduction to SAC in Sect. 2, the basic concepts of our shared memory multiprocessor implementation are outlined in Sect. 3. Preliminary performance figures are presented in Sect. 4. Finally, Sect. 5 draws conclusions and discusses future work.

2   SAC — Single Assignment C

This section is to give a very brief overview of SAC. A more detailed introduction to the language may be found in [21, 24]; its strict, purely functional semantics is formally defined in [20].

The core language of SAC may be considered a functional subset of C, ruling out global variables and pointers to keep the language free of side effects. It is extended by the introduction of arrays as first class objects. An array is represented by two vectors: a *data vector* which contains the elements of the array, and a *shape vector* which provides structural information. The length of the shape vector specifies the dimensionality of the array whereas its elements define the array's extension in each dimension. Built-in functions allow determination of an array's dimension or shape as well as extraction of array elements.

Complex array operations may be specified by means of so-called WITH-loops, a versatile language construct similar to the array comprehensions of

HASKELL or CLEAN and to the FOR-loops of SISAL. It allows the dimension-invariant, elementwise definition of operations on entire arrays as well as on subarrays selected through index ranges or strides.

WithExpr	$\Rightarrow$ **with** (*Generator*) *Operation*
Generator	$\Rightarrow$ *Expr Relop Identifier Relop Expr* $\big[$ *Filter* $\big]$
Relop	$\Rightarrow$ < | <=
Filter	$\Rightarrow$ **step** *Expr* $\big[$ **width** *Expr* $\big]$
Operation	$\Rightarrow$ **genarray** (*Expr* , *Expr*)
	| **modarray** (*Expr* , *Expr* , *Expr*)
	| **fold** (*FoldFun* , *Expr* , *Expr*)

Fig. 1. The syntax of WITH-loops.

The syntax of WITH-loops is outlined in Fig. 1. A WITH-loop consists of two parts: a *generator part* and an *operation part*. The generator part defines a set of index vectors along with an index variable representing elements of this set. Two expressions that must evaluate to vectors of equal length, define the lower and the upper bounds of a range of index vectors. This continuous range may be restricted by a filter which defines strides of arbitrary widths. For instance, with a, b, s, and w denoting expressions that evaluate to vectors of length n,
(a <= i_vec < b **step** s **width** w)   specifies the set of index vectors
$$\{i\_vec \mid \forall_{i \in \{0,\ldots,n-1\}} : a_i \leq i\_vec_i < b_i \wedge (i\_vec_i - a_i) \text{ modulo } s_i < w_i\}.$$
The operation part specifies the operation to be performed on each element of the index vector set defined by the generator. Three different operation parts exist. Let *shp* and *idx* denote SAC-expressions that evaluate to vectors, let *array* denote a SAC-expression that evaluates to an array, and let *expr* denote an arbitrary SAC-expression. Moreover, let *fold_op* be the name of a binary commutative and associative function with neutral element *neutral*. Then

- **genarray**(*shp*, *expr*) generates an array of shape *shp* whose elements are the values of *expr* for all index vectors from the specified set, and 0 otherwise;
- **modarray**(*array*, *idx*, *expr*) defines an array of shape **shape**(*array*) whose elements are the values of *expr* for all index vectors from the specified set, and the values of *array*[*idx*] at all other index positions;
- **fold**(*fold_op*, *neutral*, *expr*) allows the specification of reduction operations. Setting out with *neutral*, for each index vector from the specified set the value of *expr* is folded using *fold_op*.

The expressive power of the WITH-loop allows the specification of a comprehensive array library for SAC in the language itself. This library provides numerous dimension and shape independent high-level array operations similar to those available in APL[15] or FORTRAN-90[1] as intrinsic functions, e.g. extensions of binary scalar operations to combinations of scalars and arrays as well as to arrays of equal shape by elementwise application, various types of subarray selection, concatenation of arrays along given axes, shifting and rotating arrays, or the reduction operations sum, product, any, and all. Since this library can easily be extended by any application programmer, SAC allows high-level programming without the restriction of a fixed set of built-in operations.

3   Implementation Aspects

This section introduces the basic concepts of extending the SAC compiler in order to generate multi-threaded target code based on POSIX-THREADS. This thread API provides operations to dynamically create new threads and to synchronize them upon termination. As threads communicate with each other by means of global data, various synchronization primitives are available to ensure data integrity in the presence of simultaneous accesses by different threads. While on a uniprocessor, these are simply executed in a time-sharing mode, on a shared memory multiprocessor, the operating system scheduler may assign them to different processors for simultaneous execution. Thread scheduling is performed implicitly by the operating system; there is no means to explicitly assign threads to specific processors for execution.

For reasons already pointed out, concurrency in SAC program specifications is not to be exploited on the level of function applications but within elementwise defined array operations. Here, the design of arrays in SAC pays off. Since all high-level array operations are implemented by WITH-loops in SAC itself, we can focus entirely on this single though powerful language construct. Consequently, without any extra effort, the operations provided by the SAC array library benefit from multi-threaded execution just as any user-defined array operation.

```
A = with ( lb <= iv < ub step s width w )
    genarray( shp, e );
...
B = with ( lb <= iv < ub step s width w )
    modarray( A, iv, A[iv] + 1);
...
c = with ( lb <= iv < ub step s width w )
    fold( foldfun, neutral, B[iv]);
```

Fig. 2. SAC code example.

The compilation of WITH-loops into multi-threaded (imperative) pseudo code is outlined by means of a small example. The SAC code fragment in Fig. 2 features all three variants of the WITH-loop as introduced in Sect. 2. The variables lb, ub, s, and w that make up the generator parts as well as shp are assumed to be defined before the statements shown and to evaluate to vectors of equal length. For reasons of simplicity, the same variable names are used in all three generator parts, however, their actual values may be different. First, an array A of shape shp is generated by means of a **genarray**-WITH-loop. The variable **e** is also assumed to be defined before and to evaluate to a scalar, say int. Next, a **modarray**-WITH-loop defines an array B identical to A except for the elements selected by the generator, which are incremented by 1. Finally, a **fold**-WITH-loop is used to fold selected elements of array B by the operation **foldfun** whose neutral element **neutral** is assumed to denote a constant.

```
A = ALLOCATE_ARRAY( shp);
LOOP_NESTING( iv: shape(A), lb, ub, s, w) {
  A[iv] = ? e : 0;
}
...
B = ALLOCATE_ARRAY( shape(A));
LOOP_NESTING( iv: shape(B), lb, ub, s, w) {
  B[iv] = ? A[i]+1 : A[i];
}
...
c = neutral;
LOOP_NESTING( iv: lb, ub, s, w) {
  c = foldfun( c, B[iv]);
}
```

Fig. 3. Compilation to sequential code[1].

As a starting point, the compilation of this example code fragment into sequential (imperative) pseudo code is outlined in Fig.3. After memory for the target array is allocated, all its elements are initialized in a nesting of (**for**-) loops either with the value of **e** or with 0. The loop nesting defines a complete iteration of the variable **iv** on the target array; the concrete design however depends on lb, ub, s, and w. On this level of abstraction, the **genarray** and the **modarray** variants of the WITH-loop turn out to be identical, i.e., **modarray**-WITH-loops can be ignored from now on. The implementation of the **fold**-WITH-loop is slightly different. It starts with the initialization of the fold variable c with the neutral element of the fold operation. The loop nesting lets **iv** only iterate within the iteration space actually defined by lb, ub, s, and w. In each iteration step, the value of c is updated by folding its old value with the respective element of array B.

With this sequential implementation in mind, the basic idea of organizing the multi-threaded execution of a WITH-loop is straightforward. The corresponding iteration space has to be partitioned into several disjoint subspaces, one for each thread. In the case of the **genarray** and the **modarray** variant, each thread then

---

[1] Here A[iv] = ? e : 0; denotes that in different parts of the loop nesting the operation is either A[iv] = e; or A[iv] = 0;.

simply initializes a disjoint part of the target array. In the case of a fold-WITH-loop, each thread computes a partial fold result. Afterwards, these partial results are again folded to form the overall result.

```
A = ALLOCATE_ARRAY( shp);
MT_EXECUTION( 0 <= tid < #THREADS) {
   do {
      sb, se, cont = SCHEDULE( tid, #THREADS, shape(A), lb, ub, s, w);
      LOOP_NESTING( iv: sb, se, shape(A), lb, ub, s, w) {
         A[iv] = ? e : 0;
      }
   } while (cont);
}
```

Fig. 4. Multi-threaded implementation of the **genarray**-WITH-loop.

The multi-threaded implementation of the **genarray**-WITH-loop of the example is outlined in Fig.4. The pseudo statement **MT_EXECUTION** denotes that the following code block is to be executed concurrently by multiple threads. The exact number of threads is specified by **#THREADS** which is considered a runtime constant. Although each thread executes the same code, threads can identify themselves by means of the variable **tid** whose value in the range [0..#THREADS-1] is unique for each thread.

In the presence of subranges and strides of different widths in multiple dimensions, the actual nesting of loops can be extremely complicated. An optimization called WITH-loop-folding[22] that allows for condensing several subsequent WITH-loops into a single, more powerful variant increases this complexity even further. For reasons of efficiency in compiler design, it is therefore highly recommendable to reuse the existing sequential compilation scheme for WITH-loops as far as possible. The solution here is to completely separate from the computation, i.e. from the loop nesting, the decision of which thread actually initializes which array elements. In Fig. 4, this decision-making code is denoted by the pseudo statement **SCHEDULE** as this discipline is usually called loop scheduling.

The idea is that the loop scheduler defines a rectangular subrange of the original iteration space covered by the loop nesting, based on the total number of threads (**#THREADS**) and the thread ID (**tid**). This rectangular subspace is defined by the two vectors **sb** ('schedule begin') and **se** ('schedule end'). The original (sequential) loop nesting is only slightly modified in that each loop is restricted to the intersection between its original range and the iteration subspace defined by **sb** and **se**. Apart from reusing existing compilation schemes, strictly separating the scheduling from the computation offers the additional advantage that different scheduling strategies may easily be implemented and tested, and later on the compiler may choose the one which is most appropriate with respect to the overall array operation. Enclosing the scheduler and the loop nesting within a (do-) loop allows scheduler implementations that repeatedly assign different iteration subspaces to one thread. The scheduling code itself decides whether or not a re-scheduling is required and stores this information using the local variable cont.

The basic organizational concepts of a multi-threaded implementation of WITH-loops as outlined in the context of the genarray variant may also be be applied to modarray- and fold-WITH-loops in a more or less straightforward way. Instead of going into more details, we now focus on the aspect of organizing a whole program with respect to multiple execution threads. This concerns such issues as where and how to create and terminate additional threads, thread synchronization, and inter-thread communication.

As a result of the compilation steps described so far, all WITH-loops from the original SAC program are replaced by MT_EXECUTION blocks. These blocks exactly indicate the code sections that actually are to be executed concurrently by multiple threads. This leads straightforwardly to a fork/join execution model as depicted on the left hand side of Fig. 5. The primary thread of an application process serves as a master thread (thread ID 0). Upon program startup, the master thread begins executing the program sequentially. Each time the master thread encounters an MT_EXECUTION block, it creates #THREADS - 1 so-called worker threads. Afterwards, the master thread and the worker threads jointly execute the MT_EXECUTION block as described before. Upon completing their computation, worker threads simply terminate. The master thread, however, has to wait until the last worker thread terminates, and thereupon continues with the execution of sequential code.

This fork/join model is conceptually simple and may be implemented straightforwardly. Synchronization and communication is exactly limited to thread creation and thread termination; the worker threads do not interact with each other in any way. However, in a concrete implementation, the performance achieved by a pure fork/join model turns out to be rather poor. Sufficient speedups may only be achieved for extremely large problem sizes or with extremely costly operations per element. The reason for this is that although thread creation is relatively cheap compared to process creation, it is still expensive in terms of machine instructions. So, creating new worker threads upon each multi-threaded WITH-loop-execution and terminating them afterwards is inefficient. [2]

A solution to this problem that combines the conceptual benefits of the fork/join approach with an efficient execution scheme is graphically outlined in the centre of Fig. 5. In the enhanced fork/join model, all worker threads are created exactly once at program startup and do not terminate until the whole program does so. The necessary synchronization and communication between the threads is implemented by means of two different types of barriers: each MT_EXECUTION block is enclosed within a *start barrier* and a *stop barrier*. After creation, worker threads immediately stop at a start barrier. This barrier is lifted when the master thread encounters the first MT_EXECUTION block. The master thread and all worker threads activated thereupon share the computation

---

[2] On one of our test machines, we measured $> 10,000$ clock cycles for creating just one (kernel) thread.

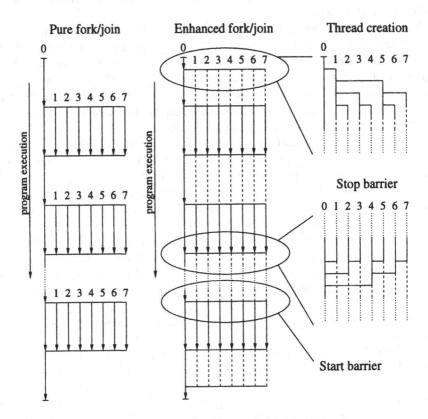

Fig. 5. Multi-threaded execution schemes.

of the WITH-loop exactly as in the pure fork/join model. Worker threads which complete their individual part of the computation, pass a stop barrier, and, with nothing else to do, immediately move on to the following start barrier. However, the master thread has to wait for the last worker thread to reach the stop barrier before it may proceed with further (sequential) computations.

Two major extensions to the compilation scheme described so far are required in order to implement this enhanced fork/join execution model. First, a function has to be specified that is executed by the worker threads upon creation, in the following called thread control function; second, the code within MT_EXECUTION blocks has to be abstracted out of its original context and lifted to a separate function definition in order to be accessible from the thread control function. These new functions are named WL-functions.

The thread control function is outlined in Fig. 6. It shows how the worker threads reach the start barrier immediately after creation. Before the master thread lifts this barrier, it stores the address of the WL-function to be executed in the global variable WL_FUN_ADDR. Upon activation, each worker thread retrieves this address and executes the respective function with its own unique thread

```
void ThreadControl( int tid)
{
  wl_fun_t *wl_fun;
  do {
    START_BARRIER_WORKER();
    wl_fun = WL_FUN_ADDR;
    *wl_fun( tid);
  } forever;
}
```

Fig. 6. Thread control function.

ID as argument. Afterwards the worker threads stop again at the start barrier waiting for further activations.

If a block of code is to be abstracted out of its original context, it must first be transformed into a combinator. For this purpose, two sets of variables have to be inferred: the set IN of all variables referenced within the block but defined outside and the set OUT of the variables assigned a value within the block that is needed outside. To actually generate a new function definition, the set LOC of all identifiers exclusively used within the block is also required. For the MT_EXECUTION block outlined in Fig.4, these sets can easily be identified as

IN = { A, e, lb, ub, s, w},   OUT = $\emptyset$,   LOC = { iv, sb, se, cont},

and for the fold-WITH-loop introduced with the initial example in Fig. 2 as

IN = { B, lb, ub, s, w},   OUT = { c },   LOC = { iv, sb, se, cont}.

With these sets of identifiers at hand, it is rather straightforward to construct a function definition and to replace the original code block by the respective function application. However, in our case, we have to observe that WL-functions are restricted in their signature since they have to be called from within the thread control function in a uniform way (see Fig. 6). As a consequence, an alternative parameter passing mechanism is required. The complete solutions for the genarray-WITH-loop of our example is outlined in Figs. 7 and 9.

At the original position of the genarray-WITH-loop, the MT_EXECUTION block is replaced by code which stores the value of each variable from the corresponding IN set within the global argument frame ARG_FRAME (Fig. 9). Afterwards, the address of the respective WL-function which actually contains the code to be executed concurrently, is stored in the global variable WL_FUN_ADDR. The master thread now activates the worker threads by reaching the start barrier and subsequently joins them in executing the WITH-loop through an ordinary call to the respective WL-function with its special thread ID 0 as argument.

In the following, all threads execute the same function (WL_FUN_1, Fig.7). This function definition has a local declaration for each variable from the corresponding IN, OUT, and LOC sets. Before any computations are done, the values of the IN variables, i.e. the 'arguments' of the WL-function, are retrieved from the global argument frame ARG_FRAME. The WL-function also contains the stop barrier. So, after returning from the application of a WL-function, the master thread may simply proceed with further (sequential) computations (Fig. 9).

```
void WL_FUN_1(int tid)
{
  int A[]  = ARG_FRAME.WL1.A;
  int e    = ARG_FRAME.WL1.e;
  int lb[] = ARG_FRAME.WL1.lb;
  ...
  int iv[], sb[], se[], cont;
  do {
    ...
  } while (cont);
  STOP_BARRIER(tid);
}
```

Fig. 7. WL-function: genarray.

```
int WL_FUN_3(int tid)
{
  int B[] = ARG_FRAME.WL3.B;
  ...
  int c, iv[], sb[], se[], cont;
  c = neutral;
  do {
    ...
  } while (cont);
  STOP_BARRIER_F(tid, foldfun, c);
  return(c)
}
```

Fig. 8. WL-function: fold.

```
A = ALLOCATE_ARRAY( shp);
ARG_FRAME.WL1.A  = A;
ARG_FRAME.WL1.e  = e;
  ...
WL_FUN_ADDR = &WL_FUN_1;
START_BARRIER_MASTER();
WL_FUN_1( 0);
```

Fig. 9. WL-context: genarray.

```
ARG_FRAME.WL3.B  = B;
ARG_FRAME.WL3.lb = lb;
ARG_FRAME.WL3.ub = ub;
  ...
WL_FUN_ADDR = &WL_FUN_3;
START_BARRIER_MASTER();
c = WL_FUN_3( 0);
```

Fig. 10. WL-context: fold.

Only minor extensions of this scheme are required for fold-WITH-loops as depicted in Figs. 8 and 10. The OUT variable c which is used to accumulate the partial fold result private to each thread is also declared a local variable. However, a special variant of the stop barrier is required that takes care of folding the partial results of the various threads, i.e., behind the stop barrier, c represents the overall fold result which then is simply returned by the WL-function. The master thread may directly use this value for further computations while the worker threads just ignore the return value of the WL-function (Fig. 6).

Some issues of particular interest have not been addressed yet: the thread creation phase and the implementation of start and stop barriers. Since these represent the administrative overhead of a multi-threaded program, their efficient implementation is crucial to achieve good speedups.

In a straightforward implementation of the thread creation phase, the master thread starts all worker threads one after another by means of a for-loop. As a consequence, the execution of the actually productive code is delayed by a time that grows linearly with the number of threads. This delay can easily be reduced if the worker threads participate in thread creation. This leads to a tree-like creation scheme which reduces this initial delay to a factor of $\lceil log_2 \text{ #THREADS} \rceil$. However, the initial delay factor may be further reduced to only 1 by excluding the master thread from the thread creation scheme as outlined on the upper right hand side of Fig. 5. The master thread creates exactly one worker thread and then immediately starts with the execution of the actual program. The first worker thread subsequently creates the other worker threads following a binary tree scheme. In this way, the administrative overhead due to thread creation overlaps with the execution of a program's (sequential) startup phase, e.g. reading input data from files.

The combination of a stop barrier and a subsequent start barrier represents a full barrier synchronization which is known to scale poorly with the number of threads [14] and, therefore, is a major cause of overhead. However, scalability can be improved by organizing the barrier as a tree-like structure of pairwise synchronizations, as depicted on the lower right hand side of Fig.5. Threads with an odd ID simply pass the stop barrier, immediately stopping at the following start barrier. Each thread with an even ID n waits for thread $n+1$ to complete. Then, it either passes the stop barrier itself if its ID is not a multiple of 4 or it continues to wait for thread $n+2$ otherwise, and so on. This concurrent synchronization scheme allows the master thread (thread ID 0) to synchronize itself with all worker threads in only $\lceil log_2 \#\textbf{THREADS}\rceil$ steps.

In the case of a fold-WITH-loop, the stop barrier is also responsible for folding the partial results of the single threads to form the overall result. Each time a thread synchronizes itself with another thread, it folds its own intermediate result with that of the other thread. This scheme is further improved by allowing threads which synchronize with several other threads to do so in any order. Then, a thread may already execute final fold operations while still waiting for other threads to complete their partial result. As in the thread creation phase, administrative overhead again overlaps with productive computation.

4   Preliminary Performance Evaluation

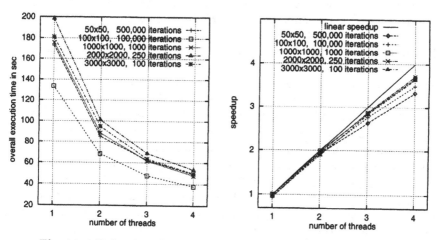

Fig. 11. 2-D Jacobi relaxation on 4-proc. Sun Ultra Enterprise 3000.

Preliminary performance tests of the current implementation described in the previous section have been made on two different machines: a Sun Ultra Enterprise 3000 with 4 processors and 512MB of memory and a Sun Ultra Enterprise

4000 featuring 12 processors and 7.5GB of memory. Both are running Solaris, versions 2.5.1 and 2.6, respectively. A simplified variant of 2-dimensional Jacobi relaxation [8] served as a benchmark kernel. Test runs for various problem sizes have been made with up to 4 threads on the Enterprise 3000 and with up to 12 threads on the Enterprise 4000. Overall execution times achieved on the two machines are depicted in Figs. 11 and 12. The respective speedups relative to a program which from exactly the same SAC source code has been compiled for sequential execution are shown in Figs. 11 and 13.

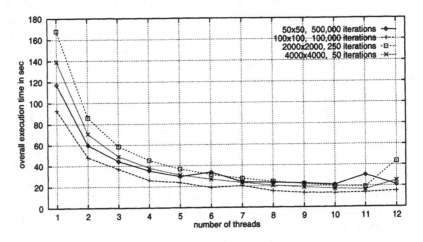

Fig. 12. 2-D Jacobi relaxation on 12-proc. Sun Ultra Enterprise 4000: execution times.

As the figures demonstrate, multi-threaded execution of the benchmark kernel yields substantial reductions in overall runtimes on both machines and for all problem sizes investigated. Speedups reach up to 3.71 on the 4-processor system and up to 8.83 on the 12-processor system. Considerable speedups are achieved even for relatively small problem sizes of only 100×100 or 50×50 array elements although they require very frequent synchronization among threads. Only for unfavourable combinations of array size and number of threads, speedups decrease due to load imbalances resulting from the simple loop scheduling mechanism.

It is important to note that multi-threading per sé produces nothing but overhead. Only when it comes to program execution on a multiprocessor does multi-threading enable the operating system scheduler to assign different threads to different processors for execution. As a consequence, speedups due to multi-threading can only be expected if different threads of an application actually run on different processors. However, the way the underlying operating system distributes runnable threads among the available processors on a given machine cannot be influenced by the application itself. Still, it is obvious that no additional speedup can be expected if the number of threads exceeds the number of available processors.

However, if exclusive access to a machine cannot be guaranteed as it is the case with the machines used for benchmarking, the execution of an application's

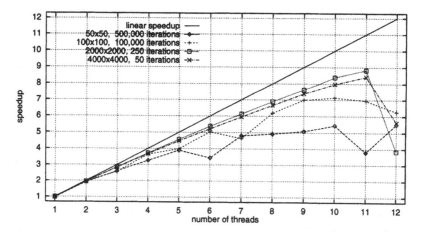

Fig. 13. 2-D Jacobi relaxation on 12-proc. Sun Ultra Enterprise 4000: speedups.

threads may interfere with other user and system processes. As soon as the total number of runnable threads in a system exceeds the number of processors available, the operating system scheduler is forced to assign several threads to the same processor for execution. In this case, a loop scheduler that statically assigns work to threads, like the one in our implementation, causes severe load imbalance, leading to a performance degradation. This is exactly what can be observed with the performance figures for the two larger test cases on the 12-processor machine. When these measurements were done, exactly one other process was constantly running in the system. Hence, up to 11 threads, execution time and speedup figures scale well, but drop dramatically if 12 threads are used.

5   Conclusions and Future Work

SAC is a programming language primarily designed with numerical applications in mind. A powerful language construct called WITH-loop allows the specification of high-level array operations independent of the operands' dimensionalities and shapes. Operations are defined elementwise on entire arrays or on subarrays selected by index ranges or strides. Despite the high level of abstraction in program specifications, sophisticated compilation schemes allow the transformation of WITH-loops into efficiently executable (sequential) code [21, 23].

The elementwise specification of operations on (sufficiently large) arrays exposes a high amount of fine-grained concurrency. This paper describes a completely implicit approach to exploit this concurrency to speed up program execution on shared memory multiprocessors. A compilation scheme which transforms WITH-loops into multi-threaded target code is outlined along with the required runtime system. By completely separating the loop scheduling facility from the loops themselves, the existing sequential compilation scheme of WITH-loops can largely be reused. Moreover, this provides the opportunity to easily exchange the loop scheduling implementation in order to adjust load balancing strategies to the program structure or target system properties. An execution model for multi-threaded programs is presented that overcomes the limitations of a simple fork/join oriented approach. Instead of repeatedly creating and terminating threads, they are created exactly once upon program startup while all synchronization is realized by a tailor-made variant of barrier synchronization.

Preliminary performance evaluations of our current implementation are made on two Sun Ultra Enterprise systems with 4 and 12 processors. A simplified version of 2-dimensional Jacobi relaxation is used as a benchmark kernel. Performance figures for various problem sizes demonstrate that even for relatively small problems substantial speedups are achieved on both systems reaching up to 3.71 or 8.83, respectively.

Future work will focus on reducing the negative performance impact of the synchronization barriers which complete each concurrently executed code segment. Since the barrier implementation itself is already highly optimized, the emphasis will be on improving the load balancing capabilities of the loop scheduler in order to cope with variations in computational complexity for different elements of the target array as well as with threads belonging to other processes on systems not used exclusively. An alternative approach is to identify larger sections of code that can be executed concurrently without intermediate synchronization, e.g., synchronization barriers between consecutive WITH-loops can be eliminated as far as there is no data dependence between them.

References

1. J.C. Adams, W.S. Brainerd, J.T. Martin, et al. *Fortran90 Handbook - Complete ANSI/ISO Reference*. McGraw-Hill, 1992. ISBN 0-07-000406-4.
2. G.M. Amdahl. Validity of the Single Processor Approach to Achieving Large-Scale Computing Capabilities. In *AFIPS Conf. Proc.*, pages 483–485. AFIPS Press, Reston, Va, 1967.
3. Arvind, K.P. Gostelow, and W. Plouffe. The ID-Report: An Asynchronous Programming Language and Computing Machine. Technical Report 114, University of California at Irvine, 1978.
4. C. Aßmann. Coordinating Functional Processes Using Petri Nets. In W. Kluge, editor, *Proc. 8th. International Workshop on the Implementation of Functional Languages*, Bad Godesberg, Germany, September 1996, volume 1268 of *LNCS*, pages 162–183. Springer-Verlag, 1997.
5. D. Bailey, E. Barszcz, J. Barton, et al. The NAS Parallel Benchmarks. RNR 94-007, NASA Ames Research Center, 1994.
6. G.E. Blelloch. NESL: A Nested Data-Parallel Language (Version 3.1). Technical Report CMU-CS-95-170, Carnegie Mellon University, Pittsburgh, PA, 1995.
7. G.E. Blelloch, S.Chatterjee, J.C. Hardwick, J. Sipelstein, and M.Zagha. Implementation of a Portable Nested Data-Parallel Language. *Journal of Parallel and Distributed Computing*, 21(1):4–14, 1994.
8. D. Braess. *Finite Elemente*. Springer-Verlag, 1996. ISBN 3-540-61905-4.
9. S. Breitinger, R. Loogen, and Y. Ortega-Mallen. Towards a Declarative Language for Parallel and Concurrent Programming. In *Proc. 1995 Glasgow Workshop on Functional Programming*. Springer-Verlag WiCS, 1995.
10. J.J. Dongarra, H.W. Meuer, and E. Strohmaier. TOP500 Supercomputer Sites, 11th edition. In *Supercomputer '98 Conference, Mannheim, Germany*, 1998.

11. M. Haines and W. Böhm. Task Management, Virtual Shared Memory, and Multithreading in a Distributed Memory Implementation of SISAL. In A. Bode, M. Reeve, and G. Wolf, editors, *Proc. PARLE '93 — Parallel Architectures and Languages Europe*, volume 694 of *LNCS*, pages 12–23, Eindhoven, The Netherlands, Spinger-Verlag, June 1991.

12. K. Hammond, H.-W. Loidl, S.L. Peyton Jones, and P. Trinder. Algorithm + Strategy = Parallelism. *Journal of Functional Programming*, 8(1), 1998.

13. J. Hicks, D. Chiou, B.S. Ang, and Arvind. Performance Studies of Id on the Monsoon Dataflow System. *Journal of Parallel and Distributed Computing*, 18(3):273–300, 1993.

14. J.M.D. Hill and D.B. Skillicorn. Practical Barrier Synchronisation. Technical Report TR-16-96, Programming Research Group, Oxford University Computing Laboratory, Oxford, England, 1996.

15. K.E. Iverson. *A Programming Language*. Wiley, New York, 1962.

16. S.L. Peyton Jones, A. Gordon, and S. Finne. Concurrent Haskell. In *Proc. 23rd ACM Symposium on Principles of Programming Languages (POPL'96)*, St. Petersburg Beach, Florida, pages 295–308, 1996.

17. J.R. McGraw, S.K. Skedzielewski, S.J. Allan, R.R. Oldehoeft, et al. SISAL: Streams and Iteration in a Single Assignment Language: Reference Manual Version 1.2. M 146, Lawrence Livermore National Laboratory, LLNL, Livermore California, 1985.

18. Institute of Electrical and Inc. Electronic Engineers. Information Technology — Portable Operating Systems Interface (POSIX) — Part: System Application Program Interface (API) — Amendment 2: Threads Extension [C Language]. IEEE Standard 1003.1c–1995, IEEE, New York, NY, 1995.

19. J.H. Reppy. CML: A higher-order concurrent language. In *Proc. 1991 ACM SIGPLAN Conf. on Programming Language Design and Implementation (PLDI 91)*, pages 293–305, 1991.

20. S.B. Scholz. **Single Assignment C** – *Entwurf und Implementierung einer funktionalen C-Variante mit spezieller Unterstützung shape-invarianter Array-Operationen*. PhD thesis, Institut für Informatik und Praktische Mathematik, Universität Kiel, 1996.

21. S.B. Scholz. On Programming Scientific Applications in SAC – A Functional Language Extended by a Subsystem for High-Level Array Operations. In W. Kluge, editor, *Proc. 8th. International Workshop on the Implementation of Functional Languages*, Bad Godesberg, Germany, September 1996, volume 1268 of *LNCS*, pages 85–104. Springer-Verlag, 1997.

22. S.B. Scholz. WITH-loop-folding: Condensing Consecutive Array Operations. In C. Clack, T. Davie, and K. Hammond, editors, *Proc. 9th International Workshop on the Implementation of Functional Languages '97*, St Andrews, Scotland, 1997, volume 1467 of *LNCS*, pages 72–91. Springer-Verlag, 1998.

23. S.B. Scholz. A Case Study: Effects of WITH-Loop Folding on the NAS Mgrid Benchmark in SAC. In *This Proceedings*.

24. S.B. Scholz. On Defining Application-Specific High-Level Array Operations by Means of Shape-Invariant Programming Facilities. In S. Picchi and M. Micocci, editors, *Proc. 1998 Array Processing Language Conference*, Rome, Italy, pages 40–45. ACM Press, 1998.

25. W. Schreiner. Parallel Functional Programming, An Annotated Bibliography (2nd edition). 93-24, Research Institute for Symbolic Computation (RISC), Johannes-Kepler-University, Linz, Austria, 1993.

26. P.R. Serrarens. Distributed arrays in Clean. In *Euro-Par '97*, LNCS. Springer, 1997.

Towards an Operational Semantics for a Parallel Non-strict Functional Language

Jon G. Hall[1], Clem Baker-Finch[2], Phil Trinder[3], and David J. King[1]

[1] Faculty of Maths and Computing, The Open University
Milton Keynes MK7 6AA
{J.G.Hall, D.J.King}@open.ac.uk
[2] Department of Computer Science, Australian National University
Clem.Baker-Finch@cs.anu.edu.au
[3] Department of Computing and Electrical Engineering
Heriot-Watt University, Riccarton, Edinburgh EH14 4AS
trinder@cee.hw.ac.uk

Abstract. Parallel programs must describe both computation and co-ordination, i.e. *what* to compute and *how* to organise the computation. In functional languages equational reasoning is often used to reason about computation. In contrast, there have been many different coordination constructs for functional languages, and far less work on reasoning about coordination.

We present an initial semantics for GpH, a small extension of the Haskell language, that allows us to reason about coordination. In particular we can reason about *work*, *average parallelism* and *runtime*. The semantics captures the notions of limited (physical) resources, the preservation of sharing, and speculative evaluation. We show a consistency result with Launchbury's well-known lazy semantics.

1 Introduction

One of the advantages of declarative languages is that it is relatively easy to reason about the values computed by programs, this being attributable to their preservation of referential transparency. Indeed, within the functional programming community there is a strong tradition of reasoning to transform, derive, and prove properties of programs.

Parallel programs must describe both computation and coordination, i.e. *what* to compute, and *how* to arrange the computation in parallel. In adding coordination constructs, many parallel functional languages are able to preserve the referential transparency of the computation language [16,3,7,17] and [4] so that standard equational reasoning techniques continue to be applicable to the values computed. Being able to reason about coordination is, however, dependent on the form its specification takes: for languages in which coordination is entirely implicit [16,3,7,15], or in which it is specified as annotations [11,17], reasoning about the coordination at the language level is not possible. It is only for languages that make the specification of coordination explicit [4,5,8] and [13], that such reasoning is possible at the language level.

H. Hammond, T. Davie, and C. Clack (Eds.): IFL'98, LNCS 1595, pp. 54–71, 1999.
© Springer-Verlag Berlin Heidelberg 1999

Our language, Glasgow Parallel Haskell (GpH) [19] is explicit about a few crucial aspects of the coordination, and so we would like to develop a semantics for reasoning about it. GpH is a modest extension to Haskell [1], adding only two coordination primitives: parallel and sequential composition, denoted **par** and **seq** respectively. By abstracting from the primitives using higher-order polymorphic functions it is possible to cleanly separate computation from coordination, and the abstractions are called *evaluation strategies* [20].

1.1 Motivation: Reasoning about Coordination

The computational meaning of **par** and **seq** is captured by the following equations; both are projections onto their second argument, but only **seq** is strict in its first argument.

$$e_0 \text{ par } e_1 = e_1$$
$$e_0 \text{ seq } e_1 = \begin{cases} \bot & \text{if } e_0 = \bot \\ e_1 & \text{otherwise} \end{cases}$$

The coordination, or operational behaviour, of **seq** is for the arguments to be evaluated in sequence: the first to weak head normal form (whnf) before the second. The coordination behaviour of **par** is for the arguments to be evaluated in parallel, potentially: the first argument is marked as a candidate for parallel evaluation by a new thread, but this will only occur if there is a free processor.

Fig. 1 shows some examples of obvious value-equivalences between terms involving the coordination primitives. We wish to be able to investigate the status of such equivalences with respect to coordination and, in particular, work, average parallelism and runtime ([6], see the discussion in Sect. 5) and the transition system we present here is a first step towards this goal. Ultimately, however, in this context the usefulness of a semantics for GpH will be measured by how it allows one to reason about programs which involve evaluation strategies, rather than just the **par** and **seq** primitives.

(I) Associativity of **seq**:

$$e_0 \text{ seq } (e_1 \text{ seq } e_2) = (e_0 \text{ seq } e_1) \text{ seq } e_2$$

(II) Idempotence of e_0 **par**:

$$e_0 \text{ par } e_1 = e_0 \text{ par } e_0 \text{ par } e_1$$

(III) Distribution of **seq** over **par**

$$e_0 \text{ seq } (e_1 \text{ par } e_2) = (e_0 \text{ seq } e_1) \text{ par } (e_0 \text{ seq } e_2)$$

Fig. 1. Some obvious value-equivalences between terms involving the coordination primitives.

1.2 Related Work

The initial motivation for our semantics comes from John Launchbury's natural semantics of lazy evaluation [12]. Readers familiar with that work will recognise a number of features here, including the normalisation process and the explicit heap of uniquely identified closures.

Launchbury presents an evaluation semantics (big-step SOS) but it is generally agreed that such an approach is inappropriate for describing parallelism [10]. Hence we build a computational semantics (small-step SOS) over structures similar to those introduced by Launchbury. The semantics is shown, in Sect. 4, to be consistent with that of Launchbury on the overlap. (Moreover, as Launchbury's semantics is shown to be consistent with Abramsky denotational semantics of the Lazy Lambda Calculus of [2], by transitivity, we have a similar consistency result.)

A distinguishing feature of the approach taken in this paper is that the computational steps are explicitly parallel, being based on lockstep synchrony ([14]). This contrasts with the common approach exemplified by many process algebras, of *representing* parallelism by interleaving computational steps [9], but allows a more natural consideration of resource usage.

The computational model we introduce for parallel non-strict evaluation is a direct extension of that of the Launchbury semantics, and we characterise their relationship in Sect. 4. In particular, the semantics captures the preservation of sharing but augments Launchbury's semantics with the notions of limited (physical) resources. We note that the current semantics does not model GpH, but models a language with speculative evaluation, a point which is discussed in Sect. 5.

1.3 Structure of the Paper

The paper is organised as follows: Sect. 2 describes the extended form of normalisation that the introduction of **par** and **seq** require, together with the rules which comprise the transition system for our parallel language. Sect. 3 gives example derivations illustrating the semantics, and in particular how it models limited resources. Sect. 4 contains a preliminary exploration of the relationship between this work and [12], and of other properties of the semantics. We end with a critique of the work which motivates our future work, together with conclusions and an outlook.

2 A Transition System for the Parallel Language

The semantics we define is a small step Plotkin-style Structured Operational Semantics [18]. In the semantics steps correspond to single (lockstep) reductions. This contrasts with the natural semantics defined in [12] in which steps correspond to full reductions to whnf. The benefits of a natural semantics are well stated in [12] with the hope there being that the high level of abstraction of a natural semantics will provide for the study of a broad spread of implementations and facilitate the proofs of properties.

Our semantic basis of a lockstep semantics could, from this point of view, be seen as a retrograde step. However, the inclusion of parallelism into the semantics appears to require it: even though we would like to be able to express parallelism between full reductions to whnf there are coordination requirements between thread creation and destruction which require consideration of behaviours at the level of single reductions.

2.1   Normalisation

The transition system is based on a lambda calculus extended with recursive **lets**, and **seq** and **par**, which we normalise to the following restricted syntax. The syntax resembles closely that of [12] in its simplicity, and shares the distinguishing features that all bound variables are distinct so that scope is irrelevant. However, whereas in [12] applications are of the form *an expression applied to a variable*, for us applications are only allowed when they are of the form *a variable applied to a variable*. Although motivation for the restrictions is shared between the two approaches—it removes the necessity to generate new closure sites when **lets** are moved into the 'heap'—we have a different form of judgement to that of [12] and must to forego the 'luxury' of an unnamed site. Because of this a function in an application must be transformable to an explicitly named site as well.

The restricted syntax for our extended lambda calculus is:

$$w, x, y, z \in Var$$
$$e \in Exp ::= \lambda\, x . e$$
$$\mid\ y\ x$$
$$\mid\ x$$
$$\mid\ \textbf{let}\ x_1 = e_1, \ldots, x_n = e_n\ \textbf{in}\ e$$
$$\mid\ x\ \textbf{par}\ e$$
$$\mid\ x\ \textbf{seq}\ e$$

(Representatives of syntactic categories will be decorated as and when necessary.)

The reader will note that **seq** and **par** are allowed expressions as their second argument; this is because of their projective nature (e_1 **par** $e_2 = e_2$ and $e_1 \neq \bot \Rightarrow$ e_1 **seq** $e_2 = e_2$), and the fact that they will be an explicitly named closure in the semantics. There projective nature implies that it is safe to reuse this name for their second argument.

Transforming an arbitrary term to the above syntax is done through the process of normalisation which is defined next. The first stage of normalisation is to produce $\hat{e}$ from e. $\hat{e}$ is e to which α-conversion has been applied renaming all bound variables to 'fresh' variable names. Although it also applies to lambda terms the main use of this step is so that, when a **let** expression is moved to the 'heap', there will be no clashes in variable names.

The second stage in the normalisation of a term is to reduce it to the restricted syntax. For a term e we define:

$$(\lambda x.e)^* = \lambda x.(e^*)$$
$$x^* = x$$
$$(\textbf{let } x_1 = e_1, \ldots, x_n = e_n \textbf{ in } e)^*$$
$$= \textbf{let } x_1 = (e_1^*), \ldots, x_n = (e_n^*) \textbf{ in } (e^*)$$

$$(e_1 \ e_2)^* = \begin{cases} e_1 \ e_2 & \text{if } e_1, e_2 \text{ are variables} \\ \textbf{let } y = (e_2^*) \textbf{ in } (e_1 \ y) & \text{if } e_1 \text{ is a variable} \\ \textbf{let } x = (e_1^*) \textbf{ in } (x \ e_2) & \text{if } e_2 \text{ is a variable} \\ \textbf{let } x = (e_1^*), y = (e_2^*) \textbf{ in } (x \ y) & \text{otherwise} \end{cases}$$

$$(e_1 \textbf{ par } e_2)^* = \begin{cases} e_1 \textbf{ par } (e_2^*) & \text{if } e_1 \text{ is a variable} \\ \textbf{let } x = (e_1^*) \textbf{ in } (x \textbf{ par } (e_2^*)) & \text{otherwise} \end{cases}$$

$$(e_1 \textbf{ seq } e_2)^* = \begin{cases} e_1 \textbf{ seq } (e_2^*) & \text{if } e_1 \text{ is a variable} \\ \textbf{let } x = (e_1^*) \textbf{ in } (x \textbf{ seq } (e_2^*)) & \text{otherwise} \end{cases}$$

where each introduced variable is 'fresh'.

Other than for the case of application (as described above), normalisation here and in [12], are the same for the core language. The extra cases of **par** and **seq** provide for the expanded syntax of the strategic extensions to the language.

2.2   Transition System

The rules which define the lockstep semantics are presented in Fig. 2, and their detail will be described in Sect. 2.4. Elements in the figure (and, more widely, the paper) follow naming conventions thus:

$$\Delta, \Gamma \in Heap = Var \nrightarrow Exp ::= \{x_1 \mapsto e_1, \ldots, x_n \mapsto e_n\}$$
$$v \in Val ::= \lambda x.e$$

A heap is a partial function from variables to expressions. A value is an expression in whnf.

A judgement in the transition system is of the form:

$$\Delta : \Gamma \longrightarrow \Delta' : \Gamma'$$

which should be read as

the *live* bindings Γ in the context of the *dead* bindings Δ in one step become the *live* bindings Γ' in the context of the *dead* bindings Δ'.

As we shall see, the concept of 'one-step' does not restrict us to a single change in the live heap as the 'one-step' is a single *lock*step, and may consist of any number of single steps (under the proviso that sufficient resources are available).

Sequential Rules

$$\Delta : (y \mapsto \textbf{let } x_1 = e_1, \ldots, x_n = e_n \textbf{ in } e)$$
$$\longrightarrow (\Delta, x_1 \mapsto e_1, \ldots, x_n \mapsto e_n) : (y \mapsto e) \qquad \textit{Let}$$

$$(\Delta, x \mapsto \lambda w.e) : (z \mapsto x \ y)$$
$$\longrightarrow (\Delta, x \mapsto \lambda w.e) : (z \mapsto e[y/w]) \quad \textit{Application}$$

$$(\Delta, x \mapsto v) : (y \mapsto x) \longrightarrow (\Delta, x \mapsto v) : (y \mapsto \hat{v}) \qquad \textit{Variable}$$

$$(\Delta, x \mapsto v) : (z \mapsto x \textbf{ seq } e) \longrightarrow (\Delta, x \mapsto v) : (z \mapsto e) \qquad \textit{Sequence}$$

$$\Delta : (z \mapsto x \textbf{ par } e') \longrightarrow \Delta : (z \mapsto e') \qquad \textit{Parallel1}$$

$$(\Delta, x \mapsto e) : (z \mapsto x \textbf{ par } e') \longrightarrow \Delta : (x \mapsto e, z \mapsto e') \qquad \textit{Parallel2}$$

Parallel Rules

$$\frac{\Delta : \tau_i \longrightarrow \Delta_i : \tau_i', \quad 1 \leq i \leq n_{red} \qquad n_{red} + m_a \leq \textbf{max}}{\Delta : \Gamma \longrightarrow \Gamma_d \cup \bigcup \Delta_i \setminus \Delta_a : \Delta_a \cup \bigcup \tau_i'} \qquad \textit{Product}$$

Fig. 2. The small-step transition system

2.3 The Parallel Abstract Machine

The transition system defines an abstract machine for the interpretation of terms in our parallel functional language. The abstract machine has explicit initial and terminal states so that we can begin and end computations from known points.

The *initial configuration* of the abstract machine is:

$$\varnothing : \{main \mapsto e\}$$

where *main* is the thread that drives the computation. *e* is likely to be a *let* expression. Note that, as we explicitly name all closures, *main* is explicit in the initial configuration.

The *terminal configuration* of a program is *not* that in which all calculation has ceased—such a scheme would allow non-terminating computations uninvolved in the determination of the value of *main* to prevent termination—rather that in which a (whnf) value has been returned for the *main* thread:

$$\Delta : (\Gamma, main \mapsto v)$$

The rules of the system are described next.

2.4   Two Rule Forms

There are two forms of rules in the system: sequential and parallel. The sequential rules apply to what we might call (in the spirit of [14, Pg. 196]) *particulate actions* or *particles*, i.e., the building blocks from which locksteps are built. Particles are characterised by the singleton nature of the live heap *on the lhs of a judgement*[1] (that before the :).

Parallel rules, of which *Product* is the only example, build locksteps from particles, in a way similar to the **Prod** rule of [14], i.e., if, in a particular state, particles can individually perform steps $s_1, \ldots, s_n$, then Product will combine these into the single lockstep $\{s_1, \ldots, s_n\}$. Because of this, applications of *Product* are justified through individual applications of the sequential rules to the constituent particles.

In addition, *Product* allows live, but whnf, terms to be switched out and dead, non-whnf, terms to have resources assigned to them, which is not the case for Milner's **Prod** rule.

Application, Variable, Let These rules allow progression in the computation associated with a single named closure in the heap.

The *Let* rule transforms the binding list of a **let** expression into named closures in the dead heap. We recall that the first normalisation step renames all bound variables to 'fresh' variables, so that this transformation will not produce name clashes.

For *Application* we assume that the function (bound to variable x in the rule) has already been reduced to whnf and appears in the dead environment. The transition associated with *Application* is to perform the β-reduction.

The *Variable* rule allows a variable whose binding is already whnf in the dead environment to be replaced by its whnf value.

Parallel and Sequence The *Sequence* rule states that if we have completed the computation of the first argument of a **seq** (i.e., it is in whnf), we should make a start on the second argument. That we require a completed reduction to whnf term for the first argument before starting the second provides the source of the strictness of **seq** in its first argument.

The *Parallel2* rule assigns a resource to the calculation of its first and second arguments. We assume that the first argument was dead. This rule will be allowed in the justification of a *Product* step if there are sufficient resources to be applied to both arguments. The *Parallel1* rule applies if there are insufficient resources: it discards its first operand. The determination of which rule to apply is made in the *Product* rule, described next.

Product The *Product* rule models our lockstep semantics of parallelism, and its resource consciousness.

---

[1] Not necessarily the rhs of a judgement.

The rule requires the following assumptions on the form of the heaps; that either:

- a live term can being reduced using one of the *Application, Variable, Let, Sequence* or one of the two parallel rules (which, in the case of the *Parallel2*, will introduce a thread into the live heap from the dead heap);
- an *irreducible* expression can be moved from the live heap to the dead heap. (In this context, by irreducible we mean that the expression is already in whnf, or is one of $x\ y$ or x **seq** e where x (or the expression bound to x) is not in whnf in the dead environment.)
- a non-whnf expression can be assigned a resource, and so moved from the dead heap to the live heap; or
- a dead thread can remain in the dead heap.

To keep the rule in Fig. 2 'page sized', we have used the following notation:

- $\Delta = \Delta_a \cup \Delta_d$ with $\Delta_a = \{y_1 \mapsto e_1, \ldots, y_{m_a} \mapsto e_{m_a}\}$ being those dead threads which become active either through the switching in of a dead thread (in which case e_i is not a whnf expression), or because of an application of the *Parallel2* rule, and $\Delta_d = \{y_{m_a+1} \mapsto e_{m_a+1}, \ldots, y_m \mapsto e_m\}$ being those dead threads that remain dead (in which case e_i may or may not be a whnf expression).
- $\Gamma = \Gamma_{red} \cup \Gamma_d$ with $\Gamma_{red} = \{\tau_1, \ldots, \tau_{n_{red}}\}$, $\tau_i = x_i \mapsto e_i$, being those active (and hence non-whnf) threads that reduce, and $\Gamma_d = \{x_{n_{red}+1} \mapsto v_{n_{red}+1}, \ldots, x_n \mapsto v_n\}$ being those alive, but irreducible, threads that become dead. Δ_i is the change wrought on the dead environment through the reduction of τ_i to τ_i'.

The indices of the variables provide as to their behaviour. Those in the live heap between 1 and n_{red} will reduce. Those in the live heap which will migrate to the dead heap can be found between indices $n_{red} + 1$ and n (this covers all indices: a thread is either reducible and reduce in the next step or is in whnf and so have its assigned resource recovered). Those in the dead heap which migrate to the live heap will be found from indices 1 and n_a.

The only other component of the rule is the proviso involving **max** which ensures that the movement of dead to live and live to dead does not exceed the level of resources available.

2.5   Building Parallel Behaviours

Because of the split between sequential and parallel rules, parallel behaviours are built solely from applications of the *Product* rule with the other rules only being used in the justification of their application. In derivations of lockstep sequences this should mean that all steps have the name *Product*, which is rather unhelpful. One might consider leaving individual steps in a derivation unlabelled; but, at least in small derivations, the reading of a derivation is facilitated by annotating *Product* rule application with its sequential justifying steps. So, for instance, the step

$$\varnothing : \{main \mapsto \mathbf{let}\ f = \lambda\,x.x, g = \lambda\,x.x, gx = g\ x\ \mathbf{in}\ gx\ \mathbf{par}\,f\ gx\}$$
$$\longrightarrow \{f \mapsto \lambda\,x.x, g \mapsto \lambda\,x.x, gx \mapsto g\ x\} : \{main \mapsto gx\ \mathbf{par}\,f\ gx\}\ Product$$

. . .

in which a *Let* step has been used to justify the *Product* will be written

$$\varnothing : \{main \mapsto \mathbf{let}\ f = \lambda\,x.x, g = \lambda\,x.x, gx = g\ x\ \mathbf{in}\ gx\ \mathbf{par}\,f\ gx\}$$
$$\longrightarrow \{f \mapsto \lambda\,x.x, g \mapsto \lambda\,x.x, gx \mapsto g\ x\} : \{main \mapsto gx\ \mathbf{par}\,f\ gx\}\ Let$$

. . .

When two or more sequential rules are used in the justification of a single application we will write them as a comma separated list. When the only steps involved in an application of *Product* are the switching-in or switching-out of threads, we will annotate an application with *Product*.

3   Example

As an example of the transition system in action, we present the derivation of the term

$$main = \mathbf{let}\ f = \lambda\,x.x, g = \lambda\,x.x, gx = g\ x\ \mathbf{in}\ gx\ \mathbf{par}\,f\ gx$$

in two situations:

1. when $\mathbf{max} = 1$, with a single processor architecture;
2. when $\mathbf{max} = 2$, with a dual-processor architecture.

The details of the term are not particularly interesting, other than for the fact that *main* contains a **par** construct. This fact should distinguish the two situations.

In the case when $\mathbf{max} = 1$ we have that:

$$\varnothing : \{main \mapsto \mathbf{let}\ f = \lambda\,x.x, g = \lambda\,x.x, gx = g\ x\ \mathbf{in}\ gx\ \mathbf{par}\,f\ gx\}$$
$$\longrightarrow \{f \mapsto \lambda\,x.x, g \mapsto \lambda\,x.x, gx \mapsto g\ x\} : \{main \mapsto gx\ \mathbf{par}\,f\ gx\}\quad Let$$
$$\longrightarrow \{f \mapsto \lambda\,x.x, g \mapsto \lambda\,x.x, gx \mapsto g\ x\} : \{main \mapsto f\ gx\}\quad\quad Parallel1(\dagger)$$
$$\longrightarrow \{f \mapsto \lambda\,x.x, g \mapsto \lambda\,x.x, gx \mapsto g\ x\} : \{main \mapsto gx\}\quad\quad\ Application$$
$$\longrightarrow \{f \mapsto \lambda\,x.x, g \mapsto \lambda\,x.x, gx \mapsto g\ x\} : \{main \mapsto g\ x\}\quad\quad Variable$$
$$\longrightarrow \{f \mapsto \lambda\,x.x, g \mapsto \lambda\,x.x, gx \mapsto x\} : \{main \mapsto x\}\quad\quad\quad Application$$

For comparison, in the case when $\mathbf{max} = 2$ we have, rather, that:

$$\varnothing : \{main \mapsto \mathbf{let}\ f = \lambda\,x.x, g = \lambda\,x.x, gx = g\ x\ \mathbf{in}\ gx\ \mathbf{par}\,f\ gx\}$$
$$\longrightarrow \{f \mapsto \lambda\,x.x, g \mapsto \lambda\,x.x, gx \mapsto g\ x\} : \{main \mapsto gx\ \mathbf{par}\,f\ gx\}\ Let$$
$$\longrightarrow \{f \mapsto \lambda\,x.x, g \mapsto \lambda\,x.x\} : \{gx \mapsto g\ x, main \mapsto f\ gx\}\quad Parallel2(\dagger)$$
$$\longrightarrow \{f \mapsto \lambda\,x.x, g \mapsto \lambda\,x.x\} : \{gx \mapsto x, main \mapsto gx\}\quad\ Application,$$
$$\qquad\qquad\qquad\qquad\qquad\qquad\qquad\qquad\qquad\qquad\qquad\qquad Application$$

$$\longrightarrow \{f \mapsto \lambda\,x.x, g \mapsto \lambda\,x.x, gx \mapsto x, main \mapsto gx\} : \varnothing\quad\ Product(*)$$
$$\longrightarrow \{f \mapsto \lambda\,x.x, g \mapsto \lambda\,x.x, gx \mapsto x\} : \{main \mapsto gx\}\quad Product(**)$$
$$\longrightarrow \{f \mapsto \lambda\,x.x, g \mapsto \lambda\,x.x, gx \mapsto x\} : \{main \mapsto x\}\quad\quad Variable$$

Notes:

1. In the case of the second derivation we provide the justification of the first
   Product step (labelled *Application, Application*) involving a lockstep between
   two *Application* applications: one on f in gx and one on g in *main*. The
   justification steps are:

   $$\{f \mapsto \lambda x.x, g \mapsto \lambda x.x\} : \{gx \mapsto g\ x\}$$
   $$\longrightarrow \{f \mapsto \lambda x.x, g \mapsto \lambda x.x\} : \{gx \mapsto x\}\ \text{Application}$$

   $$\{f \mapsto \lambda x.x, g \mapsto \lambda x.x\} : \{main \mapsto f\ gx\}$$
   $$\longrightarrow \{f \mapsto \lambda x.x, g \mapsto \lambda x.x\} : \{main \mapsto gx\}\ \text{Application}$$

2. In the second derivation, in the second *Product* application (labelled $*$) we
   have set $\Gamma_d = \{gx \mapsto x, main \mapsto gx\}$, and used *Product* to switch out all
   irreducible terms.
3. In the third application (labelled $**$) we have set $\Delta_a = \{main \mapsto gx\}$, and
   used *Product* to switch in *main*.
4. The limitation of resources to 1 in the first case prevents the application of
   the *Parallel2* rule at the step marked †; if *Parallel2* were to be applied then
   $n_{red} + m_a = 2 > \textbf{max}$. $\textbf{max} = 2$ in the second derivation so that *Parallel2*
   may be applied in this case.

3.1   On Execution Times

Clearly, the length of a computation should be proportional to the number of
reductions involved in its derivation, so that the measure of execution time is
related to the length of a derivation. This is reflected, to at least some degree,
in the presented semantics: *Product* in a single step can combine many steps
together; we should expect therefore that, at least in the general case, executions involving *Product* will be shorter. However, even though the availability of
resources will often bring with it speed-ups in a computation, there are administrative costs associated with assigning a resource so that the use of parallelism
may produce slow-downs instead. This corresponds to our real-world experiences
of parallelism.

   The lockstep nature of the rule assumes much of the timing of 'swapping-in'
and 'swapping-out' operations: *viz*, that they take the same time as each other
and, moreover, that they both take the same time as an ordinary step. This
might be an unrealistic assumption, but it simplifies the rule greatly.

4   Semantic Propriety

In this section we show consistency with the semantics of [12], and explore a little
the relationship between parallel and sequential computations. The intention of
the consistency result is to show consistency with the semantics of [2], at least
for a subset of the semantics.

To compare our semantics with that of [12] we derive rules which look like the reduction steps of that semantics from our small step rules and *vice-versa*. The translation is quite natural and is done by induction on the length of a derivation. The only real difficulty with the consistency proof is that our semantics includes parallelism. We ameliorate this problem by initially restricting ourselves to the application of rules in which **max** = 1, i.e., there is a single resource for computation (which means that, for any live heap Γ of the computation, $|\Gamma| = 1$) and then showing that, in almost all cases, parallel computations can be made equivalent to sequential ones. The implications of this will be clear to the reader on inspection of the transition system's rules in that the system begins to look very much like [12], any minor differences being only that there is a named single binding on the right of the colon.

The case for which a completely general result fails is dues to the following: although one might expect that parallelism shouldn't add anything to the values computed by a computation, there are terms for which parallelism prevents termination. An example of such a term is

let $x = x$ **par** 5 **in** x

when there are infinite resources; (after application of the *Let* rule) the term tries to use all resources — grabbing them one at a time using *Parallel2* — and hence will not terminate. Note however that, even for this term, as long as resources are finite the problem disappears: the expression stops trying to grab another resource when only one remains and gets on with the computation, eventually returning the value 5.

4.1   Consistency with Launchbury's Semantics

Manipulating a system in which bindings appear on both sides means a little extra work in our demonstration of the relationship; in particular we should show that the manipulations of such unbound thunks can be made even when bindings are involved.

To do this we prove two auxiliary properties, and derive two useful rules for *activating* and *deactivating* thunks. The first lemma states that the binding of an unused variable in the dead heap does not invalidate a computation:

Lemma 1. *Suppose that*

$$\Delta : (\Gamma, x \mapsto e) \longrightarrow^* \Delta' : (\Gamma', x \mapsto e')$$

then

$$(\Delta, w \mapsto x) : \Gamma x \mapsto e \longrightarrow^* (\Delta', w \mapsto x) : (\Gamma', x \mapsto e')$$

whenever $w \notin dom\, \Delta \cup dom\, \Gamma \cup \mathbf{FV}(e)$.

Proof   As w is not referenced in the existing heaps, it does not destroy the property of unique naming. The result follows.   □

The second lemma is slightly more complex, and states that we may arbitrarily rename binding variables, as long as they are not referenced, without invalidating a computation.

Lemma 2. *Suppose that*

$$\Delta : (\Gamma, x \mapsto e) \longrightarrow^* \Delta' : (\Gamma', x \mapsto v)$$

with v in whnf and $x \notin dom\,\Delta \cup dom\,\Gamma$. Then

$$\Delta : (\Gamma, temp \mapsto e \longrightarrow^*)\Delta' : (\Gamma', temp \mapsto v)$$

where $temp \notin dom\,\Delta \cup dom\,\Gamma$.

Proof From the assumptions we claim that e cannot depend on the value of x in reducing to v. For, suppose that it does. Then x depends directly upon its own value, and so should have the denotation $\bot$. But then e will never reach whnf in contradiction of the statement.

Hence e cannot depend directly on the value of x in the reduction. Removing x from the environment and replacing it with *temp* will not invalidate the reduction and we have the result. □

The two derived rules we introduce allow one to 'swap out' an active process, and 'swap in' an inactive process.

Lemma 3. *a. For all Δ and v*

$$\Delta : x \mapsto v \longrightarrow \Delta \cup x \mapsto v : \varnothing \quad .$$

b. For all Δ and v, when $\mathbf{max} \geq 1$,

$$(\Delta, x \mapsto e) : \varnothing \longrightarrow \Delta : x \mapsto e \quad .$$

Proof a. Set $\Delta_a = \varnothing$, $\Delta_d = \Delta$, $\Gamma_{red} = \varnothing$, $\Gamma_d = \{x \mapsto v\}$ in the *Product* rule.

b. If $\mathbf{max} \geq 1$ we may set $\Delta_a = \{x \mapsto e\}$, $\Delta_d = \Delta \setminus \Delta_a$, $\Gamma_{red} = \varnothing$, $\Gamma_d = \varnothing$ in the *Product* rule for the result. □

Theorem 1. *Let $\longrightarrow_A$ be the transition step relation based on Let, Application, Variable, In, and Out. Let $\Downarrow$ be the natural semantics relation of [12].*
Then

1. *$\Downarrow\, \subseteq\, \longrightarrow_A^*$.*
2. *suppose $[\Gamma] \longrightarrow_A^* [\Delta]$. Then for all x such that $(x \mapsto e) \in [\Gamma]$ and $(x \mapsto v) \in [\Delta]$ for some value v, there exists some Θ such that $\Gamma : x \Downarrow \Theta : v$.*

The second property in the statement is clearly the strongest that exists as, under $\longrightarrow_A^*$, we can reduce to non-whnf expressions whereas Launchbury's reductions always end in whnf expressions.

Proof

1. We will derive each of the rules of [12] from our transition step semantics. For *Lambda* and *Let* the result follows from a simple application of the rule with the same name in our system.
   Variable: Assume that

   $$\Gamma : temp \mapsto e \longrightarrow_A^* \Delta : temp \mapsto v$$

   where *temp* is as in the Launchbury convention. Then

   $$
   \begin{aligned}
   (\Gamma, x \mapsto e) &: temp' \mapsto x \\
   \longrightarrow_{Out/In} \; (\Gamma, temp' \mapsto x) &: x \mapsto e \\
   \longrightarrow_* \quad (\Delta, temp' \mapsto x) &: x \mapsto z \\
   \longrightarrow_{Out/In} (\Delta, x \mapsto z) &: temp' \mapsto x \\
   \longrightarrow_{Var} \quad (\Delta, x \mapsto z) &: temp' \mapsto \hat{z}
   \end{aligned}
   $$

   Application: Assume that

   $$\Gamma : temp \mapsto e \longrightarrow_A^* \Delta : temp \mapsto \lambda y.e'$$

   and that

   $$\Delta : temp' \mapsto e'[x/y] \longrightarrow_A^* \Theta : temp' \mapsto z \quad .$$

   Then

   $$
   \begin{aligned}
   (\Gamma, y \mapsto e) &: temp \mapsto y\,x \\
   \longrightarrow_{Out/In} \; (\Gamma, temp \mapsto y\,x) &: y \mapsto e \\
   \longrightarrow_A^* \quad (\Delta, temp \mapsto y\,x) &: y \mapsto \lambda y.e' \\
   \longrightarrow_{Out/In} (\Delta, y \mapsto \lambda y.e') &: temp \mapsto y\,x \\
   \longrightarrow_{Appl} \quad (\Delta, y \mapsto \lambda y.e') &: temp \mapsto e'[x/y] \\
   \longrightarrow_A^* \quad (\Theta, y \mapsto \lambda y.e') &: temp \mapsto z
   \end{aligned}
   $$

   as required.

2. We first introduce some auxiliary notation: suppose Γ is a heap $\{x_i \mapsto e_i\}_{i=1}^n$. We write $[\Gamma]$ to indicate an arbitrary configuration $\{x_1 \mapsto e_1, \ldots x_{j-1} \mapsto e_{j-1}, x_{j+1} \mapsto e_{j+1}, \ldots x_n \mapsto e_n\} : x_j \mapsto e_j$ for some $1 \leq j \leq n$. This helps to filter out irrelevant detail in the proof. By the *Out/In* rule, all such $[\Gamma]$ are in a sense equivalent.

   The proof of this part is by induction on the length of the derivation. Consider the last transition step in each case.
   Let: Suppose

   $$[\Gamma] \longrightarrow_A^* \Gamma' : (x \mapsto \text{let } y_1 = e_1 \ldots \text{ in } v) \longrightarrow_{Let} (\Gamma', y_1 \mapsto e_1 \ldots) : x \mapsto v$$

   The inductive hypothesis (on the $\longrightarrow_A^*$) immediately gives the result for all value bindings in Γ'. All that we need to show is that x evaluates to v in Launchbury's semantics. That's easy:

   $$
   \frac{\dfrac{(\Gamma, y_1 \mapsto e_1 \ldots) : v \Downarrow (\Gamma, y_1 \mapsto e_1 \ldots) : v}{\Gamma : \text{let } y_1 = e_1 \ldots \text{ in } v \Downarrow (\Gamma, y_1 \mapsto e_1 \ldots) : v} \; Let}{\Gamma : x \Downarrow (\Gamma, y_1 \mapsto e_1 \ldots) : \hat{v}} \; Variable
   $$

App:

$$[\Gamma] \longrightarrow_A^* (\Gamma', y \mapsto \lambda w.e) : x \mapsto y\,z \longrightarrow_{App} (\Gamma', y \mapsto \lambda w.e) : x \mapsto e[z/w]$$

Again the inductive hypothesis gives the result for all value bindings in Γ' and in particular:

$$\Gamma : y \Downarrow \Theta : \lambda w.e$$

If $e[z/w]$ is a value then we need to prove the result for x. It follows from the above by Launchbury's *Application rule*:

$$\frac{\Gamma : y \Downarrow \Theta : \lambda w.e \qquad \Theta : e[z/w] \Downarrow \Theta : e[z/w]}{\Gamma : y\,z \Downarrow \Theta : e[z/w]} \; Application$$

Out/In:

$$[\Gamma] \longrightarrow_A^* (\Gamma', x \mapsto v) : y \mapsto e \longrightarrow_{O/I} (\Gamma', y \mapsto e) : x \mapsto v$$

Immediate for all value bindings by inductive hypothesis.
Var:

$$[\Gamma, x \mapsto y] \longrightarrow_A^* (\Gamma', y \mapsto v) : x \mapsto y \longrightarrow_{Var} (\Gamma', y \mapsto v) : x \mapsto \hat{v}$$

Again the inductive hypothesis gives the result for all value bindings except x. By the inductive hypothesis we have

$$(\Gamma, x \mapsto y) : y \Downarrow \Theta : v$$

Since this deduction succeeds it must be the case that we can also derive

$$\Gamma : y \Downarrow \Theta : v$$

Otherwise y would directly depend on itself before a value was returned, and *both* proofs would have failed. Now we can simply apply the *Variable* rule:

$$\frac{\Gamma : y \Downarrow \Theta : v}{(\Gamma, x \mapsto y) : x \Downarrow \Theta : \hat{v}} \; Variable$$

$\square$

We informally discussed the relationship between parallelism and sequentiality in the context of infinite resources in the introduction to his section. A formal characterisation of this is:

Theorem 2. *If* **max** $< \infty$ *then for any computation there is an equivalent computation in a system with a single resource.*

We first define the notion of a *sequential* computation:

Definition 1. *A computation is sequential when, for all judgements $\Delta : \Gamma$ which appear in the computation, $|\Gamma| \leq 1$.*

Sequential computations can take place with as little as a single resource available.

Whence:

Proof **Idea**: By induction on the length of the proof. Base case is immediate (as initial configuration is sequential). Induction step 'flattens' a lockstep into its components (with judicious us of *In* and *Out*).   □

5   Discussion and Conclusions

We have defined a lockstep semantics of a functional language with explicit parallelism which models the effects of bounded resources during execution. We have shown that, in the case when there is a single resource, the system is the same as (to all intents and purposes) that of [12]. One useful implication is that, at least in this restricted resource case, the system correctly behaves lazily, according to Launchbury's proof of consistency with Abramsky's semantics of [2]. We have also shown that when there is more than a single resource each computation is serialisable (i.e., is equivalent to a computation on a machine with a single resource). In combination with the previous result we have that, even in the presence of parallelism, sharing is preserved, i.e., an expression is evaluated at most once.

However, the existing semantics is unsatisfactory because it does not identify what bindings should be moved from the dead heap to the live heap when resources are available. As a consequence, by selecting appropriate bindings each time it is possible to model a range of reduction strategies, including normal order and applicative order. On a machine with an unbounded number of processors it is even possible to model Knuth-Bendix reduction where every redex is reduced. An unfortunate consequence of this under-specification is that the semantics is highly speculative: it does not guarantee that a binding promoted to the live heap is needed by the program. By choosing inappropriate bindings an expression that would not be evaluated by a GpH program may be evaluated by the semantics.

Although there are many rules which could be added to the system which *reduce* the amount of speculative evaluation, we have been unable to find one that removes it completely (at least whilst preserving the resource consciousness of the semantics) without recording dependencies between active threads and the bindings needed or demanded by a thread (as occurs in the GpH run-time system!). We are actively investigating an augmented semantics that records these dependencies.

Such an augmented semantics, in removing (unplanned) speculative evaluation, will more accurately model GpH. With it, we will be in a better position to investigate the necessary notions of equivalence, such as simulation or bisimulation, which could serve for the characterisation of properties of the coordination primitives, such as those proffered in Sect. 1.1 and, ultimately, evaluation strategies themselves.

To do this we will need to consider standard performance measures such as *Work*, *Average Parallelism*, and *Runtime* ([6]) of which, in the context of Fig. 1, we make the following observations:

- **Work** (the total number of reductions performed by all threads in the computation): the right hand sides of equivalences (II) and (III) perform more work than the left hand sides because there is an additional reduction in each.
- **Average Parallelism** (the average number of active threads during the computation): the average parallelism of the right hand sides of equivalences (II) and (III) is greater than that of the left, again because extra reductions are involved.
- **Runtime** (the number of reductions for the program to complete, for conservative parallelism runtime is work divided by average parallelism): intuitively the runtime, R, of the left and right hand sides of equivalence (III) are the same because.

$$R[\![\ e_0 \ ]\!] + max(R[\![\ e_1 \ ]\!], R[\![\ e_2 \ ]\!])$$
$$= max(R[\![\ e_0 \ ]\!] + R[\![\ e_1 \ ]\!], R[\![\ e_0 \ ]\!] + R[\![\ e_2 \ ]\!])$$

The same is the case for equivalence (II), *mutatis mutandis*.

We note that, in all cases, (I) preserves its status as an equivalence.

5.1   On the *Product* Rule

The existing product rule is very complex, because it fulfils several functions simultaneously:

1. Reduce each binding in the live heap simultaneously.
2. Move whnf bindings from the live heap into the dead heap (*deactivation*)
3. Move non-whnf bindings from the dead heap into the live heap (*activation*)
4. Constrain the size of the live heap to be less than the number of processors.

It is possible to use a simplified product rule that controls only parallel reduction (function 1), if we introduce a second, *scheduling* relation that controls activation, deactivation and resource constraint (properties 2, 3 and 4). Computation is then modelled by alternating reduction and scheduling relations.

Acknowledgments

This work was produced under the APSET project, funded by The Open University.

Many thanks to David Crowe, of the Applied Mathematics Department of the Open University, for his always perspicacious comments.

References

1. J. C. Peterson, K. Hammond, L. Augustsson, B. Boutel, F. W. Burton, J. Fasel, A. D. Gordon, R. J. M. Hughes, P. Hudak, T. Johnsson, M. P. Jones, E. Meijer, S. L. Peyton Jones, A. Reid, and P. L. Wadler. *Report on the Non-Strict Functional Language, Haskell, Version 1.4*, Yale University, 1997. Available at http://haskell.org.

2. S. Abramsky. The Lazy Lambda Calculus. In D.A. Turner, editor, *Declarative Programming*. Addison-Wesley, 1990.

3. G.E. Blelloch, S. Chatterjee, J.C. Hardwick, J. Spielstein, and M. Zagha. Implementation of a portable nested data-parallel language. In *Proc. Fourth ACM Conference on Principles & Practice of Parallel Programming (PPoPP '93)*, pages 102–111. San Diego, CA, May 1993.

4. S. Breitinger, R. Loogen, Y. Ortega-Mallén, and R. Peña. The Eden Coordination Model for Distributed Memory Systems. In *Proc. HIPS '97 — High-Level Parallel Programming Models and Supportive Environments*. IEEE Press, 1997.

5. M.M.T. Chakravarty, Y. Guo, M. Köhler, and H.C.R. Lock. Goffin: Higher-Order Functions Meet Concurrent Constraints. *Science of Computer Programming*, 30(1-2):157–199, 1998.

6. D. L. Eager, J. Zahorjan, and E.D. Lazowska. Speedup Versus Efficiency in Parallel Systems. *IEEE Transactions on Computers*, 38(3):408–423, March 1989.

7. J. Feo, P. Miller, S. Skedziewlewski, S. Denton, and C. Soloman. Sisal 90. In *Proc. HPFC '95 — High Performance Functional Computing*, pages 35–47, April 1995. Denver, CO.

8. R. Halstead. MultiLisp: a Language for Concurrent Symbolic Computation. *ACM Transactions on Programming Languages and Systems*, 7(4):501–538, 1998.

9. M. Hennessy. *Algebraic Theory of Processes*. MIT Press, 1988.

10. M. Hennessy. *The Semantics of Programming Languages: An Elementary Introduction using Structural Operational Semantics*. Wiley, 1990.

11. J.M. Kewley and K. Glynn. Evaluation Annotations for Hope+. In *Proc. 1989 Glasgow Workshop on Functional Programming*, pages 329–337, Springer-Verlag WiCS, August 1989.

12. J. Launchbury. A Natural Semantics for Lazy Evaluation. In *Proc. 20th. ACM Symposium on Principles of Programming Languages (POPL '93)*, pages 144–154, Charleston, South Carolina, January 1993.

13. R. Mirani and P. Hudak. First-Class Schedules and Virtual Maps. In *Proc. Conference on Functional Programming and Computer Architecture (FPCA '95)*, pages 78–85, June 1995.

14. A.J.R.G. Milner. *Communication and Concurrency*. Prentice-Hall International, 1989.

15. G. Michaelson and N. Scaife. Prototyping a Parallel Vision System in Standard ML. *Journal of Functional Programming*, 5(3):345–382, 1995.

16. R.S. Nikhil, Arvind, and J. Hicks. pH Language Proposal. Technical report, DEC Cambridge Research Lab, 1993.

17. E.G.J.M.H. Nöcker, J.E.W. Smetsers, M.C.J.D. van Eekelen, and M.J. Plasmeijer. Concurrent Clean. In *Proc. PARLE '91 — Parallel Architectures and Reduction Languages Europe*, volume 505/506 of *LNCS*, pages 202–220. Springer Verlag, 1991.

18. G.D. Plotkin. Structured Approach to Operational Semantics. Technical Report DAIMI FN-19, Computer Science Department, Aarhus University, 1981.

19. P.W. Trinder, K. Hammond, J.S. Mattson Jr., A.S. Partridge, and S.L. Peyton Jones. GUM: a Portable Parallel Implementation of Haskell. In *Proc. 1996 ACM Conference on Programming Language Design and Implementation (PLDI '96)*, Philadelphia, pages 78–88, May 1996.
20. P.W. Trinder, K. Hammond, H.-W. Loidl, and S.L. Peyton Jones. Algorithm + Strategy = Parallelism. *Journal of Functional Programming*, 8(1):23–60, January 1998.

Concurrent Monadic Interfacing

Ian Holyer and Eleni Spiliopoulou

Department of Computer Science
University of Bristol, United Kingdom
{ian,spilio}@cs.bris.ac.uk

Abstract. In this paper we present the Brisk[1] monadic framework, in
which the usual monadic style of interfacing is adapted to accommodate a
deterministic form of concurrency. Its main innovation is to allow actions
on state components. This is a key issue which enables *state splitting*, a
technique which assigns to each new thread a part of the state, a *substate*,
to act upon. Distinct concurrent threads are restricted to access disjoint
substates. A purely functional prototype implementation is presented to
demonstrate these ideas. The resulting system acts as a basis for offering
a purely functional form of concurrency, extending the expressiveness
of functional languages without spoiling the semantics by introducing
non-determinism.

1 Introduction

The use of monads [18] has provided a new insight into the handling of stateful
computations, notably I/O and incremental arrays, as state threads in the purely
functional language Haskell [2]. Additionally, state threads have been securely
encapsulated [11, 12] and incorporated into compilers such as GHC. This framework has also been adapted to support concurrency [6] and to build reactive
systems [5, 4] in Haskell.

However, concurrency has been incorporated at the cost of introducing non-
determinism during thread creation and communication. The primitive forkIO
creates concurrent threads that mutate the same state and so non-deterministic
effects can immediately arise e.g. two threads can simultaneously access the same
file. Furthermore, threads are allowed to communicate via non-deterministic
merge operators such as mergeIO. To restore semantic properties, a compromise
called *referentially transparent non-determinism* has been adopted, where non-
determinism is pushed out of the functional program into the I/O actions and
I/O state, leaving the functional program referentially transparent. Although
the semantic properties of programs are retained, their externally visible behaviour is still non-deterministic; programs are unpredictable and unrepeatable,
and wider systems programming is not supported.

Deterministic concurrency [3, 8] is a purely declarative approach to concurrency which extends the demand driven evaluation model of functional languages
into one with multiple independent demands. The independence of demands can

---

[1] **Brisk** stands for Bristol Haskell compiler

H. Hammond, T. Davie, and C. Clack (Eds.): IFL'98, LNCS 1595, pp. 72–87, 1999.
© Springer-Verlag Berlin Heidelberg 1999

only be guaranteed by restricting distinct threads so that each acts on a different portion of the state, a *substate*, which is disjoint from the substates other threads act upon. Thus, non-deterministic effects that arise when threads mutate the same state are avoided. To achieve this, we use the technique of *state splitting*. State splitting is a mechanism which assigns at creation of each new thread a substate, disjoint from other substates, to act upon. This approach enables a concurrent setting where several independent threads access the outside world, i.e. the I/O state of the program. Under such a deterministic approach to concurrency, a processor can run one or more I/O performing operations without exhibiting any user-visible non-determinism.

In order to incorporate such a state splitting mechanism for supporting deterministic concurrency into Haskell 1.4, the underlying monadic framework needs to be extended with the ability to provide independent substates and to allow actions on such state components. In this paper, we present the Brisk monadic framework adopted in the Brisk compiler; its main innovation is that it enables the creation of independent state components and actions upon them. This framework retains all the state-based facilities provided in the existing one. Such an extended monadic framework offers two additional advantages. It provides a modularised approach to state types, where each state type and primitive operations can be defined in its own module. Furthermore, it improves some existing language features by making them deterministic, e.g. reading characters lazily from a file without unexpected effects. We also provide a lazy version of the standard Haskell function `writeFile` for writing characters lazily to a file.

2   The Existing Monadic Framework

The monadic approach for handling state has provided a new model for performing I/O, which has been incorporated into the Haskell language since version 1.3. For the GHC compiler, a generalised monadic framework has been proposed [11], which also supports other state-based facilities such as destructive array update. In this framework, any stateful computation or *state thread* is expressed as a state transformer of type `ST s a` which represents actions on a state type `s` returning results of type `a`:

```
type ST s a = s -> (a, s)
```

Single-threading is achieved by turning `ST` into an abstract data type. All primitive actions are made strict in the state to ensure that previous actions have completed. Actions can only be combined using the following generic operations:

```
returnST :: a -> ST s a
thenST :: ST s a -> (a -> ST s b) -> ST s b
```

All external state-based facilities, i.e. I/O and foreign procedure calls, are captured into a single state type called `RealWorld`, and all access to these external facilities occurs in a single global state thread, so

that a linear ordering is put on all procedure calls. A simple approach to I/O could use the type:

```
type IO a = ST RealWorld a
```

All internal facilities such as incremental arrays are bundled into a polymorphic state type **s** which notionally represents the program's heap. All access to internal state types happens via references. These are provided as pointers to ordinary values or to special state types such as arrays. A reference of type **MutVar s a** denotes an updatable location in a state of type **s**, which contains values of type **a**, introduced by:

```
newVar :: a -> ST s (MutVar s a)
```

The state type **s**, as well as representing the heap, is also used for encapsulation to ensure safety of state thread accesses. For internal facilities, the primitive **runST** has been provided, which has a rank-2 polymorphic type:

```
runST :: (forall s. ST s a) -> a
```

This takes a complete action sequence as its argument, creates an initially 'empty' state, obeys the actions and returns the result discarding the final state. Each internal state thread has a separate polymorphic state variable and the references in it are 'tagged' with this variable. For each state thread, the enclosing **runST** limits its scope and prevents its references from escaping, or references belonging to other state threads from being used within it. By forcing the state argument to be polymorphic, **runST** can only be used for internal facilities, since they refer to a polymorphic state type, and not for I/O which is applied to the specific state type **RealWorld**. This enforces a single I/O state thread, taken to exist when the program begins, by preventing further unrelated I/O state threads from being created, which could destroy referential transparency.

Both lazy and strict versions of **thenST** have been proposed:

```
thenST :: ST s a -> (a -> ST s b) -> ST s b
thenST m k s = k x s' where (x, s') = m s

strictThenST :: ST s a -> (a -> ST s b) -> ST s b
strictThenST m k s = case m s of (x, s') = k x s'
```

The strict one has been suggested for use with I/O, for efficiency. Indeed, without it, an infinite printing loop might never produce any output, for example. Lazy state threads [10], have also been considered important because they preserve laziness in the presence of imperative actions. Additionally, lazy state threads seem to be the right choice in the case of internal state, where the state is discarded at the end of the computation. Their use with I/O, although it has been hinted at in the case of interleaved I/O operations [13, 11], has so far been neglected. It turns out that they play an important role in deterministic concurrency, where evaluation of one thread should not force the main thread to terminate in order to see any results.

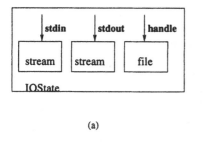

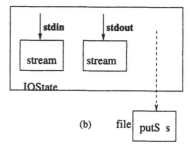

(a)   (b)   file

Fig. 1. (a) State Splitting. (b) State Forking

3   The Brisk Monadic Framework

The main issue that has permeated the design of the Brisk monadic framework is to allow states to have independent state components or substates, with separate threads acting on those substates, possibly concurrently. Specific functions are provided to create and act on substates. Each substate is associated with a reference and every access to a substate happens via this reference, as in Fig. 1. This implies that internal state types such as arrays are separated from the reference mechanism as described in [11] and they no longer need to be accessed via references, unless they happen to be substates of some other state. Thus, in the Brisk monadic framework there is no longer a distinction between internal (i.e. arrays) and external (i.e. I/O) state types. Instead, each facility has its own concrete type, so that both internal and external facilities are treated uniformly. Moreover, each state type can be defined separately in its own module. Similarly, a group of related foreign procedure calls can be encapsulated in its own module by defining a suitable state type and presenting the procedures as suitable actions.

In the next sections, the Brisk monadic framework is outlined and all the facilities that derive from it are illustrated. First, we show how all the facilities mentioned in the GHC monadic framework [11] are reproduced in the Brisk one and then we present additional features that derive from our approach.

3.1   Generic Primitives

Any stateful computation is expressed via the type Act t s a, together with operations returnAct and thenAct for accessing it:

```
type Act t s a = s -> (a,s)
returnAct :: a -> Act t s a
thenAct :: Act t s a -> (a -> Act t s b) -> Act t s b
run :: s -> (forall t. Act t s a) -> a
```

The type Act t s a is very similar to ST s a, but we have changed the name to avoid confusion between the two. The returnAct and thenAct functions have

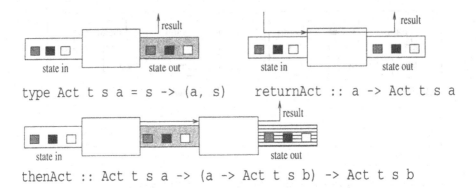

Fig. 2. Monadic Operators

the same definitions as `returnST` and the lazy version of `thenST`. As with `ST`, `Act` is made abstract for protection. An action of type `Act t s a` transforms a state of type `s` and delivers a result of type `a` together with a new state of type `s`, as can be seen in Fig. 2. However, `s` will now normally be instantiated to a specific state type. The second purpose of `s` in `ST s a`, namely to act as a tag identifying a specific state thread, is separated out into the extra type variable `t`, which is never instantiated.

As an example, we will show later that `I/O` facilities can be defined essentially as in Haskell with:

```
type IO t a = Act t RealWorld a
```

The `IO` type now has a tag `t` on it. It is possible to make this tagging less visible to the programmer, but we do not pursue that here. We will see later that specialised state-splitting facilities can be provided for safe handling of concurrent `I/O` threads.

The run function takes an initial value for the state and an action to perform. It carries out the given action on the initial state, discards the final state and returns the result. As with `runST`, the tag variable `t` identifies a particular state thread at compile-time. Forcing the action to be polymorphic in `t` encapsulates the state thread, preventing references from escaping from their scope or being used in the wrong state. To prevent run from being used in conjunction with `IO`, the `IO` module does not export any useful state value which can be used as an initial state.

The generic facilities for handling substates and references are:

```
type Ref t u s = ...
new :: s1 -> (forall u. Ref t u s1->Act t s a) -> Act t s a
at :: Ref t u s1 -> Act u s1 a -> Act t s a
```

One of the main changes in the Brisk monadic framework concerns the philosophy of references. They are treated as being independent of any specific

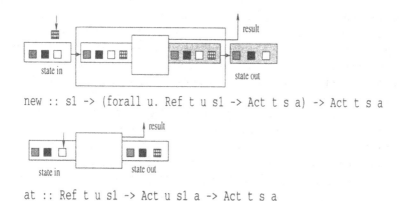

```
new :: s1 -> (forall u. Ref t u s1 -> Act t s a) -> Act t s a
```

```
at :: Ref t u s1 -> Act u s1 a -> Act t s a
```

Fig. 3. Operators for Handling Substates

substate type. References can be thought of as pointers to substates, see also Fig. 1. The reference type has two tags. The first refers to the main state and ensures that the reference is used in the state where it was created. The second tag refers to the substate, and ensures that the reference can only be used while the substate actually exists.

The **new** function is introduced to implement state splitting. The **new** function creates a new substate of type **s1** with a given initial value. It does this for any desired type **s** of main state. It also creates a reference to the new substate, as can be seen in Fig. 3. The second argument to **new** is a function which takes the new reference and performs the actions on the new extended main state. This contrasts with definitions such as the one for **openFile** where a reference is returned directly and the main action sequence continues. However, in a context where there may be substates and subsubstates and so on, this encapsulation of the actions on the extended state is needed to provide a scope for the new tag variable **u** and to protect references from misuse.

The function **at**, see also Fig. 3, carries out an action on a substate. The call **at r f** performs action **f** on the substate corresponding to the reference **r**. This is regarded as an action on the main state in which the rest of the state (the main state value and the other substates) is unaltered. In the main state, the substate accessible via **r** is replaced by the final state after the primitive actions in **f** have been performed. The actions in **f** are performed lazily, i.e. driven by demand on its result and may be interleaved with later actions in the main thread. This assumes that the substate is independent of the main state so that the order of interleaving does not matter. Consider a sequence of actions:

    a1 >> at r a2 >> a3 >> at r a4 >> a5 ...

As in Haskell, we use overloaded functions **>>=** and **>>** and **return** for monadic operations, in this case referring to **thenAct** etc. The laziness of **thenAct** means that the actions in the sequence are driven only by the demand for results. The usual convention that primitive actions should be strict in the state ensures that the actions happen in sequence. However, main state actions such as a3 are not strict in the substates of the main state. The action at r a2 replaces the substate referred to by r by an unevaluated expression; it is the next action a4 on the substate which causes a2 to be performed. Thus, the sequence of actions a1, a3, ... on the main state, and the sequence a2, a4, ... on the substate, may be executed independently. We are assuming here that the substate is independent of the main state, so that the order of interleaving does not matter. The laziness of the **thenAct** operator allows concurrency effects to be obtained in this way.

It is possible that a main state action such as a5 may cause the evaluation of the result of some previous action on a substate such as a4. In this case, there is effectively a synchronisation point, forcing all previous actions on the substate to be completed before the main state action is performed.

Now, each individual state type and its primitive actions can be defined separately in its own module. It is easy to add new state types, e.g. out of values or procedural interfaces. Furthermore, this modularised point of view can be used for providing separate interfaces to separate C libraries, instead of using a primitive **ccall**.

3.2   Semantics

The semantics of our proposed system does not require anything beyond normal lazy functional semantics. In particular, although state splitting is designed to work alongside concurrency, it is independent of concurrency and can be described in sequential terms. Thus, instead of presenting the semantics directly with a mathematical formalism, we choose to present it using a prototype implementation in Haskell. For the prototype implementation, we use Hugs which supports 2nd-order polymorphism, a common extension to Haskell at the time of writing. The principle difficulty in producing the prototype is not in capturing the correct semantics, but rather in getting around Haskell's type system. When substates are added to a state, it would seem that the type of the main state needs to change, but the type changes are too dynamic to be captured by the usual polymorphism or overloading tricks.

In the prototype implementation presented in this paper, the state type **State** s is polymorphic and describes a state with a value of type s and a list of substates. To get around Haskell's type system, substates are not described using type **State** but instead are given the substate type Sub. This is not polymorphic, but is a union of specific instantiations of the **State** type. Each type which can form a substate is made an instance of the **Substate** class, with functions **sub** and **unsub** which convert the generic state representation to and from the specific substate representation.

```
data State s = S s [Sub]

data Sub = SI Int [Sub] | SA (Array Int Int) [Sub] |
           SF File [Sub] | SW World [Sub] | ...
```

```
class Eval s => Substate s where
    sub :: State s -> Sub
    unsub :: Sub -> State s

instance Substate Int where
    sub (S n ss) = SI n ss
    unsub (SI n ss) = S n ss

instance Substate (Array Int Int) where
    sub (S ar ss) = SA ar ss
    unsub (SA ar ss) = S ar ss
...
```

This use of overloading breaks the desired modularisation of state types, but it is only necessary in this prototype. In a real implementation where state facilities are built in, none of the above is necessary. State types do not need the `State` wrapper and substates can be treated directly. In the code below, calls to `sub` and `unsub` can be ignored.

The `Act` type and the generic operations `returnAct`, `thenAct` and `run` are defined in the usual way. The definition of `run` uses `seq` to evaluate the initial state before beginning in order to prevent error values from being used as initial state values. (This is not essential, but in a real implementation, it allows compiler optimisations in which the state type is implicit rather than explicit.) In a real implementation, `Act t s a` would be a builtin abstract type, the three operations would also be builtin, with the types shown here.

```
newtype Act t s a = Act (State s -> (a, State s))

returnAct :: a -> Act t s a
returnAct x = Act (\st -> (x, st))

thenAct :: Act t s a -> (a -> Act t s b) -> Act t s b
thenAct (Act f) g =
    Act (\st->let (x,st1) = f st; Act h = g x in h st1)

run :: Eval s => s -> (forall t . Act t s a) -> a
run v act = seq v (fst (f (S v []))) where Act f = act
```

A reference is implemented as an integer for simplicity, used as an index into the list of substates. The `Ref` type is tagged with `t` and `u` tags respectively, so that actions on both the main state and the substate can be encapsulated safely. The implementation of `new` uses `seq` to prevent error values being used as initial substates, adds the new substate to the end of the list of substates, carries out the actions which use the new reference and then removes the final version of the substate. The `at` function replaces the relevant substate by the result of applying the given action on it. In a real implementation, `Ref t u s` and the two operations would be builtin; the types would be the same, with the omission of the **Substate** restriction.

```
data Ref t u s = R Int

new :: Substate s1 =>
    s1->(forall u.Ref t u s1->Act t s a)->Act t s a
new v1 f = Act g where
    g (S v ss) = seq v1 (x, S v' (init ss')) where
        (x, S v' ss') = h (S v (ss ++ [sub (S v1 [])]))
        Act h = f (R (length ss))

at :: Substate s1 => Ref t u s1 -> Act u s1 a -> Act t s a
at (R r) (Act f) = Act g where
    g (S v ss) = (x, st') where
        subst = unsub (ss !! r)
        (x, subst') = f subst
        st' = S v (take r ss ++ [sub subst'] ++ drop (r+1) ss)
```

This completes the generic facilities in the prototype. A number of examples can be demonstrated by extending the prototype.

4   Examples of State Types

In this section we demonstrate the way in which different state types can be developed in a modular way and discuss some of the issues that arise.

4.1   Values as States

State types are usually special abstract types representing updatable data structures or interfaces to procedural facilities. However, it is often convenient to carry ordinary values around in a stateful way, e.g. as substates. This can be illustrated by extending the prototype, showing how to treat **Int** as a state type. The **get** and **put** actions get and put an **Int** value held in the **StInt** state type ("stateful Int"), and **inc** increments it.

```
newtype StInt = St Int

get :: Act t StInt Int
get = action f where f (St n) = (n, St n)

put :: Int -> Act t StInt ()
put m = action f where f (St n) = ((), St m)

inc :: Act t StInt ()
inc = get >>= \n -> put (n+1)

action :: (s -> (a,s)) -> Act t s a
action f = Act g where g (S v ss) = (x,S v' ss) where (x,v')=f v
```

The function **action** converts an ordinary function of a suitable type into an action on the corresponding state type. It is a convenience function included just for the purposes of the prototype and we will also use it in later examples (it should not be made available in a real implementation because it is unsafe).

The following small example creates an **StInt** main state and an **StInt** substate of that main state.

```
eg = run (St 20) (new (St 21) (\r ->
      at r inc >> at r get >>= \n -> get >>= \m -> return (m+n)))
```

In the prototype, the example is restricted to specific types such as **StInt** in order to insert them individually into the substate union. In a real implementation, the facilities shown here can be polymorphic, using **newtype St a = St a**. The **St a** type is used rather than just **a** to prevent illegal access to, e.g., I/O states. The **get** action cannot be used during a normal I/O sequence because the type of **get** is not compatible with I/O actions. At best it has type **Act t (St RealWorld) RealWorld**. It can then only be used as part of an action sequence with state type **St RealWorld** and that sequence must have been started up with **run** or **new**. The lack of any useful values of type **RealWorld** with which to initialise **run** or **new** prevents such a sequence.

As already explained, rank-2 polymorphic types safely encapsulate actions on the state thread by forcing actions to be polymorphic in a separate type variable **t**. Actions on substates are encapsulated as well by adding an additional polymorphic type variable **u**. The following illegal example illustrates that rank-2 polymorphic types enable the secure encapsulation of state thread accesses.

```
bad = run 0 (put 41 >> new 0 (\r -> return r) >>= \r1 -> return r1)
```

The second argument to **new**, i.e. the expression (\r → return r) is of type **Ref t u s1 → Act t s (Ref t u s1)**. This is disallowed because the tag **u** is not polymorphic, since it appears in both the **Ref** and **Act** types. The second argument to **run** also breaks the rank-2 polymorphic type restriction. Similarly expressions such as the following are illegal and thus references are prevented from being imported into **run** or **new**.

```
... \r -> run (... at r act ...)
... \r -> new (\r1 -> ... at r act ...)
```

Another useful facility along similar lines would be to convert any ordinary stream function **f :: [X] -> [Y]** into a monadic form (**[X] -> [Y]**) -> **Act t s a**, for some suitable **s**, where items can be both given to **f** and taken from **f** one at a time. This generalises the emulation of **Dialogues** in terms of **IO** as described by Peyton Jones and Wadler [13]. There is a well known builtin implementation which avoids space leaks.

4.2 Arrays

As another example, we show here how to provide incremental arrays. They are
described as state types in their own right, not via references. The implementation shown here uses Haskell's monolithic array type **Array i e** as the state
type for illustration, where i is the index type and e is the element type. In practice, a built-in implementation would be provided with a separate state type,
supporting update-in-place. A minimal set of facilities might be:

```
getItem :: Int -> Act t (Array Int Int) Int
getItem n = action f where f arr = (arr ! n, arr)

putItem :: Int -> Int -> Act t (Array Int Int) ()
putItem n x = action f where f arr = ((), (arr//[(n,x)]))
```

The **getItem** function finds the array element at a given position and **putItem**
updates the element at a given position with a given value. If an array is used
as a substate via reference **r**, then its elements are accessed using calls such as
at r (getItem n) or at r (putItem n v).

Once again, specific index and element types are given for illustration in
the prototype. The **getItem** and **putItem** actions can be more general in a real
implementation.

4.3 File Handling

For handling files piecemeal rather than as a whole, a state type **File** is introduced to represent an open file.

```
newtype File = F String

getC :: Act t File Char
getC = action f where f (F (c:cs)) = (c, F cs)

putC :: Char -> Act t File ()
putC c = action f where f (F s) = ((), F (s++[c]))

eof :: Act t File Bool
eof = action f where f (F s) = (null s, F s)

contents :: Act t File String
contents = action f where f (F s) = (s, F s)
```

This is intended to be used as a substate of an input/output state.

4.4 Input and Output

In this section, we show the implementation of some common I/O facilities using
the state-splitting ideas described so far. Issues such as error handling are ignored

and facilities involving true concurrency are left until later. We treat I/O actions as actions on a global **World** state consisting of a number of files, each with an indication whether it is currently open. The type **Handle** is regarded as a reference to a **File** substate. This is like the corresponding standard Haskell type, except that in our setting it has two tag variables attached, one representing the main state and the other the **File** substate.

```
newtype World = W [(FilePath, File, Bool)]
type IO t a = Act t World a
type Handle t u = Ref t u File
data IOMode = ReadMode | WriteMode | AppendMode
```

The openFile function is one which creates a new **File** substate of the I/O state, returning a handle as a reference to it, properly encapsulated. Its implementation ensures that one cannot open a file that does not exist for reading. If a file is opened for writing, its contents are set to the null string.

```
openFile :: FilePath -> IOMode ->
              (forall u . Handle t u -> IO t a) -> IO t a
openFile name mode io = Act g where
  g (S w ss) =
   if isLocked w name then (error "locked", S w ss) else
   (x, S w2 (init ss')) where
   (x, S w1 ss')=h (S (lock w name) (ss ++ [sub (S file [])]))
   S file' [] = unsub (last ss')
   Act h = io (R (length ss))
   file = if (mode == WriteMode) then F "" else getFile w name
   w2 = unlock (putFile w name file') name

getFile :: World -> FilePath -> File
getFile w@(W ps) f = let i = find f w in thrd3 (ps !! i)
...
```

The getFile and putFile functions get and put the contents of a file with a given name. The definition of putFile is similar with the one of getFile above. The lock, unlock and isLocked functions set, unset and test the boolean flag associated with a file. In this prototype, a file cannot be reopened while already open, even for reading; in a real implementation, multiple readers could be allowed.

The openFile function can be thought of as a specialised form of the new function. Instead of creating a new substate from nothing, it uses a portion of the main state (a file) to form a new substate. While the substate is in use, the corresponding part of the main state must be locked in whatever way is necessary to ensure that the main state and the substate are independent. For example, the following is not allowed:

```
openFile "data" (\handle -> ... >> openFile "data" ...)
```

When `openFile` returns, the actions on the substate may not necessarily have been completed, since they are driven by a separate demand. However, an action which re-opens the same file after this, acts as a synchronisation mechanism, forcing all the previous actions on the substate to be completed. For example, the following is allowed:

```
openFile "data" (\handle -> ...) >> openFile "data" ...
```

The synchronisation may mean reading the entire contents of a file into memory, for example. In detecting when the same file is re-opened, care has to be taken over filename aliasing. This is where the operating system allows the same physical file to be known by two or more different names, or to be accessed via two or more different routes.

The `readFile` function now opens a file and extracts all its contents as a lazy character stream:

```
readFile :: FilePath -> IO t String
readFile name = openFile name ReadMode (\handle ->
    at handle getAll)

getAll :: Act u File String
getAll = eof >>= \b -> if b then return "" else
    getC >>= \c -> getAll >>= \s -> return (c:s)
```

This contrasts with the approach of Launchbury and Peyton Jones [11] in which unsafe generic interleaving is used. Here, we rely on the fact that `openFile` is implemented as a safe state-splitting primitive. Consider the following program in standard Haskell:

```
writeFile "file" "x\n" >> readFile "file" >>= \s ->
writeFile "file" "y\n" >> putStr s
```

One might expect the final `putStr` to print x as the result. However, the contents s of the file are read in lazily and are not needed until `putStr` is executed, which is after the second `writeFile`. On all the Haskell systems tested at the time of writing, `putStr` prints y, or a file locking error occurs (because the file happens to be still open for reading at the time of the second `writeFile`). This example is not concurrent; there are two state threads, but only one execution thread. The behaviour of the program is unacceptable in a concurrent setting because of the dependency of the behaviour on timings.

Under the state splitting approach, this program does indeed give deterministic results. The second `writeFile` forces the old version of the file to be completely read into memory (or, in a cleverer implementation, moved to a temporary location so that it is not affected by the `writeFile`).

5   Concurrency

The state-splitting proposals we have discussed are independent of the concurrency issue. However, concurrency was the main motivation for studying the problem, so we show briefly here how concurrency is implemented.

A further generic primitive **fork** can be introduced. This is the concurrent counterpart of **at** and has the same type signature:

```
fork ::  Ref t u s1 -> Act u s1 a -> Act t s a
```

The call **fork r f** has the same effect as **at r f**, carrying out an action on a substate of the main state while leaving the remainder of the main state undisturbed. However, **fork** creates a new execution thread to drive the action **f** by evaluating the final substate it produces. This new demand is additional to any other demands on **f** via its result value and the new thread executes independently of, and concurrently with, the subsequent actions on the main state, as illustrated in Fig. 1. Under the deterministic concurrency approach, a processor can run one or more I/O performing operations without including any user-visible non-determinism.

As an example of the use of **fork**, here is a lazy version of the standard Haskell function **writeFile**. The standard version, unlike **readFile**, is hyperstrict in that it fully evaluates the contents and writes them to the file before continuing with the main state actions. The lazy version shown here evaluates the contents and writes them to the file concurrently with later actions. A separate execution thread is required to drive this, otherwise there might be no demand to cause it to happen.

```
writeFile :: FilePath -> String -> IO t String
writeFile name s = openFile name WriteMode >>= \handle ->
      fork handle (putAll s)

putAll :: String -> Act u File ()
putAll s = if null s then return () else
      putC (head s) >> putAll (tail s)
```

In general, a concurrent program can be viewed as having multiple independent demands from the outside world. Each external device or service such as a file or window implicitly produces a continuous demand for output. Care needs to be taken in the implementation of concurrency if referential transparency and determinism are to be preserved. Output devices or services are regarded as substates of the outside world and their independence must be ensured. In addition, the multiple execution threads may cause independent demands on inputs to the program. To ensure fairness, a centralised approach to I/O is needed where all the inputs are merged in the sense that the first item to arrive on any input wakes up the appropriate execution thread. However, this merging is not made available to the programmer at the language level and so cannot be used to obtain non-deterministic effects.

6   Related Work

Previous work in purely functional operating systems (see Holyer and Carter [8] for a detailed overview) faced the problem of adopting non-deterministic merge operators, which destroys referential transparency. Alternatively, Stoye [16] proposed a model, adopted also by Turner [17], in which functions communicate by sending messages to a central service, called the sorting office to which non-determinism is confined. Although individual programs remain referentially transparent, the sorting office itself is non-deterministic and so is the system as a whole.

Kagawa [9] proposed compositional references in order to bridge the gap between monadic arrays [14] and incremental arrays. Compositional references can be also viewed as a means for allowing multiple state types so that a wide range of mutable data structures can be manipulated. On the other hand, they concern only internal facilities and not I/O.

The Clean I/O system [1] allows a similar mechanism to state splitting, called the multiple environment passing style. This is only possible by using the Uniqueness Type System of Clean, whereas state splitting does not require any extension to the usual Hindley-Milner type system apart from the second order polymorphism mechanism to ensure safety.

7   Conclusions and Future Work

Deterministic concurrency emerged out of the need to provide a purely declarative model of concurrency without the need for non-deterministic operators. This model has been proven expressive enough to build a single-user multi-tasking system [3] and a deterministic GUI [15] without any non-deterministic feature available to the programmer. In these systems, concurrent threads do not communicate via shared state, which immediately introduces non-determinism, but only via result streams.

In this paper we presented the Brisk monadic framework, a proposal which adapts the usual monadic style of interfacing to accommodate a deterministic form of concurrency. Its main innovation has been to introduce state splitting, a technique which assigns, to each new state thread, a substate to act upon. Deterministic concurrency arises as a natural extension of this monadic framework.

In the Brisk compiler, to complement the state splitting approach, we are investigating a freer form of communication via a safe form of message passing with timed deterministic merging of messages from different sources. This is particularly important for an object-oriented event style of programming.

As another application of deterministic concurrency we are investigating distribution [7]. Within the semantic framework that has been developed for deterministic concurrency, distribution is almost an orthogonal issue. Systems can be distributed in a trustable way, without any change to the meaning of programs – the only observable difference is the speed at which the overall system generates results. Computation, including both code and data, can be moved in response to demand.

A question that arises further in the **Brisk** monadic framework is the impact of using the lazy version of **thenST** with I/O. It affects the efficiency of I/O and disallows infinite I/O and its space behaviour needs to be investigated. On the other hand, it is essential in our setting, e.g. for writing a functional definition of reading the contents of a file lazily, which we consider more important.

References

1. P. Achten and M.J. Plasmeijer. The Ins and Outs of Clean I/O. *Journal of Functional Programming*, 5(1):81–110, 1995.
2. L. Augustsson and B. Boutel et al. *Report on the Functional Programming Language Haskell, Version 1.4*, 1997.
3. D. Carter. Deterministic Concurrency. Master's thesis, Department of Computer Science, University of Bristol, September 1994.
4. S.O. Finne and S.L. Peyton Jones. Programming Reactive Systems in Haskell. In *Proc. 1994 Glasgow Functional Programming Workshop*, Ayr, Scotland, 1994. Springer-Verlag WiCS.
5. S.O. Finne and S.L. Peyton Jones. Composing Haggis. In *Proc 5th Eurographics Workshop on Programming Paradigms in Graphics*, Maastricht, September 1995.
6. S.L. Peyton Jones, A.D. Gordon, and S.O. Finne. Concurrent Haskell. In *Proc. 23rd. ACM Symposium on Principles of Programming Languages (POPL '96)*, pages 295–308, St Petersburg Beach, Florida, January 1996. ACM Press.
7. I. Holyer, N. Davies, and E. Spiliopoulou. Distribution in a Demand Driven Style. In *1st International Workshop on Component-based Software Development in Computational Logic*, September 1998.
8. Ian Holyer and David Carter. Concurrency in a Purely Declarative Style. In J.T. O'Donnell and K. Hammond, editors, *Proc. 1993 Glasgow Functional Programming Workshop*, pages 145–155, Ayr, Scotland, 1993. Springer-Verlag WiCS.
9. K. Kagawa. Compositional References for Stateful Functional Programs. In *Proc. 1997 ACM International Conference on Functional Programming (ICFP '97)*, Amsterdam, The Netherlands, June 1997. ACM Press.
10. J. Launchbury. Lazy Imperative Programming. In *ACM SIGPLAN Workshop on State in Programming Languages*, June 1993.
11. J. Launchbury and S.L. Peyton Jones. Lazy Functional State Threads. In *Proc. 1996 ACM SIGPLAN Conference on Programming Language Design and Implementation (PLDI '96)*, Orlando, 1994. ACM Press.
12. S.L. Peyton Jones and J. Launchbury. State in Haskell. *Lisp and Symbolic Computation*, 8(4):293–341, 1995.
13. S.L. Peyton Jones and P.L. Wadler. Imperative Functional Programming. In *Proc. 20th. ACM Symposium on Principles of Programming Languages (POPL '93)*, Charleston, January 1993. ACM Press.
14. P.L. Philip. Comprehending Monads. In *Proc. 1990 ACM Conference on Lisp and Functional Programming (LFP '90)*, pages 61–78, June 1990.
15. P. Serrarens. BriX - A Deterministic Concurrent Functional X Windows System. Master's thesis, Computer Science Department, Bristol University, June 1995.
16. W.R. Stoye. A New Scheme for Writing Functional Operating Systems. Technical Report Technical Report 56, Cambridge University, Computer Lab, 1984.
17. D. Turner. Functional Programming and Communicating Processes. In J.W. Bakker, A.J. Nijman, and P.C. Treleaven, editors, *PARLE II*, volume 259 of *LNCS*, pages 54–74, Eindhoven, The Netherlands, June 1987. Springer Verlag.
18. P.L. Wadler. The Essence of Functional Programming. In *Proc. 19th. ACM Symposium on Principles of Programming Languages (POPL '92)*, Albuquerque (New Mexico, USA), January 1992. ACM Press.

A Strategic Profiler for Glasgow Parallel Haskell

David J. King[1], Jon Hall[1], and Phil Trinder[2]

[1] Faculty of Maths and Computing, The Open University
Walton Hall, Milton Keynes MK7 6AA
{d.j.king, j.g.hall}@open.ac.uk
http://mcs.open.ac.uk/{djk26,jgh23}
[2] Department of Computing and Electrical Engineering
Heriot-Watt University, Riccarton, Edinburgh EH14 4AS
trinder@cee.hw.ac.uk, http://www.cee.hw.ac.uk/~trinder/

Abstract. Execution profiling plays a crucial part in the performance-improving process for parallel functional programs. This paper presents the design, implementation, and use of a new execution time profiler (GranSim-SP) for Glasgow Parallel Haskell (GpH). Parallelism is introduced in GpH by using *evaluation strategies*, which provide a clean way of co-ordinating parallel threads without destroying a program's original structure. The new profiler attributes the cost of evaluating parallel threads to the strategies that created them. A unique feature of the strategic profiler is that the call-graph of evaluation strategies is maintained, allowing the programmer to discover the sequence of (perhaps nested) strategies that were used to create any given thread. The strategic profiler is demonstrated on several examples, and compared with other profilers.

1 Introduction

Profiling tools that measure and display the execution behaviour of a program are well established as one of the best ways of tracking down code inefficiencies. Profiling tools are particularly useful for very high-level languages where the relationship between source program and execution behaviour is far from apparent to a programmer, compared to conventional languages like C, for instance. Moreover, parallelism and laziness in a language magnifies the disparity between source program and execution behaviour by the sheer number of activities carried out in an chaotic order.

With all this in mind, a new profiler has been developed (which we're calling GranSim-SP) for the non-strict parallel functional language Glasgow Parallel Haskell (GpH)—an established parallel derivative of Haskell. The profiler allows for a direct correspondence between source program and a visualisation of its execution behaviour. This is done by allowing programmers to augment the parallel co-ordination parts of their code (known as *evaluation strategies*) with labels. Each label corresponds to a unique colour in a graphical visualisation of a program's execution behaviour, thus allowing the threads created by different strategies to be distinguished.

H. Hammond, T. Davie, and C. Clack (Eds.): IFL'98, LNCS 1595, pp. 88–102, 1999.
© Springer-Verlag Berlin Heidelberg 1999

This paper has the following structure. In Sect. 2 GPH, and evaluation strategies are briefly explained. Then in Sect. 3 a description is given of the GPH runtime system for GRANSIM that GRANSIM-SP is built on top of. In Sect. 4, the new combinator for annotating strategies is given, and a direct comparison is made with the GRANSIM profile in the previous section. In Sect. 5 the implementation of GRANSIM-SP is described, and in Sect. 6 motivating examples are given justifying why GRANSIM-SP is useful. In Sect. 7 GRANSIM-SP is compared and contrasted with GRANSIM-CC another profiler for GPH, and some imperative profilers are described. Finally, Sect. 8 discusses the paper and gives future work.

2   Glasgow Parallel Haskell

Glasgow Parallel Haskell provides parallelism by adding to Haskell a combinator for parallel composition, **par**, that is used together with sequential composition, **seq**, to control parallelism. The denotational behaviour of these combinators is described by the following equations:

$$x \text{ `seq` } y = \begin{cases} \bot, & \text{if } x \text{ is } \bot \\ y, & \text{otherwise} \end{cases} \qquad x \text{ `par` } y = y$$

Operationally, the combinator **seq** arranges for its arguments to be evaluated in sequence, **x** then **y**, and **par** arranges for its arguments to be evaluated in parallel, **x** on a separate processor from **y**. These combinators are explained in more detail elsewhere, for example, see Loidl [8].

2.1   Evaluation Strategies

Adding **par** and **seq** combinators to programs can easily obfuscate the code—mixing computation with parallel co-ordination. In view of this, Trinder et al. [15] introduced *evaluation strategies* which are lazy higher-order polymorphic functions that allow expressions to remain intact, but with suffixes that suggest their parallel behaviour. For example, an expression that maps a function over a list may be parallelised in the following way:

```
map f xs `using` strategy
```

The function **strategy** describes how to parallelise **map f xs**, and **using** is a composition function with the following definition:

```
using :: a -> Strategy a -> a
e `using` s = s e `seq` e
```

Evaluation strategies can be user-defined, but a lot of commonly occurring strategies are provided in a library module bundled with GPH.

2.2 The Need for GRANSIM-SP

When parallelising a program there are a number of different choices that can be made. Evaluation strategies make it easier to focus on the parallel co-ordination routines, but a programmer still has to choose which expressions to parallelise, and which strategies to use. The purpose of GRANSIM-SP is to give direct feedback to the programmer on the effectiveness of different choices in strategies.

3   The Runtime System for GPH

The compiler for GPH that GRANSIM-SP has been built on top of is an extension of the Glasgow Haskell compiler, GHC (Peyton Jones et al. [11]). The compiler supports parallelism using the GUM runtime system (Trinder et al. [16]) and a parallel simulator called GRANSIM (Loidl [7,8]). Our strategic profiler GRANSIM-SP is an extension of GRANSIM, and hence its name.

The runtime system that provides parallelism and parallel simulation is based on the sequential threaded runtime system for GHC that was developed to provide concurrency (Peyton Jones et al. [10]). Threads are best thought of as virtual processors. They are represented in the runtime system by TSOs (Thread State Objects) which hold a thread's registers together with various statistics about a thread. Threads are created by the **par** combinator, and die when they have completed their work. At any instant a thread will be in one of five states: running, runnable (awaiting resources to become available), blocked (awaiting for the result of evaluating another thread), fetching (awaiting the arrival of a result from another processor), or migrating (moving from a busy processor to an idle processor).

3.1   Recording Events

The parallel simulator GRANSIM (Loidl [7,8]) records information in a log file about each thread when they change from one state to another (see Fig. 1).

```
PE 18 [612386]: SCHEDULE      39
PE 17 [612288]: BLOCK         15
PE 17 [612398]: REPLY         1f
PE 17 [612410]: START         88
PE 18 [614185]: FETCH         39
PE 18 [614335]: SCHEDULE      16
PE  1 [614172]: FETCH         6a
PE  1 [614322]: SCHEDULE      68
PE 17 [614254]: RESUME(Q)     15
PE 20 [614481]: END           3c
```

Fig. 1. An extract from a GRANSIM log file.

Each line of the log file contains the processor number, the time (given in number of instructions), the state that a thread is changing to, followed by the thread number. Some other statistics about threads are also recorded, but they have been omitted here since they are of less interest to us.

3.2 Graphical Visualisations of Log Files

Log files of programs can contain so much data that it is almost impossible to discover useful information from them without a tool; such as one that can give a graphical representation of the data. GRANSIM provides tools for doing this, the most useful of which shows how many threads there are, and what state they are in (running, runnable, fetching, blocked, or migrating) at every point in time during execution. An example visualisation of a GRANSIM log file is given in Fig. 2 for the following program.

Example 1.
```
main = print ((a, b) 'using' parPair rnf rnf)
    where
        a = expA 'using' stratA
        b = expB 'using' stratB
```

Note in Example 1 that the definitions for expA, expB, stratA, and stratB have been left out for brevity, and that parPair rnf rnf is a strategy to reduce the components of a pair to normal form in parallel.

The graph in Fig. 2 plots tasks (y-axis) against time (x-axis). Two colours are shown in the graph: black representing blocked threads, and grey representing running threads. Other colours representing runnable, fetching, and migrating do not appear in the profile because the simulation was done with GRANSIM-Light (which models an idealised machine with an unlimited number of processors and zero communication cost). Note that these graphical profiles are usually viewed in colour, with detail improving with size.

4 Attributing Threads to Strategies

With the basic par and seq combinators GRANSIM records the number of threads and the state they are in, but does not attribute the created threads to any parts of the source program. There are some advanced combinators, however, such as parGlobal (see Loidl [7,8]), that provide a limited capability allowing sparks to be associated with a numerical value which is carried through to the log files. With GRANSIM-SP a more sophisticated combinator is provided, namely markStrat, for annotating all the threads created by a strategies, it has the following type:

```
markStrat :: String -> Strategy a -> Strategy a
```

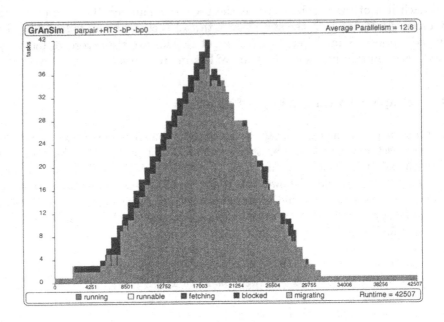

Fig. 2. A GRANSIM profile for Example Program 1.

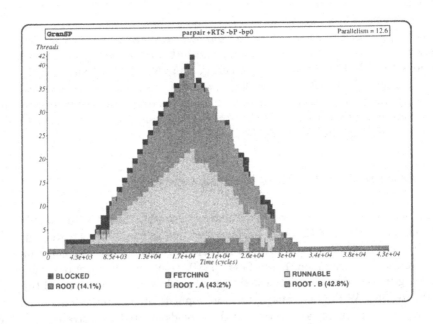

Fig. 3. A GRANSIM-SP profile for Example Program 2.

the first argument of **markStrat** is the string label that is used to annotate all the threads created in the second argument which must be a strategy. For example, taking the same program (Example 1), strategies **stratA** and **stratB** could be annotated as follows:

Example 2.
```
main = print ((a, b) 'using' parPair rnf rnf)
    where
       a = expA 'using' markStrat "A" stratA
       b = expB 'using' markStrat "B" stratB
```

Three strategies are used in this program, and two have been annotated. The graph in Fig. 3 was generated from the log file for the above program. The strategies labelled **A** and **B** are distinguished by different colours (albeit shades of grey) in this paper.

4.1   Recording the Relationships between Threads

In addition to recording a strategy name for each thread, GRANSIM-SP also records the child-to-parent relationships between threads. This information has several uses: one is to use the call-path for thread names; another, less obvious use, is to allow different call-paths of a strategy to be distinguished. But perhaps the most important use is when a thread blocks waiting for a child thread; in this case the blocked thread can trace its parentage making it possible to discover where it was created in the source program. This is useful information, since using strategies that avoid thread blocking can often give speedups. Morgan and Jarvis [9] have also had success in adding similar relationships to sequential cost centre profiling. They record *call-stacks* of names that corresponds to the function call-path of cost-centres.

The following is an example of a program where two strategies labelled F and G both use a further strategy labelled H.

Example 3.
```
main = print ((f 32, g 16)
                'using' markStrat "parPair" (parPair rnf rnf))

f x = map h [x, 2] 'using' markStrat "F" (parList rnf)
g x = map h [x, 3] 'using' markStrat "G" (parList rnf)

h x = x + sum (map loop (replicate 8 64)
                'using' markStrat "H" (parList rnf))
       where  loop n = if n==0 then 0 else loop (n-1)
```

In Example Program 3 the thread relationships that are recorded are described in Fig. 4. The relationships are also used to build the names in the

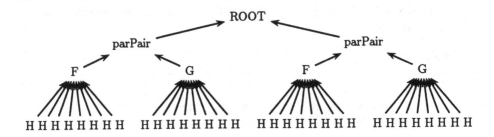

Fig. 4. The thread structure recorded by GRANSIM-SP for Example Program 3.

graphical profiles. See Fig. 5 for a per-thread activity profile, and Fig. 6 for an overall activity profile of Example Program 3.

In Fig. 4 each node corresponds to a parallel thread. The arrows are upwards, since GRANSIM-SP only records a parent name for each thread. Maintaining the reverse relationship from parent-to-child would require more storage space, and the relationship can be reproduced anyway.

Per-Thread Activity Profiles A per-thread activity profile plots threads against time, where the threads are coloured depending on their state and which strategy they correspond to. The threads are also sorted by their creation time, and by strategy. Fig. 5 is a per-thread activity profile for Example Program 3. Threads are only in two states in this example, running (shown in shades of grey), and blocked (shown in black). The two blocks of threads at the top of the graph represent the threads created by strategy H, and are named `ROOT.parPair.F.H` and `ROOT.parPair.G.H`, which describes the two call-paths of strategy H. Per-thread activity profiles are more useful with GRANSIM-SP than with GRANSIM because the threads are sorted by strategy and are labelled, making it easier to interpret the profile.

Overall Activity Profiles An overall activity profile plots thread activity against time, and is perhaps the most often used with GRANSIM. Fig. 6 depicts an overall activity profile of Example Program 3. In an overall activity graph, the threads are separated into the five thread states with the running state plotted below other states. With GRANSIM-SP the running state is broken down into different coloured areas representing each strategy, and again these are sorted by strategy name. The advantage of an overall activity profile over a per-thread activity profile is that it is easier to see the amount of a particular type of activity (e.g. parallelism, or blocking) at any given point in time. The disadvantage is that it is not possible to see which threads are blocking at any point in time.

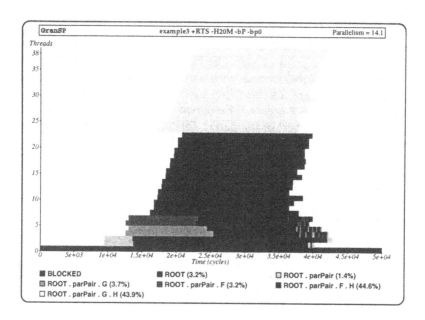

Fig. 5. A GRANSIM-SP per-thread activity profile for Example Program 3.

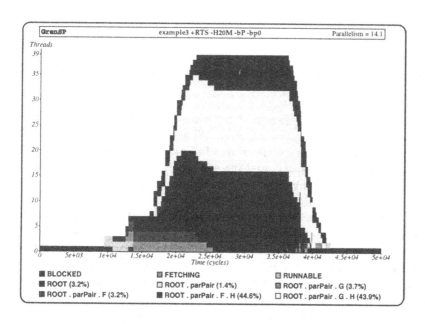

Fig. 6. A GRANSIM-SP profile for Example Program 3.

5   Implementation

Our implementation of markStrat is a small addition to the on-going GpH project. From a user's point of view the function markStrat has been added, whose behaviour is to label threads with a given strategy name. When running a program the log files are the same as before (see Fig. 1), but with a name and parent identifier on START events. The parent identifier is the thread name (a unique hexadecimal number) of the parent thread. For example, the start of the log file for the program in Sect. 4.1 is given in Fig. 7:

```
PE  0 [0]:      START      0       (ROOT , -1)
PE  0 [10519]: START      1       (parPair , 0)
PE  0 [10540]: START      2       (parPair , 0)
PE  0 [11790]: BLOCK      0
PE  0 [13632]: START      3       (G , 2)
PE  0 [13653]: START      4       (F , 1)
PE  0 [14040]: START      5       (F , 1)
PE  0 [14563]: RESUME     0
PE  0 [14693]: BLOCK      2
PE  0 [14040]: START      6       (G , 2)
PE  0 [15333]: BLOCK      0
PE  0 [14765]: BLOCK      1
PE  0 [17094]: START      7       (H , 4)
PE  0 [17669]: START      8       (H , 4)
PE  0 [18081]: START      9       (H , 5)
PE  0 [18656]: START      a       (H , 5)
```

Fig. 7. A log file extract for Example Program 3 that is used by GRANSIM-SP.

GRANSIM-SP was implemented by changing the runtime system for GpH, and by writing new visualisation tools. What follows is a sketch of the implementation in the runtime system. First of all extra fields were added to the data structures representing sparks and threads for (i) strategy name, and (ii) parent identifier. Whenever markStrat is evaluated the accompanying label is recorded in the currently active thread's data structure (i.e. the TSO described in Sect. 3). When a spark is created the strategy name and thread identifier of the current thread is saved in the spark data structure. At the point when sparks are turned into threads the name and thread identifier, held in the spark data structure, are passed to the new thread; this thread identifier being that of the parent thread. Finally, the strategy name and parent identifer are output on the START event, which is the most convenient place for the visualisation tools.

The overheads incurred by our implementation are negligible. Indeed, when simulating, no overheads are recorded in the log file. The implementation has not yet been tested on a real parallel machine, but again the overheads should be minor and consistent (i.e. the same overhead is incurred for each thread).

6   Is GRANSIM-SP Useful?

The bottom-line is: *does* GRANSIM-SP *help a programmer to track down in-efficiencies?* A question like this can only be answered properly after many programmers have used GRANSIM-SP on many different applications over a reasonable period of time. So far, however, the signs are good. GRANSIM-SP has shown to be useful in understanding the behaviour of a number of non-trivial examples including: a canny edge detector, a ray tracer for spheres, a naughts-and-crosses program, and a word-search program. The word-search program is a good example to look at closely, because it has been well-studied by Runciman and Wakeling ([12], Ch. 10), and it uses non-trivial forms of parallelism. The program searches for a number of words in a grid of letters. The words may appear horizontally, vertically, or diagonally, and either forwards or backwards. The program is made parallel by producing different orientations of the grid in parallel, and then by searching these orientations in parallel. A GRANSIM profile of the (version 6) program produced by Runciman and Wakeling is given in Fig. 8. Originally, Runciman and Wakeling used the HBC-PP compiler, which is a version of the Chalmers HBC compiler that provides a parallel simulator. The profile in Fig. 8 is not identical to the original, since GRANSIM was used to produce it, but it is pleasingly similar, which demonstrates a consistency between the simulators GRANSIM and HBC-PP.

Taking the original soda program it was re-written to use strategies, and then profiled with GRANSIM-SP. Using GRANSIM-SP revealed that the peaks in Fig. 8 corresponded to searching the grid in different orientations in turn, i.e. sequentially. This was perhaps not the intention of Runciman and Wakeling, but was caused by a subtlety in their code. By searching all the orientations in parallel it was possible to increase the parallelism and reduce the runtime by approximately 25%, as depicted in Fig. 9.

One feature of our profiler that is particularly useful is the recording of parent/child relationships. A common inefficiency is that there is more blocking going on than there needs to be. Blocking is caused by a thread waiting for a result from a child thread, and this can sometimes be avoided by changing a program's evaluation order. Since the parent/child relationships between threads are recorded by GRANSIM-SP it is possible to locate precisely where the blocking occurs.

7   Related Work

In this section a comparison is given with GRANSIM-CC a parallel cost centre profiler, and some imperative profilers are discussed.

7.1   Comparing GRANSIM-SP with GRANSIM-CC

Independently, Hammond et al. [5] have been working on GRANSIM-CC, a parallel cost-centre profiler. Their work combines sequential cost centre profiling (Sansom and Peyton Jones [13]) with the Glasgow Parallel Haskell runtime system.

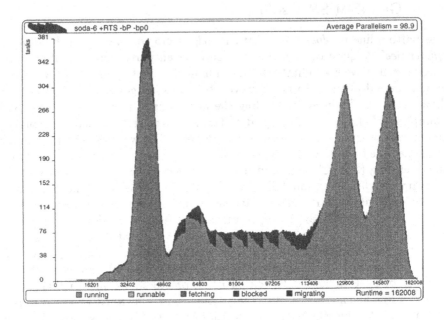

Fig. 8. A GRANSIM profile for the original soda program.

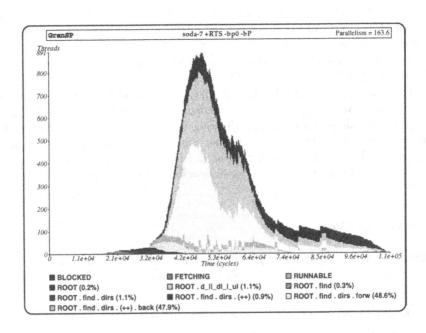

Fig. 9. A GRANSIM-SP profile for an improved version of the soda program.

GRANSIM-CC uses the set-cost-centre primitive _scc_ to annotate expressions. When an expression with _scc_ is evaluated the given label is recorded in the log file. It is then possible to produce a profile that divides up activity by the cost of these expressions, and attributes them to the expression labels. An example of a GRANSIM-CC profile for Example Program 3 is shown in Fig. 10. This profile should be compared with 2, which is a GRANSIM-SP profile of the same example. The program had to be modified for GRANSIM-CC, which involved using _scc_ around expressions instead of markStrat on strategies. In this instance there is a similarity between the GRANSIM-CC and GRANSIM-SP profiles which shows a consistency between the two systems. There is a difference, however, which is that GRANSIM-SP is giving more detail because it is able to distinguish between two separate call-paths to the same function, whereas GRANSIM-CC is unable to. This highlights one advantage of GRANSIM-SP over GRANSIM-CC which is that it records parent-to-child relationships between threads, and makes good use of them. GRANSIM-CC is also a much more complex system, and as noted by Hammond et al. [5], it hasn't been fully developed. The main advantage of GRANSIM-CC is that any expression can be annotated, whereas GRANSIM-SP only allows strategies to be annotated. Therefore, both systems are useful in their own right, and both can provide different and useful information.

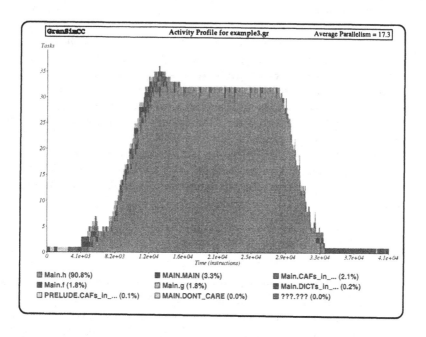

Fig. 10. A GRANSIM-CC profile for Example Program 3.

Lexical Scoping Versus Evaluation Scoping Another difference between using markStrat in GRANSIM-SP and _scc_ in GRANSIM-CC is in their scoping rules. For example, in the following expression:

```
map f xs 'using' _scc_ "A" strat
```

The cost of evaluating map f xs would be attributed to the enclosing cost centre, and not to A, because a form of *lexical scoping* is used with GRANSIM-CC (see Clack et al. [2] for a full explanation of lexical profiling). Essentially, lexical scoping attributes costs to the enclosed expression. If markStrat was used in the above example instead of _scc_, then all the threads that are sparked when the strategy strat is applied to the map expression are labelled. This form of scoping is *evaluation scoping*, and is precisely the semantics one would want for markStrat. See the cost centre work of Sansom and Peyton Jones [13] for a discussion about different scoping rules. Sansom and Peyton Jones found that a hybrid of lexical scoping was the most appropriate for the sequential cost centre profiling of Haskell.

7.2   Imperative Profiling Tools

There are several profiling tools available for imperative parallel languages. One example is *Jumpshot* which is provided with an implementation of MPI (Message Passing Library) called mpich (Gropp and Lusk [3]). Jumpshot is an interactive tool written in Java^{TM}, that animates a program's execution displaying parallel time lines with process states (e.g. running, or communicating) for each processor. Another tool is XPVM (Kohl and Geist [6]) which provides a graphical monitor and console to PVM. XPVM is written in Tcl/Tk and is similar to Jumpshot in that it provides an interactive environment showing an animation of the activity on each processor. It's also possible to use XPVM to trace which instruction caused a particular activity. XPVM and Jumpshot differ from GRANSIM-SP in that they don't relate a section of program source to the displayed histogram. This is perhaps because with imperative parallel languages the evaluation order is static, and the parallelism is explicit, so it is easier to relate source to profile.

8   Discussion and Future Work

Discussion GRANSIM-SP has been described in this paper which is an addition to the available profiling tools for Glasgow Parallel Haskell. Its purpose is to help a programmer understand, and thereby improve their parallel Haskell program. The implementation of the profiler was straightforward and fits comfortably into the runtime system for the parallel simulator GRANSIM. GRANSIM-SP enables the programmer to annotate threads giving a direct correspondence between program and profile. The usefulness of GRANSIM-SP was demonstrated on several simple examples, as well as some moderately sized ones.

Future Work One obvious improvement is to get GRANSIM-SP working with the parallel runtime system, so far our efforts have been concentrated on the parallel simulator GRANSIM. There should not be any major obstacles with this. GRANSIM-SP has been tested on several examples, and this experimentation plays a crucial role in uncovering shortcomings and ideas for improvement. One improvement is to provide a compiler option to automatically annotate strategies. Automatic annotation has shown to be useful with sequential cost centre profiling, especially for large examples, where the programmer wants to get results quickly without having to make lots of annotations. The only real usefulness of using markStrat instead of an automatic name generator is that the programmer is given freedom to use any desired name, and he or she may want to use a common name for more than one strategy.

One unique feature of the sequential cost centre profiling work of Sansom and Peyton Jones [14], is that they give a formal specification for attributing costs to costs centres, and show it equivalent to an operational semantics. The same could be done to justify the behaviour of markStrat. First of all though, an operational semantics is needed to model GPH, which is far from trivial. Hall et al. [4] are currently working on such a semantics.

Producing better visualisations of profiles is also of interest to us. The two forms of profile that are shown here, namely the per-thread activity profile, and the overall activity profile, are useful, but why restrict ourselves to these? For example, it may be useful to mask away some strategies, or to zoom in on one part of a profile. This may be of particular value for large scale parallel programs, where there are thousands of active threads. It would also be useful to provide a programmer with the actual call-graph. The call-graph information is currently provided in the log files, and it is used to generate the profiles, but the complete graph is not displayed.

All the above features would best be provided by an interactive graphical interface like those provided by *Jumpshot* and *XPVM*. Charles and Runciman [1] have begun work on such a project for GPH. Their particular interest is to translate log files to a database format, and then to query the information. This high-level interactive approach appears to be a good way forward, and may be of use for profiling other languages, sequential or imperative.

Acknowledgements

This work has been supported by the Research Development Fund at The Open University under the project title APSET (A Parallel Software Engineering Tool). We would also like to thanks everyone that has helped to improve our work, especially the GPH gurus Kevin Hammond and Hans-Wolfgang Loidl.

References

1. N. Charles and C. Runciman. An Interactive Approach to Profiling Parallel Functional Programs. In *This Proceedings*.
2. C. Clack, S. Clayman, and D. Parrott. Lexical Profiling: Theory and Practice. *Journal of Functional Programming*, 5(2):225–277, Apr. 1995.
3. W. Gropp and E. Lusk. *User's Guide for mpich, a Portable Implementation of MPI.* Mathematics and Computer Science Division, Argonne National Laboratory, University of Chicago, July 1998.
4. J. G. Hall, C. Baker-Finch, P. Trinder, and D. J. King. Towards an Operational Semantics for a Parallel Non-Strict Functional Language. In *This Proceedings*.
5. K. Hammond, H.-W. Loidl, and P. Trinder. Parallel Cost Centre Profiling. In *Proc. 1997 Glasgow Workshop on Functional Programming*, Ullapool, Scotland, Sept. 1997.
6. J. A. Kohl and G. A. Geist. *XPVM 1.0 User's Guide.* Oak Ridge National Laboratory, Nov. 1996.
7. H.-W. Loidl. *GranSim's User Guide.* Department of Computing Science, University of Glasgow, 0.03 edition, July 1996.
8. H.-W. Loidl. *Granularity in Large-Scale Parallel Functional Programming.* PhD thesis, Department of Computing Science, University of Glasgow, Mar. 1998.
9. R. G. Morgan and S. A. Jarvis. Profiling Large-Scale Lazy Functional Programs. *Journal of Functional Programming*, 8(3), May 1998.
10. S. L. Peyton Jones, A. Gordon, and S. Finne. Concurrent Haskell. In *Proc. 23rd ACM Symposium on Principles of Programming Languages (POPL '96)*, pages 295–308, St Petersburg Beach, Florida, Jan. 1996.
11. S. L. Peyton Jones, C. Hall, K. Hammond, W. Partain, and P. Wadler. The Glasgow Haskell compiler: A technical overview. In *Proc. UK Joint Framework for Information Technology, Technical Conference (JFIT '93)*, pages 249–257, Keele, Mar. 1993.
12. C. Runciman and D. Wakeling. *Applications of Functional Programming.* UCL Press Ltd, 1995.
13. P. M. Sansom and S. L. Peyton Jones. Time and Space Profiling for Non-Strict, Higher-Order Functional Languages. In *Proc. 22nd. ACM Symposium on Principles of Programming Languages (POPL '95)*, pages 355–366, San Francisco, California, Jan. 1995. ACM SIGPLAN-SIGACT.
14. P. M. Sansom and S. L. Peyton Jones. Formally-Based Profiling for Higher-Order Functional Languages. *ACM Transactions on Programming Languages and Systems*, 19(1), Jan. 1997.
15. P.W. Trinder, K. Hammond, H.-W. Loidl, and S.L. Peyton Jones. Algorithm + Strategy = Parallelism. *Journal of Functional Programming*, 8(1):23–60, January 1998.
16. P.W. Trinder, K. Hammond, J.S. Mattson, A.S. Partridge, and S.L. Peyton Jones. GUM: a Portable Parallel Implementation of Haskell. In *Proc. 1996 ACM SIGPLAN Conference on Programming Language Design and Implementation (PLDI '96)*, pages 79–88, 1996.

Implementing Eden – or: Dreams Become Reality*

Ulrike Klusik[1], Yolanda Ortega[2], and Ricardo Peña[2]

[1] Philipps-Universität Marburg, D-35032 Marburg, Germany
klusik@mathematik.uni-marburg.de
[2] Universidad Complutense de Madrid, E-28040 Madrid, Spain
{yolanda,ricardo}@sip.ucm.es

Abstract. The parallel functional programming language Eden was specially designed to be implemented in a distributed setting. In a previous paper [3] we presented an operational specification of DREAM, the distributed abstract machine for Eden. In this paper we go a step further and present the imperative code generated for Eden expressions and how this code interacts with the distributed RunTime System (RTS) for Eden. This translation is done in two steps: first Eden is translated into PEARL (Parallel Eden Abstract Reduction Language), the parallel functional language of DREAM, and then PEARL expressions are translated into imperative code.

1 Introduction

The parallel functional language Eden [6,5], with its explicit notion of process, represents an alternative to annotated parallel functional languages [14,16] and to the automatic parallelization of functional programs [9]. The advantages of having explicit processes have been extensively discussed elsewhere [4]. Moreover, Eden processes are autonomous closed entities producing results to be consumed by other processes without any notion of central manager or coordinator, or common shared memory. Thus, the language facilitates the programming of distributed systems. Correspondingly, Eden is specially suited for a distributed implementation.

Actually, Eden extends the lazy functional language Haskell [10] with a coordination language to explicitly express parallelism. There exist already very good and efficient compilers for Haskell. Thus, we decided to use the Glasgow Haskell compiler (GHC) [12] as a basis for the implementation of the computational language, and to concentrate our efforts in the distributed implementation of the coordination features.

Our first step towards an efficient distributed implementation for Eden has been the definition of DREAM (DistRibuted Eden Abstract Machine), consisting of a set of multithreaded abstract machines, each of which executes an Eden

---

* Work partially supported by German-Spanish Accion Integrada HA1997–0107 and the Spanish projects CAM-06T/033/96 and CICYT-TIC97-0672.

H. Hammond, T. Davie, and C. Clack (Eds.): IFL'98, LNCS 1595, pp. 103–119, 1999.

process. In [3] a formal definition of the operational semantics of DREAM in terms of a transition system, in the same spirit as the STG machine description in [11], was given. Our next step has been the construction of a distributed runtime system (RTS), i.e. a compiled version of DREAM. The RTS is explained in [2].

The main contribution of this paper is the translation of each Eden feature into imperative code calling the RTS routines. This translation is done in two phases: first, Eden expressions are *desugared* and translated into a much simpler parallel functional language we call PEARL (Parallel Eden Abstract Reduction Language); then, PEARL expressions are translated into imperative code. We discuss in detail the interaction between the compiled code and the RTS by using scenarios describing the main activities taking place at runtime (i.e. how processes are instantiated, etc).

Outline of the paper: we begin with a short presentation of the coordination features in Eden. Then, in Sect. 3, we explain the characteristics of PEARL and give translation schemes from Eden expressions into PEARL expressions. Sect. 4, contains a brief overview of the runtime system. Translation schemes from PEARL expressions into a sequence of RTS routine calls are given in the next section. Then, the most important scenarios are presented. We conclude with some references to related work.

2   An Overview of Eden

In this section, the language Eden is presented very briefly. For details, the interested reader is referred to [6] and [5]. Eden extends the lazy functional language Haskell with a set of *coordination* features, aimed to express parallel algorithms.

Coordination Features of Eden They are based on two principal concepts: *explicit management of processes* and *implicit communication*.

Functional languages distinguish between function definitions and function applications. Similarly, Eden offers *process abstractions*, i.e. abstract schemes for process behaviour, and *process instantiations* for the actual creation of processes and of the corresponding communication channels. A process mapping input variables $x_1, \ldots, x_n$ to output expressions $exp_1, \ldots, exp_k$ can be specified by the following process abstraction:

$$\textbf{process } (x_1, \ldots, x_n) \rightarrow (exp_1, \ldots, exp_k)$$
$$\textbf{where } equation_1 \ldots equation_r$$

The output expressions can reference the input variables, as well as the auxiliary functions and common subexpressions defined in the optional **where** part. A process can communicate to other processes through tuples of channels and arbitrary data structures of channels. The latter are explained in [1].

A process instantiation expression has the form:

$$(y_1, \ldots, y_k) = p \ \# \ (exp_1, \ldots, exp_n)$$

From now on, we will refer to the new instantiated process as the *child* process, while the process where the instantiation takes place, is called the *parent*. The process abstraction bound to p is applied to a tuple of input expressions, yielding a tuple of output variables. The child process uses k independent threads of control in order to produce these outputs. Correspondingly, the parent process creates n additional threads for evaluating $exp_1, \ldots, exp_n$.

Communication is unidirectional, from one producer to exactly one consumer. In order to provide control over where expressions are evaluated, only fully evaluated data objects are communicated. This also facilitates a distributed implementation of Eden. But retaining the lazy nature of the underlying computational functional language, lists are transmitted in a *stream*-like fashion, i.e. element by element.

Concurrent threads trying to access not yet available input will be suspended. This is the only way of synchronizing Eden processes.

New communication channels can be established at runtime by means of *dynamic reply channels*, which are specially useful for the description of reactive concurrent systems. A process may generate a new input channel by executing the following expression:

$$\texttt{new } (var_{cn}, \; var_c) \; exp$$

where the value var_c of the created channel can be used in the expression exp, and the channel name var_{cn} can be sent to another process. A process receiving var_{cn} can use it to output a value through the channel[1] referenced by this name by executing:

$$var_{cn} \;\texttt{!*}\; exp_1 \;\texttt{par}^2\; exp_2$$

Before exp_2 is evaluated, a new concurrent thread for the evaluation of exp_1 is generated, whose result is transmitted via the received reply channel.

Nondeterminism constitutes a controversial point in language design. On the one hand, it is an essential feature for some program applications but, on the other hand, it spoils the purity of functional languages. In Eden, nondeterminism is gently introduced by means of a predefined process abstraction **merge** which is used to instantiate nondeterministic processes, each one fairly merging a list of input channels into a single list.

The following table summarizes Eden's coordination constructs:

$exp \rightarrow$	**process** *pattern* **->** *exp*	
	where *equations*	process abstraction
	$\mid exp_1 \# exp_2$	process instantiation
	$\mid$ **new** $(var_{cn}, \; var_c) \; exp$	dynamic channel creation
	$\mid var_{cn} \;\texttt{!*}\; exp_1 \;\texttt{par}\; exp_2$	dynamic channel connection
	$\mid$ **merge**	merge process abstraction

---

[1] To ensure that channels connect unique writers to unique readers, it is checked at runtime that no other process is already connected (see Sect. 5.3).

[2] This construction in Eden is not related to the homonymous function in [14].

The Evaluation Model for Eden Process Systems The evaluation of an Eden process is driven by the evaluation of its output expressions, each of which constitutes an independent thread of execution. Although this overrules lazy evaluation to some extent, in order to speed up the generation of new processes and the distribution of the computation all *top level* process instantiations are immediately evaluated. Therefore, if the demand driven evaluation of inner process instantiations hinders the unfolding of the parallel process system, the programmer has the possibility to lift them to the top level where they are immediately evaluated. Nevertheless, the system evolution is still controlled by the demand for data, so that a process without output terminates immediately and its input channels are eliminated. This implies the abolition of the corresponding output channels in sender processes, and the propagation of process termination.

Example: The following Eden program specifies a parallel mergesort algorithm, where a parameter h controls the granularity by specifying the desired height of the process tree to be generated (h=0 for one process, h=1 for three processes, etc):

```
parMsort h = process xs -> ys
   where ys | h == 0 = seqMsort xs
            | h > 0  = ordMerge (parMsort (h-1) # x1, parMsort (h-1) # x2)
                       where (x1,x2) = unshuffle xs
seqMsort []  =  []
seqMsort [x] =  [x]
seqMsort xs  =  ordMerge (seqMsort x1, seqMsort x2)
                where (x1,x2) = unshuffle xs
```

Notice the difference between the parameter h, which must be known at instantiation time, and the input xs, i.e. the list of values to be sorted, which will be gradually provided during the execution of the process. Ignoring the height parameter h, the similarity between the sequential and parallel versions is remarkable. While the former makes two function applications —function seqMsort—, the latter produces two process instantiations —process abstraction parMsort. Sequential functions unshuffle (splitting a list into two by putting odd position elements into one list and even position ones into another) and ordMerge (merging two ordered lists into a single ordered list) are written in plain Haskell and are not shown here.

3   First Translation Phase: Eden into PEARL

PEARL is the language of DREAM, the abstract machine for Eden. Before going into the details of the translation from EDEN into PEARL, we give a brief description of the syntax for PEARL.

$$
\begin{array}{lll}
prog & \rightarrow & binds \\
binds & \rightarrow & bind_1 \; ; \ldots ; bind_n & \quad n \geq 1 \\
bind & \rightarrow & var \; = \; lf \\
lf & \rightarrow & vars_f \backslash\pi \; vars_a \; \text{->} \; expr \\
\pi & \rightarrow & u \mid n \\
expr & \rightarrow & literal \\
& \mid & constr \; atoms & \quad \text{constructor application} \\
& \mid & primOp \; atoms & \quad \text{primitive application} \\
& \mid & var \; atoms & \quad \text{application} \\
& \mid & \textbf{let} \; binds \; \textbf{in} \; expr & \quad \text{local definition} \\
& \mid & \textbf{letrec} \; binds \; \textbf{in} \; expr & \quad \text{local recursive definition} \\
& \mid & \textbf{case} \; expr \; \textbf{of} \; alts & \quad \text{case expression} \\
vars & \rightarrow & \{var_1, \ldots, var_n\} & \quad n \geq 0, \text{variable list} \\
atoms & \rightarrow & \{atom_1, \ldots, atom_n\} & \quad n \geq 0, \text{atom list} \\
atom & \rightarrow & var \mid literal
\end{array}
$$

$$
\begin{array}{lll}
bind & \rightarrow & vars_o = var_p \; \# \; var_i & \qquad \textbf{process instantiation} \\[2mm]
lf & \rightarrow & vars_f \; \backslash\textbf{proc} \; vars_a \; \text{->} \; expr & \qquad \textbf{process abstraction} \\[2mm]
expr & \rightarrow & \{|var_1||\ldots||var_k|\} & \qquad k \geq 1, \textbf{parallel expression} \\
& \mid & \textbf{new} \; \{var_{cn}, var_c\} \; var_e & \qquad \textbf{dynamic channel creation} \\
& \mid & \textbf{write} \; var_{cn} \; var_{e1} \; var_{e2} & \qquad \textbf{dynamic channel use} \\[2mm]
primOp & \rightarrow & \textbf{sendVal} \mid \textbf{sendHead} \mid \textbf{closeStrm} & \textbf{communication primitives}
\end{array}
$$

Fig. 1. Syntax of STGL (above) and PEARL extensions (below)

3.1   PEARL

PEARL extends the language of GHC, called STGL (Spineless Tagless G-machine Language), by incorporating constructs for the coordination features in Eden. A summary of the syntax of STGL, as it has been defined in [11], is presented in the upper part of Fig. 1, while PEARL extensions are shown in the lower part. An STGL program is a non-empty sequence of bindings of variables to lambda forms: $vars_f \backslash\pi \; vars_a \; \text{->} \; expr$, i.e. lambda abstractions with additional information about the free variables $vars_f$ appearing in the body, and a flag π indicating whether the corresponding closure should be updated or not after its evaluation. PEARL introduces a new binding expression for defining process instantiations: $vars_o = var_p \; \# \; var_i$, where $vars_o$ denotes the list of variables receiving the output of the process, var_p is bound to a process abstraction, and var_i is bound to the input expression. Process instantiations can only occur in the binding part of **let** and **letrec** expressions.

Lambda forms in PEARL can be either original STGL lambda forms defining functions, or process abstractions defining Eden processes. In this latter case, the arguments $vars_a$ represent the formal input variables of the process, and the process body is an expression which evaluates the tuple of output expressions. As outputs are evaluated in parallel, the whole body eventually evaluates to a parallel expression $\{|var_1|| \ldots ||var_k|\}$, where each component expression will give rise to a different concurrent thread. Parallel expressions are used too when instantiating new processes, because the actual inputs for the child process are also evaluated by independent threads in the parent process. Both situations are reflected in the translation schemes of Sect. 3.2.

Other PEARL expressions are introduced for dynamic channel handling: **new** for the creation and **write** for using it. In the expression for creating a channel, var_{cn} and var_c represent, respectively, the channel name and the channel value, and var_e is bound to a lambda abstraction ChanName a -> a -> b expecting the channel name and the channel value to produce a result of type b. In the **write** expression, var_{cn} corresponds to the channel name, and var_{e1} and var_{e2} are supposed to be respectively bound to the message expression and to the continuation expression.

At the PEARL level, communication is more explicitly handled. The primitive function **sendVal** is used to send a single value of any type, **sendHead** sends the next value of a stream and **closeStrm** closes a stream. However, the actual process intercommunication remains implicit, i.e. the use of these primitives is not required to provide a particular channel or receiver. These primitive functions form the basis of the overloaded function **sendChan**, shown below, which transmits values on a channel. In the translation schemes of the next subsection, the compiler inserts an application of **sendChan** to any expression to be evaluated by a parallel thread. The class **Transmissible** contains all the types whose values can be transmitted from one process to another. The compiler provides *derived* instances of this class for any user defined type.

```
class NFData a => Transmissible a where
  sendChan :: a -> ()
  sendChan x = rnf x 'seq' sendVal x        -- default definition

instance Transmissible [a] where
  sendChan []     = closeStrm
  sendChan (x:xs) = rnf x 'seq' sendHead x 'seq' sendChan xs
```

sendChan uses the overloaded function rnf :: a -> () to reduce elements to normal form. This is defined in the implementation of *Glasgow Parallel Haskell* [14]. The class definition follows:

```
class Eval a => NFData a where
  rnf :: a -> ()
  rnf a = a 'seq' ()                        -- default definition
```

The function seq :: a -> b -> b evaluates its first argument to head normal form and then returns its second argument.

```
x 'seq' y = case x of _ -> y
```

3.2 Translating Eden Expressions into PEARL

We present the translation schemes for the new expressions introduced by Eden with respect to Haskell, in the form of a recursive function $tr_1 :: Eden \rightarrow PEARL$. For the rest of the computational language, i.e. normal Haskell expressions, this function provides the original Haskell to STGL translation, and it is not shown here.

Process Abstraction

$tr_1(\text{ process } (x_1, \ldots, x_n) \text{ -> } e \text{ where } eqns) \overset{\text{def}}{=}$
    $\text{let } f = \{frees\} \setminus n \{x_1, \ldots, x_n\} \text{ -> } tr_1(\text{let } eqns \text{ in } e)$
      $\text{in let } p = \{f\} \setminus \text{proc } \{x_1, \ldots, x_n\} \text{ -> } \text{case } f \{x_1, \ldots, x_n\} \text{ of}$
        $(y_1, \ldots, y_k) \text{ -> } \text{let } v_1 = \{y_1\} \setminus u \{\} \text{ -> } \text{sendChan } y_1 \text{ in}$
          $\cdots$

          $\text{let } v_k = \{y_k\} \setminus u \{\} \text{ -> } \text{sendChan } y_k \text{ in}$
          $\{|v_1 || \ldots || v_k|\}$
      $\text{in } p$

We assume the type of the process abstraction to be **Process** $(t_1, \ldots, t_n)(t'_1, \ldots, t'_k)$ and *frees* to be the free variables in the body e and in the auxiliary equations *eqns*. The whole expression reduces to a variable p bound to a process abstraction which evaluates its outputs in parallel. The body is just a lambda abstraction applied to the inputs.

Process Instantiation

$tr_1(e_1 \# e_2) \overset{\text{def}}{=}$
    $\text{letrec } p = \{frees_1\} \setminus u \{\} \text{ -> } tr_1(e_1)$
        $v = \{frees_2\} \setminus u \{\} \text{ -> } \text{case } tr_1(e_2) \text{ of}$
          $(x_1, \ldots, x_n) \text{ -> } \text{let } v_1 = \{x_1\} \setminus u \{\} \text{ -> } \text{sendChan } x_1 \text{ in}$
            $\cdots$

            $\text{let } v_n = \{x_n\} \setminus u \{\} \text{ -> } \text{sendChan } x_n \text{ in}$
            $\{|v_1 || \ldots || v_n|\}$
      $(y_1 \ldots, y_k) = p \# v$
    $\text{in } (y_1, \ldots, y_k)$

We assume the type of e_1 to be **Process** $(t_1, \ldots, t_n)(t'_1, \ldots, t'_k)$, the type of e_2 to be $(t_1, \ldots, t_n)$, and *frees$_i$* to be the free variables in e_i ($i = 1, 2$). The translation specifies that a process abstraction expression p will be evaluated and that its inputs will be fed in parallel with the result of evaluating the tuple e_2. The result of the whole evaluation is the tuple of outputs produced by the instantiated process.

Actually, process instantiations are not translated one by one. Instead, they are collected in a single **letrec** expression. This feature is crucial for the eager distribution of the computation.

Dynamic Channel Creation and Use

$tr_1(\text{ new } (cn, c) \ e) \overset{\text{def}}{=}$
    $\text{let } v = \{frees\} \setminus n \{cn, c\} \text{ -> } tr_1(e)$
    $\text{in new } \{cn', c'\} \ v$

$$tr_1(\ cn\ !*\ e_1\ \textbf{par}\ e_2) \stackrel{\text{def}}{=}$$
$$\textbf{let }\ v_1 = \{frees_1\}\ \backslash u\ \{\} \rightarrow tr_1(e_1)$$
$$v_2 = \{frees_2\}\ \backslash u\ \{\} \rightarrow tr_1(e_2)$$
$$\textbf{in write }\ cn\ v_1\ v_2$$

The translation in these two last cases is quite straightforward and requires little explanation. As usual, *frees*, *frees*$_1$ and *frees*$_2$ are the free variables in their respective expressions. Let us note, in the channel creation case, that the free variables cn and c in Eden's expression are changed to lambda-bound variables in the translation. This facilitates the further translation of this expression into imperative code, as we only have to apply v to the fresh variables cn' and c'.

4   A Distributed Runtime System for Eden

The environment to execute an Eden program consists of a set of distributed abstract machines, each machine executing an instance of an Eden process abstraction. DREAM refers to the whole set of machines, while each single abstract machine is referred to as a *Dream*. Recall that an Eden process consists of one or more concurrent threads of control. These evaluate different output expressions which are independent of each other and use a common heap that contains shared information. The destination of the value produced by the thread is called an *outport*. In essence, an outport is a global address consisting of a destination processing element together with a unique local identifier in this processor called an *inport*. The state of a Dream includes information common to all threads, and the individual state of each thread. As input is shared among all threads, the shared part in a Dream includes an *inport table* as well as the heap. The inport table maps inport identifiers to the respective heap addresses, where received messages are to be stored. These heap addresses point to queueMe closures which represent not yet received messages. Should a thread enter a queueMe closure, it would get blocked into a queue where all threads needing a not received value wait until the value arrives.

The state of a thread comprises the state of a sequential abstract machine and a specification of the associated outport referencing the connected inport. Therefore, the interface of a process is visible in the following way: The inports are enumerated in the inport table and the outports are associated to threads (either runnable or blocked). Communication channels are only represented by inports and outports which are connected to each other. There are no explicit channel buffers. Instead, the data is transferred from the producer's heap to the consumer's heap using the inport table to find the location where the data should be stored.

Let us now obtain a compilable version of our DREAM abstract machine in terms of a distributed runtime system consisting of a set of *processor elements* (PE), each containing a pool of runnable threads, each represented by a heap-allocated Thread State Object (TSO) containing the thread's registers and pointers to the heap-allocated argument and return stacks.

Mapping of Several Dreams to one PE: As we allow more Eden processes than we have PEs available, several Eden processes need to share a PE. We can easily map several Dreams onto one abstract machine, by joining their interface representations, threads, heaps, and code. This enables a cheap dynamic creation of Eden processes, whereas the process system of the underlying message passing system is static: one abstract machine process per available PE.

Runtime Tables: In order to be able to reference inports and outports of other PEs, we need immutable global references of the form *(PEId,Id)*, where *Id* is a locally unique identifier. We cannot simply use the heap addresses of the queueMe closures and TSOs — for inports and outports, respectively — because they may change under garbage collection. Therefore, each PE keeps one *inport* and one *outport* runtime table, where the current heap addresses are stored, and indexes to these tables are used as local *Ids*. For termination purposes, the global reference to the sender thread is saved, together with the queueMe closure address, in the inport table; while outport identifiers are mapped to TSOs. As several Eden processes share the same inport and outport tables, each PE also needs a separate *process* table, with the lists of the current inports and outports of each process.

Communication Unit and Protocol: The communication unit is responsible for communicating with other PEs, providing sending and receiving routines for the following messages:

Data messages concerning the communication of values through channels:

- *VAL* for sending a value over a one value channel.
- *HEAD* for sending an element of a stream.
- *CLOSE-STRM* for closing a stream.

System messages implying modifications on the runtime tables of a remote PE. Messages of this kind always include the identification of the sending PE, to be used appropriately at the receiver PE.

- *CREATE-PROCESS*: Is sent by the parent to a remote PE[3] to instantiate a new process there. The process abstraction and the new local inports and outports of the parent are included in the message.
- *ACK*: Is the response to a *CREATE-PROCESS* message, acknowledging the creation of the child process and including information to properly connect the inports and outports of the child in the parent process.
- *DCH*: When a process uses a dynamic channel, it must communicate to the creator of the channel the new connection.
- *TERM-THREAD*: For terminating a remote thread, represented by its associated outport.

---

[3] The specific remote PE will be decided by the RTS of the parent PE, depending on the global scheduling and load balancing policies.

Termination When a thread has completed its computation and has sent its output value, it terminates closing the corresponding outport. If the last outport in a process is closed — this can be looked up in the process table — the whole process is terminated by closing all its inports. When an inport is closed, the sending thread is informed that its results are not longer needed. This is done via a *TERM-THREAD* message. Inports may also be closed at garbage collection, when it is detected that the input is not referenced anymore.

Only a brief overview of the runtime system for Eden has been given here. It suffices to understand the second translation phase described in the next section and its interaction with the RTS. For a more detailed presentation and a discussion on topics not adressed here, e.g scheduling, process distribution, garbage collection, etc., the interested reader is referred to [2].

5   Second Translation Phase and Runtime Scenarios

In this section we present the translation of PEARL expressions into imperative code, i.e. a sequence of calls to the procedures of the RTS. As we did it in Sect. 3.2 for the first translation phase from Eden to Pearl, we present the translation schemes in the form of a recursive function $tr_2 :: PEARL \to RTS$. Function tr_2 is here only described for the new expressions introduced by PEARL with respect to STGL.

In order to better understand the runtime behaviour of Eden programs, we present the translation schemes grouped into two "scenarios": *process creation* and *dynamic channel handling*. In each scenario, we explain the interaction between the code generated by PEARL expressions and the code executed by the RTS upon the reception of system messages. In this way, the reader can get a whole picture of what happens at runtime.

In the following, we will assume that process abstractions always have type **Process** $(t_1, \ldots, t_n)$ $(t'_1, \ldots, t'_k)$, i.e. they have n inports and k outports. The following notation and conventions will also be used:

inport (outport) identifiers Local inport (outport) identifiers will be denoted by $i_1, \ldots, i_n$ $(o_1, \ldots, o_k)$ in the child process and by $i'_1, \ldots, i'_k$ $(o'_1, \ldots, o'_n)$ in the parent process. The *destination* of a thread (*origin* of an inport) is its corresponding remote inport (outport), and it is represented by a global inport (outport) identifier, i.e. a tuple (idp, i) $((idp, o))$ where idp is a remote PE and i (o) is a local inport (outport) in that PE. Destinations (origins) may also be denoted by D (O).

closure addresses $a, b, p, q, e, \ldots$

thread state objects are distinguished from other closure addresses and denoted by tso.

procedure calls are of the form $o_1, \ldots, o_r \leftarrow name(i_1, \ldots, i_s)$, where $o_1, \ldots, o_r$ are the output parameters, *name* is the name of the called procedure and $i_1, \ldots, i_s$ are the input parameters.

5.1 Interface between the Imperative Code and the RTS

The self-explanatory procedure names and the accompanying text will, in general, suffice to understand the translation. The less obvious procedures offered by the RTS are explained in advance.

$tso \leftarrow createThread(e, D)$ Creates a thread tso, where e is the heap address of the expression to be executed, and D is the destination of the thread. If this is not known yet, or if the thread has no destination, the value $undefD$ is used.

$idp \leftarrow sendCreateProcess(p, o_{tso}, i'_1, \ldots, i'_k, o'_1, \ldots, o'_n)$ The RTS will compose and send a $CREATE\text{-}PROCESS$ message to some remote PE, and return the identifier idp of the chosen remote machine. The parameter p represents a closure that will eventually evaluate to a process abstraction, and o_{tso} is the outport associated with the thread (in parent's PE) responsible for spawning the threads feeding the inports of the child process. It is passed around in order to have a handle to this thread and to be able to activate it after the corresponding acknowledgement message arrives. The rest of the parameters are the inports —$(i'_1, \ldots, i'_k)$— and the outports —$(o'_1, \ldots, o'_n)$— at the parent's side, which correspond to outports, respect. inports, in child's PE.

$sendAck(idp, o, i'_1, \ldots, i'_k, o'_1, \ldots, o'_n, i_1, \ldots, i_n, o_1, \ldots, o_k)$ Sends an ACK message to the matching thread for outport o in PE idp, acknowledging that the process instantiated from that thread has been created with inports $i_1, \ldots, i_n$ and outports $o_1, \ldots, o_k$. The rest of the parameters are just a repetition of the remote inports and outports received in the corresponding $CREATE\text{-}PROCESS$ message.

5.2 Scenario 1: Process Creation

A graphical description of this scenario is shown in Fig. 2. The parent and the child side, and the messages exchanged between both are represented there. As we will see in the generated code, newly created inports in both sides are initially bound to **queueMe** closures so that threads trying to consume values not yet produced by the remote process will be suspended. Outports should be matched to their corresponding threads, but in many cases these are not already known at the moment of creating the outport. Thus, outports are usually initially matched to $undefT$ threads.

Translation of the Process Instantiation Expression

The environment at the parent's side has to be created in order to be able to feed the inports of the remote process and to receive the values delivered by it through its outports. Therefore, k inports and n outports are created. However, at instantiation time of a new process not all the information is at hand at the parent's side to create the new outports. In fact, the output expressions which will feed each outport and the destinations of the new threads are not yet

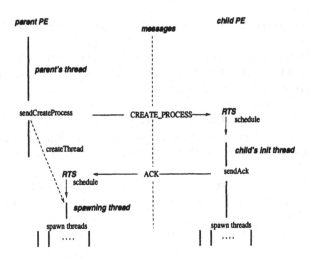

Fig. 2. Process creation scenario

known. Therefore, instead of directly matching the outports to their corresponding threads, a *spawning thread* is created that will eventually reduce to a parallel expression. When this happens, threads are spawned and matched to the previously created outports (see translation of the parallel expression below). Notice that, at this moment, this spawning thread is created but not yet activated. Then, the remote process creation is initiated —by sending the corresponding message—, and the tuple of new input channels is delivered to the continuation stack as the result of the whole instantiation. The addresses of the newly created **queueMe** closures form this tuple.

$$tr_2 \ (p\#e) \overset{\text{def}}{=}$$
$$a_1 \leftarrow createQM(); \ldots; a_k \leftarrow createQM();$$
$$i'_1 \leftarrow createInport(a_1); \ldots; i'_k \leftarrow createInport(a_k);$$
$$o'_1 \leftarrow createOutport(undefT); \ldots; o'_n \leftarrow createOutport(undefT);$$
$$tso \leftarrow createThread(e, undefD);$$
$$o_{tso} \leftarrow createOutport(tso);$$
$$idp_{child} \leftarrow sendCreateProcess(p, o_{tso}, i'_1, \ldots, i'_k, o'_1, \ldots, o'_n);$$
$$returnTuple(a_1, \ldots, a_k)$$

Arrival of the Process Creation Message

When the RTS of the PE where the child process must be instantiated, receives the message $CREATE\text{-}PROCESS(idp_{parent}, p, o_{tso}, i'_1, \ldots, i'_k, o'_1, \ldots, o'_n)$, it first unpacks the closure p and copies it to the local heap — let p' denote the address of the copied closure— then, it creates the initial thread:

$$tso \leftarrow createThread(p', undefD);$$
$$initArg(tso, idp_{parent}, o_{tso}, i'_1, \ldots, i'_k, o'_1, \ldots, o'_n);$$
$$scheduleThread(tso)$$

Before scheduling the initial thread, all parameters in the message, except p, are saved in the argument stack, so that the code generated for the process abstraction (see below) can use them.

Translation of the Process Abstraction Expression
The code generated for a process abstraction assumes that the executing thread's stack contains the arguments mentioned above. This is safe as we call it only in this setting.

Now, the environment of the new instantiated process must be established: n inports and k outports are created. As the origins of the inports are already known, the connection is completed. Thereafter, the destinations and the outports of the future parallel threads are saved — in a table associated to the spawning thread state, an ACK message is sent, and the body of the process abstraction is executed. The arguments $x_1, \ldots, x_n$ are free in the body of the process abstraction, and the values bound to them are supposed to be in the argument stack. That is the reason for pushing there the addresses of the queueMe closures.

$$tr_2\left(\{\mathit{frees}\}\ \backslash\texttt{proc}\ \{x_1, \ldots, x_n\} \to \mathit{body}\right) \stackrel{\text{def}}{=}$$

$\quad idp_{parent} \leftarrow popArg();$
$\quad o_{tso} \leftarrow popArg();$
$\quad i'_1 \leftarrow popArg(); \ldots; i'_k \leftarrow popArg();$
$\quad o'_1 \leftarrow popArg(); \ldots; o'_n \leftarrow popArg();$
$\quad b_1 \leftarrow createQM(); \ldots; b_n \leftarrow createQM();$
$\quad i_1 \leftarrow createInport(b_1); \ldots; i_n \leftarrow createInport(b_n);$
$\quad o_1 \leftarrow createOutport(undefT); \ldots; o_k \leftarrow createOutport(undefT);$
$\quad connectInport(i_1, (idp_{parent}, o'_1)); \ldots; connectInport(i_n, (idp_{parent}, o'_n));$
$\quad tso \leftarrow ownTSO():$
$\quad saveDestinations(tso, (idp_{parent}, i'_1), \ldots, (idp_{parent}, i'_k));$
$\quad saveOutports(tso, o_1, \ldots, o_k);$
$\quad sendAck(idp_{parent}, o_{tso}, i'_1, \ldots, i'_k, o'_1, \ldots, o'_n, i_1, \ldots, i_n, o_1, \ldots, o_k);$
$\quad pushArg(b_n); \ldots; pushArg(b_1);$
$\quad tr_2(body)$

Arrival of the Acknowledgement Message
When a message $ACK(idp_{child}, o_{tso}, i'_1, \ldots, i'_k, o'_1, \ldots, o'_n, i_1, \ldots, i_n, o_1, \ldots, o_k)$ arrives to the parent's PE, the outports and destinations of the threads, which will be later created by the parallel expression, are stored in the state of the spawning thread. Inports are connected, and the spawning thread is scheduled:

$\quad tso \leftarrow getThread(o_{tso});$
$\quad saveDestinations(tso, (idp_{child}, i_1), \ldots, (idp_{child}, i_n));$
$\quad saveOutports(tso, o'_1, \ldots, o'_n);$
$\quad connectInport(i'_1, (idp_{child}, o_1)); \ldots; connectInport(i'_k, (idp_{child}, o_k));$
$\quad scheduleThread(tso)$

Translation of the Parallel Expression
The executing thread will spawn a set of m parallel threads and thereafter die. The translation below is valid both for parallel expressions in process instantiations (parent's side) and for parallel expressions in process abstractions (child's side). It is assumed that the destinations and the outports associated to the spawned threads have been previously saved in the state of the executing thread.

$$tr_2 \left(\{ | e_1 | | \ldots | | e_m | \} \right) \stackrel{\text{def}}{=}$$
$$D_1, \ldots, D_m \leftarrow getDestinations();$$
$$o_1, \ldots, o_m \leftarrow getOutports();$$
$$tso_1 \leftarrow createThread(e_1, D_1); \ldots; tso_m \leftarrow createThread(e_m, D_m);$$
$$matchOutportThread(o_1, tso_1); \ldots; matchOutportThread(o_m, tso_m);$$
$$scheduleThread(tso_1); \ldots; scheduleThread(tso_n);$$
$$exitThread()$$

5.3   Scenario 2: Dynamic Channel Handling

Translation of the Channel Creation Expression
A new inport is created in the current machine, bound to a `queueMe` closure and the global address of this inport is saved in a `ChanName` closure which, in essence, is a tuple. Then, the main expression is entered, having previously pushed in the stack the arguments of this lambda abstraction.

$$tr_2 \ (\texttt{new} \ \{cn, c\} \ e) \stackrel{\text{def}}{=}$$
$$idp_{creator} \leftarrow ownPE();$$
$$q \leftarrow createQM();$$
$$i \leftarrow createInport(q);$$
$$a \leftarrow createCHN(idp_{creator}, i);$$
$$pushArg(q);$$
$$pushArg(a);$$
$$enter(e)$$

Let us note that the binding variables c and cn are ignored and replaced by the fresh heap addresses q and a. The first one, i.e. q, is bound to a `queueMe` closure, representing the new channel, whereas the second one, a, is bound to a `ChanName` closure containing the global address of the channel.

Translation of the Channel Use Expression
The message expression v_1 and the main expression v_2 are evaluated by independent threads. Therefore, a new thread is created and scheduled for the message evaluation, whereas the current thread continues with the evaluation of the main expression. A new local outport o matching the new thread is created. Then a DCH message is sent to communicate the new connection to the creator of the dynamic channel.

$tr_2 \, (\texttt{write} \ cn \ v_1 \ v_2) \overset{\text{def}}{=}$
  $idp_{creator}, i \leftarrow accessCHN(cn);$
  $tso \leftarrow createThread(v_1, (idp_{creator}, i));$
  $o \leftarrow createOutport(tso);$
  $sendDch(idp_{creator}, i, o);$
  $scheduleThread(tso);$
  $enter(v_2)$

Arrival of the Dynamic Channel Connection Message
When the message $DCH(idp_{user}, i, o)$ arrives to the dynamic channel creator's
PE, the RTS will just connect the local inport i to its new established origin
(idp_{user}, o), by executing:

$connectInport(i, (idp_{user}, o));$

The fact that no other process has connected to this channel before can be
checked by looking up in the inport table.

6   Related and Future Work

The specialized code generation defined here instantiates Eden processes, each
one consisting of a number of threads and a complex communication structure,
whereas languages like Concurrent ML [13] or Facile [8] use explicit message passing primitives on the language level, and they treat these primitives as ordinary
functions during code generation. Other systems like GpH [14] and *Concurrent
Clean* [16] handle communication implicitly by relying on a virtually shared
memory. Their parallel annotations are also implemented in a straightforward
manner by primitive operations. Closer to our approach is Caliban [7], which
extracts topology information from the program text and needs a special code
generation, but it is restricted to static process networks.

The starting point for the implementation of Eden has been the Glasgow
Haskell Compiler (GHC) [12]. Only small modifications to the parser were needed
in order to accept the new expressions Eden has with respect to Haskell. As a
consequence, our abstract machine DREAM is an extension of the STG machine [11] on which GHC is based. The extensions concern multithreading and
communication features. The current runtime system for Eden has much profited
from the runtime system GUM for Glasgow Parallel Haskell [15]. The implementation status is as follows: a compiler for the basic features of Eden is running
and producing C code; PEARL constructions have been implemented by a set
of predefined C functions called from this code; the RTS has been coded and
the whole system is being integrated. In brief, we will present efficiency results
with this compiler. Preliminary figures were obtained with a first distributed
prototype directly calling MPI from Haskell, and they were published elsewere
[2]. They promise good speedups for the actual implementation. Eden features
not covered up to now are channel structures and implementation optimizations
such as channel bypassing.

Acknowledgements We thank Luis Antonio Galán, Rita Loogen, Cristóbal Pareja, Steffen Priebe, Fernando Rubio and Clara Segura for useful discussions, and comments provided while preparing this paper.

References

1. S. Breitinger, U. Klusik, and R. Loogen. Channel Structures in the Parallel Functional Language Eden. In *Proc. 1997 Glasgow Workshop on Functional Programming*, 1998. revised version.
2. S. Breitinger, U. Klusik, and R. Loogen. From (Sequential) Haskell to (Parallel) Eden: An Implementation Point of View. In *Proc. Programming Languages: Implementations, Logics and Programs (PLILP'98)*, volume 1490 of *LNCS*, pages 318–334, Springer-Verlag, 1998.
3. S. Breitinger, U. Klusik, R. Loogen, Y. Ortega-Mallén, and R. Peña. DREAM - the DistRibuted Eden Abstract Machine. In C. Clack, A.J.T. Davie and K. Hammond, editors, *Proc. 9th. International Workshop on the Implementation of Functional Languages (IFL '97), St Andrews, Scotland, September 1997*, volume 1467 of *LNCS*, pages 250–269. Springer-Verlag, 1998.
4. S. Breitinger, U. Klusik, R. Loogen, and Y. Ortega-Mallén. Concurrency in Functional and Logic Languages. In *Proc. Fuji International Workshop on Functional and Logic Programming, Japan*. World Scientific Publishing Company, 1995. ISBN 981-02-2437-0.
5. S. Breitinger, U. Klusik, R. Loogen, Y. Ortega-Mallén, and R. Peña. Eden — Language Definition and Operational Semantics. Technical Report 96-10, Philipps-Universität Marburg, 1996.
6. S. Breitinger, R. Loogen, Y. Ortega-Mallén, and R. Peña. The Eden Coordination Model for Distributed Memory Systems. In *Proc. HIPS '97 — High-Level Parallel Programming Models and Supportive Environments*. IEEE Press, 1997.
7. S. Cox, S.-Y. Huang, P.H.J. Kelly, J. Liu, and F. Taylor. An Implementation of Static Functional Process Networks. In *Proc. PARLE '92 — Parallel Architectures and Languages Europe*, pages 497–512. Springer-Verlag, 1992.
8. A. Giacalone, P. Mishra, and S. Prasad. Facile: A Symmetric Integration of Concurrent and Functional Programming. *Journal of Parallel Programming*, 18(2), 1989.
9. G. Hogen, A. Kindler, and R. Loogen. Automatic Parallelization of Lazy Functional Programs. *Proc. 1992 European Symposium on Programming (ESOP '92)*, Springer-Verlag *LNCS*, 1992.
10. J.C. Peterson, K. Hammond, L. Augustsson, B. Boutel, F. W. Burton, J. Fasel, A. D. Gordon, R. J. M. Hughes, P. Hudak, T. Johnsson, M. P. Jones, E. Meijer, S. L. Peyton Jones, A. Reid, and P. L. Wadler. *Report on the Non-Strict Functional Language, Haskell, Version 1.4*, 1997.
11. S.L. Peyton-Jones. Implementing lazy functional languages on stock hardware: the Spineless Tagless G-machine, version 2.5. *Journal of Functional Programming*, 2(2):127–202, April 1992.
12. S. L. Peyton Jones, C. Hall, K. Hammond, W. Partain, and P. Wadler. The Glasgow Haskell compiler: A technical overview. In *Proc. UK Joint Framework for Information Technology, Technical Conference (JFIT '93)*, pages 249–257, Keele, Mar. 1993.

13. J.H. Reppy. CML: A higher-order concurrent language. In *Proc. 1991 ACM SIG-PLAN Conf. on Programming Language Design and Implementation (PLDI 91)*, pages 293–305, 1991.

14. P.W. Trinder, K. Hammond, H.-W. Loidl, and S.L. Peyton Jones. Algorithm + Strategy = Parallelism. *Journal of Functional Programming*, 8(1):23–60, January 1998.

15. P.W. Trinder, K. Hammond, J.S. Mattson, A.S. Partridge, and S.L. Peyton Jones. GUM: a Portable Parallel Implementation of Haskell. In *Proc. 1996 ACM SIGPLAN Conference on Programming Language Design and Implementation (PLDI '96)*, pages 79–88, 1996.

16. M.C.J.D. van Eekelen and M.J. Plasmeijer. *Functional Programming and Parallel Graph Rewriting*, Addison-Wesley, 1993.

Efficient Combinator Parsers

Pieter Koopman[*] and Rinus Plasmeijer

Computer Science
Nijmegen University, The Netherlands
pieter@cs.kun.nl, rinus@cs.kun.nl

Abstract. Parser combinators enable the construction of recursive descent parsers in a very clear and simple way. Unfortunately, the resulting parsers have a polynomial complexity and are far too slow for realistic inputs. We show how the speed of these parsers can be improved by one order of magnitude using continuations. These continuations prevents the creation of intermediate data structures. Furthermore, by using an exclusive or-combinator instead of the ordinary or-combinator the complexity for deterministic parsers can be reduced from polynomial to linear. The combination of both improvements turn parser combinators from a beautiful toy to a practically applicable tool which can be used for real world applications. The improved parser combinators remain very easy to use and are still able to handle ambiguous grammars.

1 Introduction

Parser combinators [3, 6, 5, 8] are a beautiful illustration of the use of higher order functions and currying. By using a small set of parser combinators it becomes possible to construct parsers for ambiguous grammars in a very elegant and clear way. The basis of parser combinators is the list of successes method introduced by Wadler [13]. Each parser yields a list of results: all successful parsings of the input. When the parser fails this list is empty. In this way it is very easy to handle ambiguous parsers that define multiple ways to parse a given input.

Despite the elegant formulation and the ability to handle ambiguous grammars, parser combinators are rarely used in practice. For small inputs these parsers work nice and smoothly. For realistically sized inputs the parsers consume extraordinary amounts of time and space due to their polynomial complexity.

In this paper we show that the amounts of time and memory required by the combinators parsers can drastically be reduced by improving the implementation of the parser combinators and providing a little more information about the grammar in the parser that is written. This additional information can reduce the complexity of the parser from polynomial to linear. Although the implementation of the parser combinators becomes more complex, their use in combinator parsers remains as simple as in the original setting.

This paper starts with a short review of classical parser combinators. The proposed improvements are presented hereafter. We use a running parsing example to measure the effect of the improvements.

---

* Sponsored by STW project NWI.4411

H. Hammond, T. Davie, and C. Clack (Eds.): IFL'98, LNCS 1595, pp. 120–136, 1999.

2   Conventional Parser Combinators

There are basically two approaches to construct a parser for a given grammar[1]. The first approach is based upon the construction of a finite state automaton determining the symbols that can be accepted. This approach is used in many parser generators like *yacc* [7, 1, 10], *Happy* [4] and *Ratatosk* [9]. In general the constructed parsers are efficient, but cumbersome to achieve and there might be a serious distance between the automaton accepting input tokens and the original grammar. If we use a generator there is a barrier between parsing and using the parsed items in the rest of the program.

The second approach to achieve a parser is to create a recursive descent parser. Such a parser follows the rules of the grammar directly. In order to ensure termination the grammars should not be left-recursive. Parser combinators are a set of higher order functions that are convenient in the construction of recursive descent parsers. The parser combinators provide primitives to recognize symbols and the sequential or alternative composition of parsers.

The advantages of parser combinators are that they are easy to use, elegant and clear. Due to the fact that the obtained parsers directly correspond to the grammar there is no separate parser generator needed. Since parser combinators are ordinary functions they are easy to understand and use. It is easy to extend the set of parser combinators with new handy combinators whenever this is desired. The full power of the functional programming language is available to construct parsers, this implies for instance that it is possible to use second order grammars. Finally, there are no problems to transfer parsed items from the parser to the manipulation functions.

Conventional parser combinators are described at many places in the literature e.g. [3, 6, 5, 8]. Here we follow the approach outlined in [8], using the functional programming language Clean [11]. We restrict ourselves to a small, but complete set of parser combinators to illustrate our improvements.

A `Parser` is a function that takes a list of input symbols as argument and produces a `ParsResult`. A `ParsResult` is the list of successes. Each success is a tuple containing the rest of the list of input symbols and the item found. The types `Parser` and `ParsResult` are parameterized by the type of symbols to be recognized, `s`, and the type of the result, `r`.

```
:: Parser s r :== [s] -> ParsResult s r
:: ParsResult s r :== [([s],r)]
```

In the examples in this paper we will use characters, `Char`, as symbols in the lists of elements to be parsed, but in general they can be of any datatype.

2.1   Basic Parser Combinators

The basic combinator to recognize a given symbol in the input is `symbol`. This parser combinator takes the symbol to be recognized as its argument. When the first token in the input is equal to this symbol there is a single success. In all other situations the list of successes is empty indicating that the parser failed. It is of course requested that the equality is defined for the type of symbols to be recognized, this is indicated by the phrase | == s in the type definition.

```
symbol :: s -> Parser s s | == s
symbol sym = p
where   p [s:ss] | s==sym = [(ss,sym)]
        p _              = []
```

A related combinator is called satisfy. This combinator takes a predicate on the first input symbol as its argument. When the first symbol satisfies this predicate the parser combinators succeeds, otherwise it fails.

```
satisfy :: (s->Bool) -> Parser s s
satisfy pred = p
where   p [s:ss] | pred s = [(ss,s)]
        p _              = []
```

To complete the set of basic parser combinators there is a combinator, called fail, that always fails (i.e. yields the empty list of successes) and the combinator yield that always succeeds with the given item.

```
fail :: Parser s r
fail = \_ -> []

yield :: r -> Parser s r
yield r = \ss -> [(ss,r)]
```

2.2   Combining Parsers

Given two parser it is possible to create new parsers by combining them using parser combinators. For instance, the or-combinator indicates a choice between two parsers. Using the list of successes, the implementation just concatenates the results of both parsers. To enhance readability this parser combinator is defined as an infix operator named <|>.

```
(<|>) infixr 4 :: (Parser s r) (Parser s r) -> Parser s r
(<|>) p1 p2 = \ss -> p1 ss ++ p2 ss
```

There are several ways to compose parsers sequentially. Here we restrict attention to the so-called *monadic style* where the result of the first parser is given as an argument to the second parser. This and-combinator, named <&=>, is defined as:

```
(<&=>) infixr 6 :: (Parser s r) (r -> Parser s t) -> Parser s t
(<&=>) p1 p2 = \ss -> [ tuple
                  \\ (ssRest,result1) <- p1 ss
                  , tuple            <- p2 result1 ssRest
                  ]
```

The next parser combinator applies a function to the parsed item. This combinator, called `<@`, is again an infix operator. It is defined in terms of the combinators defined above as the sequential composition of two parsers. The first parser recognize the item. The second parser is the function composition of the item transformation function `f` and the parser that yields the transformed item.

```
(<@) infixl 5 :: (Parser s r) (r->t) -> Parser s t
(<@) p f = p <&=> yield o f
```

Although the introduced set of combinators is sufficient to construct all parsers, it appears to be convenient to introduce additional combinators for repetition. In the BNF description of grammars the notation `p*` means zero or more times `p`. The parser combinator `<*>` applies a parser as often as it can. The results of repeated applications of the parser are accumulated in a list. For the definition we observe that `<*>` `p` is either `p` followed by `<*>` `p`, or the empty list.

```
<*> :: (Parser s r) -> Parser s [r]
<*> p = (    p        <&=> \r  ->
           <*> p <@   \rs -> [r:rs])
       <|> yield []
```

There is a related notion, `p+` in BNF, to applies a parser at least once. It is defined as the parser `p` followed by zero or more applications of the parser `p`.

```
<+> :: (Parser s r) -> Parser s [r]
<+> p = p <&=> \r -> <*> p <@ \rs -> [r:rs]
```

2.3   Examples and Measurements

In order to illustrate the use of parser combinators we will show some examples. Our first parser, `aANDbORc`, recognize a character `'a'` followed by a `'b'` or a `'c'`. The result of the parser is a tuple containing the parsed items.

```
aANDbORc :: Parser Char (Char,Char)
aANDbORc = symbol 'a'                      <&=> \x ->
           (symbol 'b' <|> symbol 'c') <@    \y -> (x,y)
```

We illustrate the use of this parser by applying it to some inputs.

The program	yields
Start = aANDbORc ['abc']	[(['c'],('a','b'))]
Start = aANDbORc ['acb']	[(['b'],('a','c'))]
Start = aANDbORc ['cba']	[]

Our next example is the ambiguous parser `alphaORhex`. It recognizes characters from the alphabet and hexadecimal characters.

```
alphaORhex :: Parser Char Char
alphaORhex = alpha <|> hex
```

```
alpha :: Parser Char Char
alpha = satisfy (\c -> isMember c (['a'..'z']++['A'..'Z']))

hex :: Parser Char Char
hex = satisfy (\c -> isMember c (['0'..'9']++['A'..'F']))
```

Again we illustrate the use of the parser by applying it to some inputs.

The program	yields
`Start = alphaORhex ['abc']`	`[(['bc'],'a')]`
`Start = alphaORhex ['ABC']`	`[(['BC'],'A'),(['BC'],'A')]`
`Start = alphaORhex ['123']`	`[(['23'],'1')]`

The characters from the range ['A'..'F'] are accepted by the parsers hex and alpha. Hence alphaORhex is ambiguous and yields both results. Here the parser alphaORhex recognizes an alpha, an alpha and a hex, and a hex respectively.

As a more serious example we turn to a parser that recognize a sentence. A sentence is defined as a sequence of words separated by white space and/or comma's and terminated by a full stop. The result of the parser sentence is the list of words in the sentence. Each words is represented by a string.

```
word :: Parser Char String
word = <+> satisfy isAlpha <@ toString

sep :: Parser Char [Char]
sep = <+> (satisfy isSpace <|> symbol ',')

sentence :: Parsers Char [String]
sentence = word                       <&=> \w ->
          <*> (sep <&=> \_ -> word) <&=> \r ->
          symbol '.'                 <@   \_ -> [w:r]
```

The function isAlpha from the standard library checks whether a character is an element from the alphabet. Similarly, the test for white space (space, tab, newline ..) is done by isSpace. Note that the parser word is ambiguous. It does not only find the entire word, but also all non-empty initial parts.

The program	yields
`Start = word ['Hello world']`	`[((' world'],"Hello")`
	`,(['o world'],"Hell")`
	`,(['lo world'],"Hel")`
	`,(['llo world'],"He")`
	`,(['ello world'],"H")`
	`]`

The parser sentence looks clear and simple. It is not ambiguous since trailing parts of a word are not recognized as separators and the sentence has to end in a full stop. To investigate its efficiency we apply it to a sentence of 50,000 characters (the size of a reasonable file). As comparison we use a hand written ad-hoc parser which is described in Appendix A. This ad-hoc parser uses a state automaton and accumulators to construct the words and is pretty efficient. As a consequence it is harder to determine which syntax is accepted by the parser by looking at the definition. Measurements in this paper are done on a 266 MHz Pentium II, using 10 Mb of heap space and 500 Kb of stack space. The execution time includes the generation of the input list and the consumption of the result.

Parser used	execution time (s)	garbage collect (s)	total time (s)	minimal heap (Kb)
sentence	120	345	465	7070
ad-hoc	0.06	0.03	0.09	625

These measurements show that the performance of the parser **sentence** is rather disappointing. It consumes one order of magnitude more memory than the ad-hoc parser and is about 5000 times slower. This disappointing performance is the reason that many people turn to parser generators, like yacc, Happy and Ratatosk mentioned above, forbid ambiguity [12], or use an ad-hoc parser. In this paper we will investigate how we can improve the performance of parsers within the given framework of potential ambiguous parser combinators. In general the time and memory needed by a parser is dependent on the parser and its input. We will use the parser **sentence** as running example.

3   Avoiding Intermediate Data Structures

As a first step to increase the speed of parser combinators we focus on the traditional implementation of these combinators. Although the list of successes method is conceptual nice and clear, it introduces a very large overhead. Each result must be packed in a list of tuples. Usually, this list of tuples is immediately taken apart in the next action of the parser.

Using continuations [2] in the implementation of the parser combinators it is possible to avoid these superfluous intermediate lists and tuples. The parser combinators will handle all continuations. The only thing that changes for the user of these parser combinators is that a parser should be initiated by **begin parser input**, instead of **parser input**.

The parser combinators using continuations can replace the combinators introduced in the previous section completely. Nevertheless, in this paper we use new names for the version of the combinators using continuations such we can identify the different implementations of the combinators.

The type of a continuation parser reflects the fact that there are two continuations. The first continuation handles the item recognized by the parser. This first continuation is very similar to the second argument of the **<&=>** operator. The second continuation contains all remaining results.

```
:: ParserC s r t :== (Success s r t) (NextRes s t) -> Parser s t
:: Success s r t :== r (NextRes s t) -> Parser s t
:: NextRes s t   :== ParsResult s t
```

The type `ParserC` has three arguments. The first argument, s, denotes the type of symbols parsed. The next argument, r, is the type of the result of parsing. The success continuation transforms this to the type t of the total result. One can regard this success continuation as a function applied by the apply-combinator `<@`. The type variables s and r correspond to the type variables we have for ordinary parser combinators, the total type variable, t, is new.

The parser combinator that always fails is now defined as the function that yields the next continuation.

```
failC :: ParserC s r t
failC = \succ next ss -> next
```

The parser combinator `yieldC`, that yields the given element r applies the success continuation to this element, the next continuation and the input.

```
yieldC :: r -> ParserC s r t
yieldC r = \succ next ss -> succ r next ss
```

The parser that recognizes the given symbol s, checks whether the first element of the input stream is equal to this symbol. If it is, the success continuation is applied to the symbol, the next continuation and the rest of the input stream. If the first element is not equal to the given symbol, the parser fails and hence yields the next continuation.

```
symbolC :: s -> ParserC s s t | == s
symbolC sym = p
where  p sc nc [s:ss] | s==sym = sc sym nc ss
       p sc nc _               = nc
```

The new definitions of the and-combinator and or-combinator are trivial. In the and-combinator the second parser is used as success continuation. This parser is applied to the item found by the first parser and the original success continuation.

```
(>&=<) infixr 6 :: (ParserC s u t) (u->ParserC s v t) -> ParserC s v t
(>&=<) p1 p2 = \sc -> p1 (\t -> p2 t sc)
```

In the or-combinator the next continuation is replaced by applying the second parser to the success continuation, the original next continuation and the input.

```
(>|<) infixr 4 :: (ParserC s r t) (ParserC s r t) -> ParserC s r t
(>|<) p1 p2 = \sc nc ss -> p1 sc (p2 sc nc ss) ss
```

In the combinators `<@`, `<*>` and `<+>` we replace the original combinators by the introduced versions. The new operators are called `@<`, `>*<` and `>+<` respectively.

Finally we introduce the function `begin` that provides the initial continuations for a parser. As success continuation we provide a function that constructs an element in the list of successes. The next continuation is initially the empty list.

```
begin :: (ParserC s t t) -> Parser s t
begin p = p (\r nc ss -> [(ss,r):nc]) []
```

To determine the effect of using continuations we apply a modified parser
sentence again to the same input. Inside the definition of the parser we have
replaced all parser combinators by the corresponding version using continuations.

Parser used	execution time (s)	garbage collect (s)	total time (s)	minimal heap (Kb)
original **sentence**	120	345	465	7070
sentence with continuations	9.6	36.6	46.2	5940
ad-hoc	0.06	0.03	0.09	625

From these measurements we see that using continuations improves the execution speed by a factor of ten. Also the minimal amount of memory needed
to run this program is reduced a little bit. This effect is caused by omitting the
construction of intermediate data structures. On the other hand it is clear that
this improvement is not enough, the difference between this parser and the hand
written parser is still a factor of 500.

4   Limit Backtracking

Since it looks impossible to speed up the parser combinators much more, we
must turn our focus to the behaviour of the parsers. As we have seen in the
word ['Hello world'] example in Sect. 2.3 above, the parser **word** is ambiguous.
Apart from the whole word, it yields also all initial fragments of this word. This
implies that there are n results for a word of n characters. The same holds for
the separations of words recognized by the parser **sep**. In the current application
we are only interested in the most eager parsing of words and separations. All
other results will not yield a successful parsing of a sentence.

This behaviour is determined by the or-combinator, **<|>**, used in the defini-
tion of the repeat-combinator, **<*>**. The or-combinator yields the results of both
alternatives inside the definition of **<*>**. Even when **p <&=> \r -> <*> p <@ \rs
-> [r:rs]** succeeds, the or-combinator also yields the empty list. In the current
situation we require an exclusive or-combinator that only applies the second
parser when the first one fails.

In the plain list of successes approach the definition of the xor-combinator is
very direct. The parser **p2** is only applied to the input **ss** if applying **p1** to the
input yields the empty list of successes. If applying **p1** to the input produces a
non-empty result, this is the result of the entire construct.

```
(<!>) infixr 4 :: (Parser s r) (Parser s r) -> Parser s r
(<!>) p1 p2 = \ss -> case p1 ss of
                      [] -> p2 ss
                      r  -> r
```

Using continuations we can achieve the same effect by replacing the next continuation of the new success-continuation by the original next continuation. This excludes the results of p2 from the result when p1 succeeds.

```
(>!<) infixr 4 :: (ParserC s r t) (ParserC s r t) -> ParserC s r t
(>!<) p1 p2 = \sc nc ss -> p1 (\r _ -> sc r nc) (p2 sc nc ss) ss
```

Now we can define eager versions of the repeat-combinators by replacing the ordinary or-combinator in the body of <*> by the xor-combinator. For the version using continuations we obtain:

```
>!*< :: (ParserC s r t) -> ParserC s [r] t
>!*< p = (      p       >&=< \r ->
                >!*< p   @< \rs -> [r:rs])
          >!< yieldC []


>!+< :: (ParserC s r t) -> ParserC s [r] t
>!+< p = p >&=< \r -> >!*< p @< \rs -> [r:rs]
```

It is important to note that the previous optimization, using continuations, does not have any semantically influence on the parser combinators. In the current optimization we turn an ambiguous parser for words into an eager and deterministic parser for words. In the context of parsing a sentence this is allowed, but there might be (rare?) occurrences where the ambiguous nature of the parser word is used. So, it depends on the context whether this optimization can be applied. In general we need the deterministic parser combinators >!< and >!*< as well as the ambiguous combinators >|< and >*<. It is advisable to use the deterministic versions whenever the context allows this.

We repeat the measurements of parsing the sentence of 50,000 characters in order to determine the effect of the eager repeat-combinators.

Parser used	execution time (s)	garbage collect (s)	total time (s)	minimal heap (Kb)
original sentence	120	345	465	7070
<!*> in word and sep	12.4	21.0	33.4	4925
<!*> everywhere	0.30	0.19	0.49	4712
sentence with continuations	9.6	36.6	46.2	5940
>!*< in word and sep	1.19	1.12	2.31	1872
>!*< everywhere	0.28	0.14	0.43	1740
ad-hoc	0.06	0.03	0.09	625

These measurements show that using xor-combinators instead of ordinary or-combinators make a tremendous differences. The difference in speed between the ad-hoc parser and the best combinator parser is less than a factor 5. Even when the xor-combinator is used only at a limited number of places it has a huge effect. In fact we obtain the effect of an old-fashioned tokenizer when we use the eager repeat combinators in word and sep.

It is mainly the memory usage that makes it preferable to use the continuation version of the parser combinators when we use xor-combinators and eager repeats everywhere. If there is ambiguity on the parser, the ordinary or-combinator (<|>), the version using continuations is an order of magnitude more efficient.

5   Reducing the Memory Requirements

As a last improvement we try to reduce the memory requirements of the parser. As a side effect of the other optimizations introduced above, the memory requirements are reduced by a factor of four. We can improve this by observing that in many applications of the xor-combinator we can decide that the second alternative will not apply before the first alternative does succeed. Currently, the second alternative is not thrown away before the first alternative succeeds.

Consider again the repeat combinator. The version using continuations is:

```
>!*< :: (ParserC s r t) -> ParserC s [r] t
>!*< p = (      p      >&=< \r  ->
               >!*< p   @< \rs -> [r:rs])
         >!< yieldC []
```

As soon as the parser p is successfully applied, it is clear that the alternative yieldC [] will not be used. However, this alternative is kept until the first alternative of >!< succeeds. This alternative succeeds after the completion of >!*< p, which can be a huge amount of work. By adding primitives to throw the xor-alternatives away the programmer can improve the memory requirements of the parser. In order to do this we introduce a new continuation, XorCont s t, containing the xor-alternatives.

```
:: CParser s r t :== (SucCont s r t) (XorCont s t) (AltCont s t)
                        -> Parser s t
:: SucCont s r t :== r (XorCont s t) (AltCont s t) -> Parser s t
:: XorCont s t   :== (AltCont s t) -> ParsResult s t
:: AltCont s t   :== ParsResult s t
```

The xor-continuation is a function that takes the ordinary alternative continuation as argument and yields the remaining parse results. Of course we have to adopt the definitions of all parser combinators to this new continuation. Again, the parsers which use these combinators remain unchanged. In order to distinguish the various versions of the combinators we introduce again new names. The basic parser combinators are:

```
Cfail :: CParser s r t
Cfail = \sc xc ac ss -> xc ac

Cyield :: r -> CParser s r t
Cyield x = \sc -> sc x
```

```
Csymbol :: s -> CParser s s t | == s
Csymbol sym = p
where   p sc xc ac [s:ss] | s==sym = sc sym xc ac ss
        p sc xc ac _              = xc ac
```

In the and-combinator the second parser, p2, is inserted in the first continuation, the success continuation sc, of the first parser, p1.

```
(<<&=>>) infixr 6 :: (CParser s u t) (u->CParser s v t) -> CParser s v t
(<<&=>>) p1 p2 = \sc -> p1 (\t -> p2 t sc)
```

For the xor-combinator we insert the second parser in the xor-continuation, xc, of the first parser.

```
(<<!>>) infixr 4 :: (CParser s r t) (CParser s r t) -> CParser s r t
(<<!>>) p1 p2
 = \sc xc ac ss -> p1 (\x xc2 -> sc x xc) (\ac3 -> p2 sc xc ac3 ss) ac ss
```

For the ordinary or-combinator we insert the second parser in the alternative continuation, ac, of the first parser.

```
(<<|>>) infixr 4 :: (CParser s r t) (CParser s r t) -> CParser s r t
(<<|>>) p1 p2 = \sc xc ac ss -> p1 sc (\ac2 -> ac2) (p2 sc xc ac ss) ss
```

Again there is a function Begin that provides the initial continuations to construct a parse result for the successful parsings.

```
Begin :: (CParser s t t) -> Parser s t
Begin p = p (\x xc ac ss -> [(ss,x):xc ac]) (\ac -> ac) []
```

After the definition of the basic combinators we can define the combinator cut that removes xor-alternatives by replacing the corresponding continuation, xc, by an identity function.

```
cut :: (CParser s r t) -> CParser s r t
cut p = \sc xc ac -> p sc (\ac -> ac) ac
```

The scope of the cut is all xor-combinators up to the first ordinary or-combinator. Multiple cuts, or cuts in a context without xor-alternatives are harmless. It appears to be convenient to combine the cut-combinator with an and-combinator.

```
(<<!&=>>) infixr 6 :: (CParser s u t) (u->CParser s v t) -> CParser s v t
(<<!&=>>) p1 p2 = \sc -> p1 (\t ac2 -> p2 t sc (\ac -> ac))
```

The semantics of this combinator reads: iff p1 succeeds, the xor-alternatives are thrown away and we continue parsing with p2. If p1 fails, we turn to the xor- and or-alternatives as usual.

An obvious application of this combinator is the eager repeat-combinator <!*> discussed above. When p succeeds we can remove the xor-alternative Cyield []. We use the operator <<!&=>> to achieve this. The definition of the eager repeat-combinator doing this is:

```
<<!*>> :: (CParser s r t) -> CParser s [r] t
<<!*>> p = (      p         <<!&=>> \r  ->
                  <<!*>> p <<@      \rs -> [r:rs])
           <<!>> Cyield []
```

To determine the effects of this optimization we repeat our measurements.

Parser used	execution time (s)	garbage collect (s)	total time (s)	minimal heap (Kb)
>!*< everywhere	0.28	0.14	0.43	1740
<<!*>> everywhere	0.27	0.11	0.38	937
ad-hoc	0.06	0.03	0.09	625

Although the improvements (12% for speed 46% for minimal memory) are of another range than the previous optimizations we consider them useful. The gain of this optimization depends on the amount of storage that is claimed by the alternative that is thrown away and the moment it is thrown away. For huge alternatives that are thrown away after a very complex (time and memory consuming) first alternative, the gain will be larger.

6   Using Accumulators

Finally, we can consider implementing the repeat-combinator outside the framework of parser combinators. For the implementation of the combinator <*>, it might be useful to employ an accumulator like we have used in the ad-hoc parser. This can look like:

```
<<!!*>> :: (CParser s r t) -> CParser s [r] t
<<!!*>> p = ClistP p []

<<!!+>> :: (CParser s r t) -> CParser s [r] t
<<!!+>> p = p <<&=>> \r -> ClistP p [r]

ClistP :: (CParser s r t) [r] -> CParser s [r] t
ClistP p l = clp l
where  clp l sc xc ac ss
       = p
         (\r xc2 -> clp [r:l] sc (\ac3 -> ac3))
         (\ac4 -> sc (reverse l) xc ac4 ss)
         ac
         ss
```

This new implementation is transparent for the user of the repeat combinators. We measure the value of this modification in our running example.

Parser used	execution time (s)	garbage collect (s)	total time (s)	minimal heap (Kb)
<<!*>> everywhere	0.27	0.11	0.38	937
<<!!*>> everywhere	0.26	0.08	0.34	887
ad-hoc	0.06	0.03	0.09	625

Using this implementation shows again a small improvement. Due to the use of accumulators and the changed form of recursion, this version also requires less stack space. It appears that the xor-continuation is necessary to implement this efficiently. For the repeat-combinator such an implementation might be used. However, we cannot expect a user of the parser combinators to write such an implementation. Fortunately, the price to be paid by using parser combinators instead of tailor-made functions using accumulators is limited (about 10%).

7   Complexity

Parsers constructed by using conventional parser combinators only work well for small inputs. For larger inputs the execution time increases very rapidly. This is a strong indication that there is a problem with the complexity of the parsers.

It is impossible to make useful statements about all, potentially ambiguous, parsers created by parser combinators. However, we can investigate the complexity of a specific parser constructed using parser combinators. We will again take the parser for sentences as example. A large part of the discussion is based on the behaviour of the repeat-combinators and the recognition of tokens. This part of the discussion will apply to almost any parser written.

As shown in Sect. 2.3 parsing words is ambiguous. The ambiguity is caused by using the standard repeat-combinator <+>. Apart from the longest possible word, all initial fragments of this word are also recognized as a word. The recognition of the characters in the word is shared among the various results. But, for each result a spine of the list of characters has to be constructed. These lists of characters are later transformed to strings. For each individual result the parser continues with the remaining part of the input. In our example, parsing the rest of the input will fail on the first input character for all but the most eager result of **word**. Nevertheless, there are n results for parsing a word of length n. For each of these results a list of characters of average length $n/2$ is constructed and the next character after that result is parsed. This indicates that parsing words, and hence parsing a sentence, in this way is $O(n^2)$.

In Sect. 4 we showed how we can get rid of partial words by introducing an xor-combinator. When we construct the repeat-combinator using this xor-combinator, the parser **word** has only a single result. Parsing a word of length n implies parsing n characters and constructing a single list of length n to hold these characters. The parser is now linear, $O(n)$, in the length of the word.

When we also apply the eager repeat-combinator in the parser **sentence**, the entire parser will be linear in the length of the input. This holds for all implementations of the parser combinators. Various implementations of the same combinator result in parsers of the same complexity, only the constants are different. When we apply the ordinary or-combinators the parser **sentence** will be polynomial. Using xor-combinators the parser will be linear.

In order to verify this we measure the time consumed by our best implementation of the combinators (Sect. 5) as function of the length of the input.

length	or-combinators			xor-combinators			speed-up
	execution time(s)	garbage collect(s)	total time(s)	execution time(s)	garbage collect(s)	total time(s)	total time
1000	0.02	0.01	0.01	0.01	0.00	0.01	1
2000	0.05	0.02	0.07	0.01	0.00	0.01	7
4000	0.12	0.04	0.16	0.02	0.01	0.03	5
10,000	0.45	0.27	0.72	0.04	0.03	0.07	10
20,000	1.46	1.73	3.19	0.09	0.05	0.15	21
40,000	5.54	16.87	22.41	0.21	0.09	0.30	75
100,000	heap full			0.46	0.35	0.81	-
200,000	heap full			0.96	1.15	2.11	-
400,000	heap full			1.92	5.56	7.48	-

These measurements show clearly that the time consumed by the version using the ordinary or-combinator grows polynomially. Also for the xor-combinator version there seems to be some slight super-linear effect, especially in the garbage collection times. To understand this it is important to note that the parser cannot yield any result before the full stop indicating the end of the sentence is encountered. If the full stop is not found, it is not a proper sentence and the parser should yield an empty result. Since parsers of larger inputs have to handle larger data structures, the garbage collector will reclaim less memory. Hence we need a larger number of garbage collections. This explains the super-linear growth of the garbage collection time in the parser using xor-combinators.

The changed complexity caused by using the eager repeat-combinators, like <!*>, instead of the usual repeat combinators, like <*>, explains the enormous increase of efficiency for the running example of this paper. In fact the efficiency gain of more than a factor of 1000 is just an example. If we increase the size of the input, the speed-up figure grows rapidly.

8   Conclusion

Parser combinators are a nice and clear way to define ambiguous recursive descent parser in functional programming languages. Unfortunately, the parsers that are usually constructed are not suited for large inputs since they consume enormous amounts of time and memory. This is caused by a polynomial complexity and an implementation that generates many intermediate data structures.

In this paper we have introduced a new implementation technique for parser combinators based on continuations. This improves the speed of the parser by one order of magnitude and reduces the amount of memory required significantly by eliminating intermediate data structures.

By introducing an exclusive or-combinator we are able to reduce the complexity of deterministic parsers from polynomial to linear. This makes it possible to use the parsers constructed by parser combinators for large inputs. However, we stay within the framework of ambiguous parser combinators. This implies that it is always possible to use ambiguity, introduced by the ordinary or-combinator, whenever this is desired.

As a result the example parser in this paper is only four times slower for large inputs than an efficient ad-hoc parser for the same problem. Using the standard parser combinators it was 5000 times slower. This indicates that the proposed changes turn the parser combinators from a nice toy for small problems, into a beautiful and useful tool for real world parsing problems.

9   Related and Future Work

More people have experienced that parser combinators are attractive, but not suited for large inputs. Doaitse Swierstra and his group follow a different approach to tackle the problem. They exclude ambiguity from the beginning and construct parser combinators for deterministic grammars. Our work is more general since it allows ambiguity whenever the user wants it. The user can indicate that the parser is not ambiguous by using the xor-combinator instead of the or-combinator. If the parser is known to be non-ambiguous the complexity decreases from polynomial to linear. In our xor-combinator it is allowed that alternatives overlap partially. In their approach the alternatives should be distinguished at the first symbol. Moreover, our combinator satisfy enables the use of a conditional function on the input symbols, while the Swierstra combinators require that all allowed symbols are listed explicitly by a symbol combinator. Hence, our combinators are easier to use than Swierstra's unambiguous grammars. Swierstra combinators enables the generation of error messages. It is simple and cheap to extend our combinators in a similar way. In order to compare the speed of both approaches, we implemented their combinators in Clean and applied them to the running example, 2000 simple function alternatives and a huge expression.

parser	old-combinators			new-combinators			Swierstra-combinators		
	ex (s)	gc (s)	tot (s)	ex (s)	gc (s)	tot (s)	ex (s)	gc (s)	tot (s)
sentence	120	345	465	0.26	0.08	0.34	0.55	0.28	0.83
functions	5.5	50.5	56.0	0.43	0.22	0.65	0.98	0.37	1.35
expression	73	104	177	0.36	0.19	0.55	0.51	0.33	0.84

As a conclusion we state that our combinators are more powerful (since they allow ambiguity), easier to use (since they allow alternatives to overlap partially and conditions on input symbols) and seems to be more efficient.

Currently the user has to indicate whether the or-combinator or the xor-combinator has to be used. It would be convenient if the parser uses the xor-combinator whenever this is possible. In principle it is possible to detect this automatically in a number of situations. If the branches of the or-combinators excludes each other (i.e. the parser in unambiguous) the or-combinator can be replaced by the xor-combinator. It looks feasible and seems attractive to construct such an automatic parser optimizer.

References

1. A. Aho, R. Sethi and J.D. Ullman. *Compilers: Principles, Techniques and Tools.* Addison-Wesley, 1986.
2. A. Appel. *Compiling with Continuations.* Cambridge University Press. 1992.
3. J. Fokker. Functional Parsers. In *Advanced Functional Programming, 1st. International School on Functional Programming Techniques, Båstad, Sweden,* volume 925 of *LNCS,* pages 1–23. Springer-Verlag, 1995.
4. A. Gill and S. Marlow. The Parser Generator for Haskell. University of Glasgow. 1995.
5. S. Hill. Combinators for Parsing Expressions. *Journal of Functional Programming,* 6(3):445–463, 1996.
6. G. Hutton. Higher Order Functions for Parsing. *Journal of Functional Programming,* 2:323–343, 1992.
7. S.C. Johnson. Yacc: Yet Another Compiler Compiler. *UNIX On-Line Documentation.* 1978.
8. P. Koopman. Parser Combinators. Chapter II.5 of *Functional Programming in Clean* In preparation (draft available at http://www.cs.kun.nl/\homedirclean).
9. T. Mogensen. Ratatosk: A Parser Generator and Scanner Generator for Gofer. University of Copenhagen (DIKU), 1993.
10. S.L. Peyton Jones. Yacc in SASL, an Exercise in Functional Programming. *Software: Practice and Experience,* 15(8):807–820, 1995.
11. M.J. Plasmeijer and M.C.J.D. van Eekelen. The Concurrent Clean Language Report, Version 1.3. Nijmegen University, The Netherlands. 1998. http://www.cs.kun.nl/\homedirclean.
12. D. Swierstra and L. Duponcheel. Deterministic, Error-Correcting Combinators Parsers. In *Advanced Functional Programming.* volume 1129 of *LNCS,* pages 185–207, Springer-Verlag, 1996
13. P.L. Wadler. How to Replace Failure by a List of Successes: a Method for Exception Handling, Backtracking, and Pattern Matching in Lazy Functional Languages. In J.P. Jouannaud, editor *Proc. 1985 Conference on Functional Programming Languages and Computer Architecture (FPLCA '85).* volume 201 of *LNCS,* pages 113–128, Springer-Verlag, 1985.

A   The Ad-Hoc Parser

For the sake of completeness we include the ad-hoc parser used in the measurements listed above. The parser has three states called **word**, **sep** and **dot**. In the state **word** the parser accepts characters for the current word. When the character cannot be part of this word we go to that state **sep**. In this state we read separations. When the separation is empty and the input character is not part of the separation the parser enters state **dot**. Otherwise the parser returns to **word**. The parser uses accumulators to construct the current word **w** and the sentence **s**. The accumulators are constructed in reversed order to avoid polynomial complexity. When accumulation is finished the accumulator is reversed to obtain the right order.

```
manParse :: [Char] -> [([Char],[String])]
manParse input = word [] [] input
where word w  s [c:r] | isAlpha c = word [c:w] s r
      word w  s input              = sep [] [toString (reverse w):s] input

      sep l  s [c:r] | isSpace c || c == ',' = sep [c:l] s r
      sep []  s input = dot s input
      sep _   s input = word [] s input

      dot [] input   = []
      dot s  ['.':r] = [(r,reverse s)]
      dot _  _       = []
```

On the Unification of Substitutions in Type Inference

Bruce J. McAdam

Laboratory for Foundations of Computer Science
The University of Edinburgh
bjm@dcs.ed.ac.uk

Abstract. The response of compilers to programs with type errors can be unpredictable and confusing. In part this is because the point at which type inference fails may not be the point at which the programmer has made a mistake. This paper explores a way of making type inference algorithms fail at different locations in programs so that clearer error messages may then be produced.

Critical to the operation of type inference algorithms is their use of substitutions. We will see that the way in which substitutions are applied in type inference algorithm W means that errors are detected towards the right-hand side of expressions. This paper introduces a new operation — unification of substitutions — which allows greater control over the use of substitutions so that this bias can be removed.

1 Introduction

One benefit of having a type system for a programming language is that programs which do not have types can be rejected by the compiler. This is of help to programmers as it assures them of one aspect of program correctness, however a difficulty many programmers find in programming is that when their program is rejected by a compiler they are not given enough information to easily locate and repair the mistakes they have made.

This paper deals with *Hindley-Milner* type systems such as that of Standard ML. Programmers using these type systems frequently complain about the poor quality of type error messages. We will see in Sect. 2 that one complaint is that the part of the program highlighted by the compiler is generally not the part of the program in which the programmer made the mistake. In Sect. 3 we examine the type inference algorithm and see that it has a *left-to-right bias* towards detecting problems late in the code and this bias is caused by the way unification and substitutions are used.

The solution to this problem with the conventional inference algorithm is a new type inference algorithm designed from a pragmatic perspective. The key idea here is that the algorithm should be *symmetric*, treating subexpressions identically so that there is no bias causing errors to tend to be reported in one part of a program rather than another. The new algorithm rests upon the novel concept of the *unification of substitutions* to allow the symmetric treatment of

H. Hammond, T. Davie, and C. Clack (Eds.): IFL'98, LNCS 1595, pp. 137–152, 1999.

subexpressions. Sect. 4 introduces the operation of unifying substitutions and discusses how it will remove the left-to-right bias from type inference. Sect. 5 presents a variation of the classic type inference algorithm for Hindley-Milner type systems which uses this substitution unifying procedure.

Further uses of unifying substitutions are given in Sect. 6. Issues in implementing these ideas are discussed in Sect. 7. A summary of the conclusions of this paper is in Sect. 8.

2   Motivation

Type systems play two important roles in software development. The programmer has simple static properties of programs machine-checked and the compiler can optimise on the basis of types. We are concerned with the first of these roles, and in particular that the compiler rejects untypeable programs as they are not guaranteed to have a meaningful interpretation in the language semantics.

The problem with this is that the burden of correcting the program lies in the programmer's hands and often there is little help the compiler can give. Compilers typically tell the programmer at which point in the program the error was found, but generally this is not the part of the program in which the programmer made the mistake and it is unclear why type checking failed at this point.

2.1   An Inherent Problem with Hindley-Milner

Two key features of Hindley-Milner type systems are of particular interest to this paper.

Implicit typing means that the programmer need not say what type an expression or identifier should have, the type system (and inference algorithm) can infer most types with only a small number of typing assertions necessary.

Polymorphic typing means that types can be flexible. For example, a function might take a value of any type and return a value of the same type. In this case the function can have type $\tau \to \tau$ for any type τ. We denote this with the polymorphic type scheme $\forall \alpha . \alpha \to \alpha$. It is not necessary for the programmer to specify that a function is polymorphic, type inference will discover this fact.

From the point of view of finding the location of mistakes in a program, these features are weaknesses. The only way to detect a mistake is to find an inconsistency between two parts of the program. This is in contrast to explicit type systems in which the inconsistencies are typically between the use of identifiers and the declarations of their types. So with Hindley-Milner based languages, rather than being able to establish that either the use of an identifier or its declaration is incorrect, there are three possibilities: the first expression may be incorrect, the second may be incorrect, or the problem may lie in the context. Because of polymorphism some program fragments which contain mistakes will have still have a type — but not the type the programmer expected. This can lead to a cascading effect: spurious errors are announced later when newly derived types are found to be in conflict with the type derived for the mistake.

2.2 Examples of Untypeable Expressions

Let us first consider a simple λ-calculus example of a Hindley-Milner untypeable expression. This function should take a real number and return the sum of the original number and its square root:

$$\lambda a.\text{add } a \text{ (sqrt } a)$$

A typical error message from a type checker would read:

Cannot apply sqrt : real $\rightarrow$ real to a : int.

A programmer, seeing this message, may be confused as a is intended to be real. So the mistake cannot be that sqrt is being applied to a, it must be that something else causes a to appear to be an int. The source of the problem will become apparent if we look at the type environment the expression is checked inside:

$$\text{add : int} \rightarrow \text{int} \rightarrow \text{int}$$
$$\text{sqrt : real} \rightarrow \text{real}$$

The mistake has been to use integer addition where real number addition is required.

Clearly in this case the error message is inappropriate as there is equal evidence that a should be a real as there is that it should be an int. The type checker has incorrectly given priority to the information derived from the leftmost subexpression — it has a left-to-right bias. It would have been more informative in the example if the type checker had pointed out that there was an inconsistency *between* the two subexpressions, instead of falsely claiming that either was internally inconsistent.

A classic example used to illustrate the monomorphism of function arguments is

$$\lambda I.(I \text{ 3, } I \text{ true})$$

The programmer has written a function which expects the identity function as an argument, this is not possible in Hindley-Milner type systems as arguments cannot be used polymorphically. When a compiler is faced with this expression it type checks from left to right, first establishing that I must have a type of the form int $\rightarrow$ α and then finding that I cannot, therefore, be applied to true of type bool. The programmer will be given an error message of the form

Cannot apply I : int $\rightarrow$ α to true : bool.

This message implies that there is an inconsistency inside I true. In fact there is an inconsistency in the use of I between the two subexpressions. The algorithm in this paper will find this inconsistency in the uses of I between the subexpressions of $(I \text{ 3, } I \text{ true})$ instead of finding an apparent mistake in I true.

2.3   Alternative Approaches to the Problem

A number of other authors have looked into the problem of generating error messages about the appropriate parts of programs. Johnson and Walz [7] looked at the difficulty in working out how unification fails. They applied their method to the classic inference algorithm, so it still suffers from a left-to-right bias. It is likely that their ideas could be applied to unification of substitutions to both eliminate the left-to-right bias in the point at which unification fails, and generate improved error messages about why unification failed.

Duggan and Bent [6] provided another system for recording why substitutions were made during unification. Their interest is in producing meaningful messages after some unification fails, whereas this paper is interested in making unification fail at the appropriate point. Beaven and Stansifer [1] provided another explanation facility.

Bernstein and Stark [2] provide a novel type inference algorithm based on the unification of *type environments*. Like the algorithm in this paper, their's is symmetric and has no left-to-right bias. Lee and Yi [9] discuss a folklore algorithm. They prove that it can reject programs sooner than the classic algorithm. One might suppose that this will eliminate left-to-right bias, but this is not the case. Given an untypeable application, $e_0 e_1$, the folklore algorithm may reject during the recursive call for e_1 when e_0 and e_1 are incompatible. In order to remove the left-to-right bias rejection must be *delayed* until the entire expression $e_0 e_1$ is being examined.

3   Type Systems and the Classic Inference Algorithm

This section begins by summarising the language and type system used in the remainder of the paper. An introductory discussion of type systems and their inference algorithms can be found in [3]. Proofs of algorithm W's correctness can be found in [4].

3.1   Types, Type Schemes and Type Environments

In this paper we will consider types which are built from type variables ($\alpha, \beta \ldots$) (hence types are polymorphic); type constants (int, real and others); and the function type constructor $\rightarrow$.

The form of polymorphism in Hindley-Milner type systems arises from the use of *type schemes*. These are types with some (or all) of their type variables universally quantified, for example $\forall \alpha. \alpha \rightarrow \beta$. A type, τ', is a *generic instance* of a type scheme, $\forall \alpha_1 \cdots \alpha_n. \tau$, if τ' can be obtained from τ by substituting types for the type variables $\alpha_1 \cdots \alpha_n$. In this paper, we are not particularly concerned with type schemes as substitutions refer to type variables which are not universally quantified.

Type inference starts from a type environment, Γ, which is a map from identifiers to type schemes. Γ can be augmented with new terms, for example after a declaration, and can have terms removed from it (Γ_x is Γ with any term for x removed).

Type schemes are obtained from types by *closing* a type under a type environment. $\overline{\Gamma}(\tau)$ (the closure of τ under Γ) is the type scheme $\forall \alpha_1 \cdots \alpha_n.\tau$ where $\alpha_1 \cdots \alpha_n$ are the type variables occurring in τ but which do not occur free in Γ. In particular, closing a type under a type environment with no free type variables results in every type variable in the type being universally quantified.

Component	Values
Type Variables	$\alpha, \beta, \ldots$
Types	$\tau ::= \alpha \mid \tau_0 \rightarrow \tau_1 \mid \mathsf{int} \mid \mathsf{real} \mid \cdots$
Type Schemes	$\sigma = \forall \alpha_0 \cdots \alpha_n.\tau$
Type Environments	$\Gamma = \{x_0 : \sigma_0, \cdots, x_n : \sigma_n\}$

Table 1. Components of type systems.

3.2 Language and Type System

Hindley-Milner type systems are formulated as non-deterministic transition systems. In this paper, we will look at a simple λ-with-let-calculus (as in Fig. 1) and will be particularly interested in the rule for deriving types of applications. The type system is in Fig. 2.

$$
\begin{aligned}
e ::= \ &x \\
\mid \ &e_0 e_1 \\
\mid \ &\lambda x.e \\
\mid \ &\mathsf{let}\ x = e_0\ \mathsf{in}\ e_1
\end{aligned}
$$

Fig. 1. Syntax of the λ-with-let-calculus.

The type inference rule APP states that if (given the type environment Γ) subexpression e_0 has type $\tau' \rightarrow \tau$ (it is a function), and similarly that e_1 has type τ' under the same type environment (it is a suitable argument for the function), then the application of e_0 to e_1 has type τ. The non-determinism in this case arises from the function argument type τ'. If we are attempting to show $\Gamma \vdash e_0 e_1 : \tau$, there is no way of knowing what τ' to use in the sub-derivation for each of e_0 and e_1.

Note that the inference rule tells us that in order for $e_0 e_1$ to be typeable, three conditions must be satisfied. e_0 must be typeable, e_1 must be typeable

$$\frac{\Gamma(x) > \tau}{\Gamma \vdash x : \tau} \text{ VAR}$$

$$\frac{\Gamma \vdash e_0 : \tau' \to \tau \qquad \Gamma \vdash e_1 : \tau'}{\Gamma \vdash e_0 e_1 : \tau} \text{ APP}$$

$$\frac{\Gamma_x \cup \{x : \tau_0\} \vdash e : \tau_1}{\Gamma \vdash \lambda x.e : \tau_0 \to \tau_1} \text{ ABS}$$

$$\frac{\Gamma \vdash e_0 : \tau_0 \qquad \Gamma_x \cup \{x : \overline{\Gamma}(\tau_0)\} \vdash e_1 : \tau_1}{\Gamma \vdash \text{ let } x = e_0 \text{ in } e_1 : \tau_1} \text{ LET}$$

Fig. 2. Type derivation rules.

and the types of the two must be compatible for application. It is, therefore, desirable for error messages to describe a mistake as being in e_0 or e_1, or as an incompatibility between them. We saw in Sect. 2.2 that this does not happen with current type checkers. Sometimes they announce an incompatibility as if it was a problem inside e_1.

3.3 Substitutions

In addition to types, type schemes and type environments, type inference algorithms make extensive use of *substitutions*. A substitution is a finite mapping from type variables to types. Substitutions are denoted by a set of mappings, $\{\alpha_1 \mapsto \tau_1, \cdots \alpha_n \mapsto \tau_n\}$. A substitution represents a means of refining types. If we know that a certain type (containing type variables) is associated with an expression, and that a substitution is also associated with it then we can apply the substitution to the type to refine it. Both the classic algorithm and the new algorithm in this paper work by refining types using substitutions.

All substitutions must meet a well-formedness criteria.

Definition 1 (Well-formedness). *A substitution S is said to be well-formed whenever* $\text{dom}(S) \cap FV(S) = \{\}$.

This restriction prevents us from getting 'infinite' types (types which contain themselves).

Substitutions can be composed. $S_1 S_0$ is the substitution which has the same effect as applying first S_0 and then S_1. $S_1 S_0$ exists iff it is well formed, so as well as both conjuncts being well formed it is necessary that $FV(S_1) \cap \text{dom}(S_0) = \{\}$.

We define an ordering on types: $\tau > \tau'$ iff $\exists S : S\tau = \tau'$. Also, a type environment, Γ, has an instance, Γ', iff $\exists S : S\Gamma = \Gamma'$.

3.4 The Classic Inference Algorithm

The classic inference algorithm, W, is a deterministic simulation of the derivation rules. For a particular type environment and expression, it attempts to find a type for the expression and a substitution of types for type variables such that the expression has the type under the substituted type environment. The algorithm traverses the structure of the expression building up substitutions and types as shown in Fig. 3. This paper is concerned with the case of the algorithm which handles function applications.

$$
\begin{aligned}
W(\Gamma, x) = \;&\textbf{let} \\
&\forall \alpha_1 \cdots \alpha_n . \tau = \Gamma(x) \\
&\textbf{in} \\
&(\{\}, \tau[\beta_1/\alpha_1, \cdots, \beta_n/\alpha_n]) \;\textbf{for new}\; \beta_1 \cdots \beta_n \\
W(\Gamma, e_0 e_1) = \;&\textbf{let} \\
&(S_0, \tau_0) = W(\Gamma, e_0) \\
&(S_1, \tau_1) = W(S_0 \Gamma, e_1) \\
&\tau_0' = S_1 \tau_0 \\
&V = U(\tau_0', \tau_1 \to \beta) \;\textbf{for new}\; \beta \\
&\textbf{in} \\
&(V S_1 S_0, V\beta) \\
W(\Gamma, \lambda x.e) = \;&\textbf{let} \\
&(S, \tau) = W(\Gamma_x \cup \{x : \beta\}, e) \;\textbf{for new}\; \beta \\
&\textbf{in} \\
&(S, S\beta \to \tau) \\
W(\Gamma, \textbf{let}\; x = e_0 \;\textbf{in}\; e_1) = \;&\textbf{let} \\
&(S_0, \tau_0) = W(\Gamma, e_0) \\
&(S_1, \tau_1) = W(S_0 \Gamma_x \cup \{x : \overline{S_0 \Gamma}(\tau_0)\}, e_1) \\
&\textbf{in} \\
&(S_1 S_0, \tau_1)
\end{aligned}
$$

Fig. 3. The classic type inference algorithm, W.

The most significant part of this case is the use of *unification*. The algorithm U returns the most general substitution which when applied to each of its argument types will produce the same type, for example $U(\text{int} \to \alpha, \; \beta \to \text{real}) = \{\alpha \mapsto \text{real}, \; \beta \mapsto \text{int}\}$. A survey of applications and techniques for unification can be found in [8]. Type inference fails if no unifier exists. When inference fails because of a failure to unify, implementations produce error messages indicating a problem with the subexpression of current interest.

The result of type inference shown to the programmer (when it succeeds) is a polymorphic type scheme. If W returns (S, τ) then the type scheme is $\overline{S\Gamma}(\tau)$. Since Γ typically does not have any free type variables, all type variables in the result type will normally be universally bound.

The action of the algorithm satisfies a soundness theorem and a completeness theorem.

Theorem 1 (Soundness of W). *If $W(\Gamma, e)$ succeeds with (S, τ) then there is a derivation of $S\Gamma \vdash e : \tau$.*

Theorem 2 (Completeness of W). *Given (Γ, e) let Γ' be an instance of Γ and η be a type scheme such that $\Gamma' \vdash e : \eta$. Then*

1. *$W(\Gamma, e)$ succeeds*
2. *If $W(\Gamma, e) = (P, \pi)$ then for some R: $\Gamma' = RP\Gamma$, and η is a generic instance of $\overline{RP\Gamma}(\pi)$.*

Proofs of these theorems can be found in [4]. We will revisit these theorems after the algorithm is modified later in the paper.

3.5   Source of Left-to-Right Bias

The left-to-right bias arises in application expressions because the first substitution, S_0, is applied to the type environment, Γ, before type checking e_1. This means that if an identifier is used incorrectly in e_0 and used correctly in e_1 inference on e_1 could fail and wrongly imply that e_1 contains an error.

Table 2 shows the different ways in which the application case of W can fail, and how these can be interpreted. The concern of this paper is that it is not possible to differentiate inconsistencies between e_0 and e_1 from inconsistencies inside e_1.

Point of failure	Possible meanings
Recursive call $W(\Gamma, e_0)$	There is an internal inconsistency in e_0. e_0 is incompatible with Γ.
Recursive call $W(S_0\Gamma, e_1)$	There is an internal inconsistency in e_1. e_1 is incompatible with Γ. There is an inconsistency between e_0 and e_1.
Unification $U(S_1\tau_0, \tau_1 \to \beta)$	e_0 cannot be applied to e_1.

Table 2. Ways in which W can fail to type check an application expression.

It is the third cause of failure of $W(S_0, \Gamma, e_1)$ which we wish to eliminate. The solution proposed in this paper is to delay applying the substitutions to Γ by having some means for combining substitutions. Such a means is described in the next section.

4   An Algorithm for Unifying Substitutions

We have already seen some examples demonstrating the left-to-right bias of W. We have also seen how the algorithm works and know why the bias arises in the case of application. The objective of the new algorithm is to allow us to infer types and substitutions for each subexpression independently. The new algorithm U_S deals with combining substitutions, the next section shows how to modify W to make use of it and Sect. 6 shows how to further extend the algorithm and to apply it to other type inference algorithms and other type systems.

4.1   The Idea — Unifying Substitutions

To treat the subexpressions e_0 and e_1 independently in a modified version of W, the recursive calls must be $W(\Gamma, e_0)$ and $W(\Gamma, e_1)$. This will yield two result pairs: (S_0, τ_0) and (S_1, τ_1). It is necessary then to

- check that the two substitutions are consistent
- apply terms from S_0 to τ_1 and from S_1 to τ_0 so that the resulting types have no free type variable in the domain of either substitution, and
- return a well-formed substitution containing entries from both S_0 and S_1.

The second of these requirements is not simply $S_0\tau_1$ and $S_1\tau_0$, because these could have unwanted free type variables. Likewise the third of these is not simply S_1S_0 or S_0S_1. The essence of these three operations can be summarised in these two requirements:

- check the substitutions are consistent, and if they are
- create a substitution which contains the effect of both.

We must *unify* the two substitutions.

4.2   Examples

Before we look at the algorithm for unifying substitutions, it will be worthwhile seeing some examples.

The simplest case is where the two substitutions are completely independent.

$$S_0 = \{\alpha \mapsto \text{int}\}$$
$$S_1 = \{\beta \mapsto \gamma\}$$
$$U_S(S_0, S_1) = \{\alpha \mapsto \text{int}, \beta \mapsto \gamma\}$$

If the domains of S_0 and S_1 contain a common element, we must unify the relevant types:

$$S_0 = \{\alpha \mapsto \text{int} \to \beta\}$$
$$S_1 = \{\alpha \mapsto \gamma \to \text{real}\}$$
$$U_S(S_0, S_1) = \{\beta \mapsto \text{real}, \gamma \mapsto \text{int}\}$$

Note that equivalent results cannot be obtained simply by composing the substitutions (S_0S_1 or S_1S_0). The previous example would have occurred inside the lambda term $\lambda f.\lambda x.(f\,1) + ((f\,x) + 0.1)$. S_0 is the substitution produced from $f\,1$ and S_1 comes from $(f\,x) + 0.1$ (α is the type variable for f).

Substitution unification can fail, for example with

$$S_0 = \{\beta \mapsto \alpha \to \mathsf{real}\}$$
$$S_1 = \{\beta \mapsto \mathsf{real} \to \mathsf{real}, \alpha \mapsto \mathsf{int}\}$$

There is an inconsistency between the instantiations of α in this case.

Unification can also fail with an *occurs* error.

$$S_0 = \{\alpha \mapsto \mathsf{int} \to \beta\}$$
$$S_1 = \{\beta \mapsto \mathsf{int} \to \alpha\}$$

Clearly the two substitutions here imply that α and β should map to infinite types, hence the two substitutions cannot be unified.

4.3   Formal Definition

A substitution, S', unifies substitutions, S_0 and S_1, if $S'S_0 = S'S_1$. In particular the most general unifier of a pair of substitutions is S' such that

$$(S'S_0 = S'S_1) \wedge (\forall S'' : (S''S_0 = S''S_1) \Rightarrow (\exists R : S'' = RS'))$$

i.e. S' unifies S_0 and S_1, and S' can be augmented to be equivalent to any other unifying substitution.

The unified substitution, $S'S_0$, has the effect of both S_0 and S_1 since $S'S_0\alpha < S_0\alpha$ and $S'S_0\alpha < S_1\alpha$, for all α.

4.4   Algorithm U_S

Algorithm U_S computes the most general unifier of a pair of substitutions.

To see how the algorithm works, note that the domain of the result consists of three parts as shown in Fig. 4. The algorithm to be introduced here deals with each of the three parts of the domain separately. The free variables in the range of the unifier are free in either S_0 or S_1 and are in the domains of neither.

The algorithm, commented in italics, is in Fig. 5. Note that it can terminate with an occurs error as indicated, or if U fails.

4.5   Verification of U_S

It must be shown that U_S does indeed compute the most general unifier of a pair of substitutions. Two theorems define this property.

Theorem 3. *For any pair of substitutions, S_0 and S_1, if $U_S(S_0, S_1)$ succeeds then it returns a unifying substitution.*

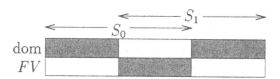

Fig. 4. The domain of $U_S(S_0, S_1)$ consists of three parts (shaded). The disjoint parts of the domains of S_0 and S_1, and the free variables in their ranges where their domains overlap.

$U_S(S_0, S_1) = $ **let**

> *First split the domains into three disjoint parts:*
>
> $D_0 = \text{dom}(S_0) - \text{dom}(S_1)$ $T_0 = \{\alpha \mapsto S_0\alpha : \alpha \in D_0\}$
>
> $D_1 = \text{dom}(S_1) - \text{dom}(S_0)$ $T_1 = \{\alpha \mapsto S_1\alpha : \alpha \in D_1\}$
>
> $D_\cap = \text{dom}(S_0) \cap \text{dom}(S_1)$
>
> *Note: $FV(T_0) \cap \text{dom}(S_0) = \{\}$, similarly for T_1.*
>
> *Start with T_0 and add terms for D_1 one at a time,*
>
> *always producing well formed substitutions:*
>
> $S'_0 = T_0$ $\{\alpha_1 \mapsto \tau_1 \cdots \alpha_n \mapsto \tau_n\} = T_1$
>
> $S'_{i+1} = $ **let**
>
> > *Remove elements of $\text{dom}(S'_i)$ from τ_{i+1},*
> >
> > *and remove α_{i+1} from S'_i:*
> >
> > $\tau'_{i+1} = S'_i\tau_{i+1}$
> >
> > **If** $\alpha_{i+1} \in FV(\tau'_{i+1})$ **terminate (occurs error)**
> >
> > **in** $\{\alpha_{i+1} \mapsto \tau'_{i+1}\}S'_i$
>
> S'_n *is the unifier for T_0 and T_1.*
>
> *Now deal with items in $D_\cap = \{\beta_1 \cdots \beta_m\}$:*
>
> $V_0 = S'_n$
>
> $V_{i+1} = $ **let**
>
> > $\tau_0 = V_i S_0\beta_{i+1}$ $\tau_1 = V_i S_1\beta_{i+1}$
> >
> > **If** $\beta_{i+1} \in FV(\tau_0) \cup FV(\tau_1)$ **terminate (occurs error)**
> >
> > **in** $U(\tau_0, \tau_1)V_i$

in V_m

Fig. 5. Algorithm U_S commented in italics.

Theorem 4. *If S'' unifies S_0 and S_1 then*

1. *$U_S(S_0, S_1)$ succeeds returning S', and*
2. *there is some R such that $S'' = RS'$.*

Proofs of both these propositions can be found in the extended version of this paper [10].

5   The New Version of W

Now that we know what it means to unify two substitutions and have seen that this is possible, let us now look at the new type inference algorithm, W', in Fig. 6. This differs from W only in the case for applications

$$W'(\Gamma, e_0 e_1) = \textbf{let}$$
$$(S_0, \tau_0) = W'(\Gamma, e_0)$$
$$(S_1, \tau_1) = W'(\Gamma, e_1)$$
$$S' = U_S(S_0, S_1)$$
$$\tau_0' = S'\tau_0 \qquad \tau_1' = S'\tau_1$$
$$V = U(\tau_0', \tau_1' \to \beta) \textbf{ for new } \beta$$
$$\textbf{in}$$
$$(VS'S_0, V\beta)$$

Fig. 6. Algorithm W', case for application.

As stated earlier, the algorithm treats e_0 and e_1 symmetrically and features U_S in an analogous manner to (and in addition to) U.

5.1   Correctness of W'

Algorithm W' should produce the same results as W. To verify this it is necessary to prove the soundness and completeness theorems for W'. These theorems are analogous to those which Damas proved for W.

The algorithm is sound if every answer it gives is a type for the parameter expression under the type environment obtained from applying the substitution to the original type environment.

Theorem 5 (Soundness of W'). *If $W'(\Gamma, e)$ succeeds with (S, τ) then there is a derivation of $S\Gamma \vdash e : \tau$.*

This theorem is proved in [10]. The completeness result states that if a type exists for an expression, then W' returns a type which is at least as general as the type known to exist.

Theorem 6 (Completeness of W'). *Given Γ and e, let Γ' be an instance of Γ and η be a type scheme such that $\Gamma' \vdash e : \eta$.*
Then

1. *$W'(\Gamma, e)$ succeeds*
2. *If $W'(\Gamma, e) = (P, \pi)$ then for some R: $\Gamma' = RP\Gamma$, and η is a generic instance of $\overline{RP\Gamma}(\pi)$.*

The proof of this theorem can also be found in [10].

Because W' satisfies the same soundness and completeness theorems as W, and we know that the solutions of these theorems are unique (from the principal type scheme theorem of [5]) we know that W' always produces the same results as W.

Corollary 1 (W' and W are equivalent). *For any pair, (Γ, e), $W(\Gamma, e)$ succeeds and returns (S, τ) if and only if $W'(\Gamma, e)$ succeeds and returns (S, τ).*

5.2   Interpreting the Failure of W'

The argument for using W' is that it is possible to create better error messages when it fails than is possible with W. First, recall the ways in which the application case of W can fail and the possible causes of this as given in Table 2. In particular when $W(S_0\Gamma, e_1)$ fails this may be caused by e_1 being incompatible with a mistake in e_0. This is the sort of error message which programmers find so frustrating as it is not easy to find the original source of the problem from it.

Now consider the possible causes of failure of the application case of W', given in Table 3.

Point of failure	Possible meanings
Recursive call $W(\Gamma, e_0)$	There is an internal inconsistency in e_0.
	e_0 is incompatible with Γ.
Recursive call $W(\Gamma, e_1)$	There is an internal inconsistency in e_1
	e_1 is incompatible with Γ.
Substitution unification $U_S(S_0, S_1)$	There is an inconsistency between e_0 and e_1.
Unification $U(S_1\tau_0, \tau_1 \to \beta)$	e_1 is not a suitable argument for e_0.

Table 3. Ways in which W' can fail to type check an application expression.

Clearly from this, type checkers using W' can produce more informative error messages than those using W.

6   Other uses of U_S

This section explores further uses of U_S. It can be used to type check larger expressions than simple applications symmetrically (for example curried expressions and tuples); and it can be used in other type inference algorithms.

6.1 Larger Syntactic Structures

The type inference algorithm given earlier treated application expressions symmetrically. Similarly, the treatment of tuples and records is typically asymmetric and U_S can be used to eliminate this asymmetry.

Not only can U_S be used to treat simple application expressions symmetrically — it can also be used for curried applications of the form $e_0 e_1 \cdots e_n$. Each of the subexpressions must be type checked, then all the resulting substitutions are unified and the type of the curried expression is found. The advantage of this technique is that it allows type checking to follow the structure of the program in the way the programmer views it.

6.2 Another Type Inference Algorithm, M

An alternative type inference algorithm for Hindley-Milner type systems is M, [9]. This is a top-down algorithm which attempts to check that an expression has a type suitable for its context. The algorithm takes type environment, Γ, expressions, e, and target type, τ, and returns substitution, S, such that $S\Gamma \vdash e : S\tau$. The case of the algorithm for application expressions is shown in Fig. 7.

$$M(\Gamma, e_0 e_1, \tau) = \textbf{let}$$
$$S_0 = M(\Gamma, e_0, \beta \to \tau)$$
$$S_1 = M(S_0 \Gamma, e_1, S_0 \beta)$$
$$\textbf{in } S_1 S_0$$

Fig. 7. The application case of algorithm M.

It is clear that this algorithm suffers from the same left-to-right bias as W but it is a simple matter to change M to remove the bias as can be seen from Fig. 8.

$$M'(\Gamma, e_0 e_1, \tau) = \textbf{let}$$
$$S_0 = M'(\Gamma, e_0, \beta \to \tau)$$
$$S_1 = M'(\Gamma, e_1, \beta)$$
$$\textbf{in } (U_S(S_1, S_0)) S_0$$

Fig. 8. The application case for the modified M.

If the inference $M'(\Gamma, e_0, \beta \to \tau)$ fails, this implies that e_0 is not a function, or does not have the correct return type. The inference $M'(\Gamma, e_1, \beta)$ will fail if and only if Γ and e_1 are inconsistent (there is no typing for $\Gamma \vdash e_1$). If the unification fails then either e_1 is not a suitable argument for e_0, or there is some other inconsistency between them.

7   Implementation

The modified version of W has been implemented for a simple λ-with-let calculus. The implementation has also been extended to deal with curried expressions as described in Sect. 6.1.

One difficulty in implementing type inference using U_S for a full programming language is that it prevents substitutions from being implemented using references. In most compilers, instead of storing explicit substitutions, a type variable, α, is represented as a reference which can refer to a type, τ, to implement the substitution term $\alpha \mapsto \tau$. It has been suggested [11] that this style of implementation is more efficient for large projects (though [12] suggests that explicit substitutions are equally efficient for smaller implementations). Because updating global references represents a greedy strategy it is in conflict with the cautious taken in this paper approach of waiting until as late as possible to apply substitutions.

The ideal for further investigating the ideas in this paper is an implementation in a full-scale compiler. This should be experimentally tested by comparing how programmers deal with problems using modified and unmodified versions of the compiler. An issue not dealt with in this paper which will become relevant in doing this is the actual generation of error messages. Most compilers use *ad hoc* methods which lead to idiosyncratic messages. It is not clear how this would affect experimental testing of this paper's ideas, but it seems that the choice of compiler would be important.

8   Conclusions

This paper introduced the concept of *unifying substitutions* in type inference. An algorithm, U_S, for this was defined. Proofs of properties of U_S can be found in [10].

The classic inference algorithm, W, was modified so that the recursive calls when type checking application expressions are independent of each other. This was achieved using U_S. Proofs that the modified version of W is correct can be found in [10]. The new type inference algorithm has the advantage that it has no left-to-right bias in the locations in which type errors are found (when type checking application expressions). This means that an type inconsistency between the function and argument will never be detected as if it is an internal inconsistency in the argument. Thus, one form of error message confusing to programmers has been removed.

The new inference algorithm can be extended to deal with more complex syntactic structures such as curried expressions and tuples. U_S can also be used to remove the left-to-right bias in other type inference algorithms.

The algorithm has been implemented for a toy language, and issues for a large scale implementation have been discussed.

Acknowledgements

Thanks to Ian Stark and Stephen Gilmore for commenting on early versions of this paper. This work is supported by an EPSRC research studentship.

References

1. M. Beaven and R. Stansifer. Explaining Type Errors in Polymorphic Languages. *ACM Letters on Programming Languages and Systems*, 2(1):17–30, March 1993.
2. K.L. Bernstein and E.W. Stark. Debugging Type Errors (Full version). Technical report, State University of New York at Stony Brook, Computer Science Department, November 1995. `http://www.cs.sunysb.edu/~stark/REPORTS/INDEX.html`.
3. L. Cardelli. Basic Polymorphic Type-Checking. *Science of Computer Programming*, 8(2):147–172, 1987.
4. L.M.M. Damas. *Type Assignment in Programming Languages*. PhD thesis, Department of Computer Science, The University of Edinburgh, April 1985. CST-33-85.
5. L.M.M. Damas and A.J.R.G. Milner. Principal Type-Schemes for Functional Programs. In *Proc. 9th. ACM Symposium on Principles of Programming Languages (POPL '82)*, pages 207–212, 1982.
6. D. Duggan and F. Bent. Explaining Type Inference. *Science of Computer Programming*, (27):37–83, 1996.
7. G.F. Johnson and J.A. Walz. A Maximum-Flow Approach to Anomaly Isolation in Unification-Based Incremental Type-Inference. In *Proc. 13th. ACM Symposium on Principles of Programming Languages (POPL '86)*, pages 44–57, 1986.
8. K. Knight. Unification: A Multidisciplinary Survey. *ACM Computing Surveys*, 21(1):93–124, 1989.
9. O. Lee and K. Yi. Proofs About a Folklore Let-Polymorphic Type Inference Algorithm. *ACM Transactions on Programming Languages and Systems*, 1999. To Appear.
10. B.J. McAdam. On the Unification of Substitutions in Type-Inference. Technical Report ECS-LFCS-98-384, Laboratory for Foundations of Computer Science, The University of Edinburgh, James Clerk Maxwell Building, The Kings Buildings, Mayfield Road, Edinburgh, UK, March 1998.
11. S.L. Peyton Jones and P.L. Wadler. Imperative Functional Programming. In *Proc. 20th. ACM Symposium on Principles of Programming Languages (POPL '93)*, pages 71–84, January 1993.
12. M. Tofte. Four Lectures on Standard ML. Technical Report ECS-LFCS-89-73, Laboratory for Foundations of Computer Science, The University of Edinburgh, March 1989.

Higher Order Demand Propagation

Dirk Pape

Department of Computer Science
Freie Universität Berlin
pape@inf.fu-berlin.de

Abstract. A new denotational semantics is introduced for realistic non-strict functional languages, which have a polymorphic type system and support higher order functions and user definable algebraic data types. It maps each function definition to a demand propagator, which is a higher order function, that propagates context demands to function arguments. The relation of this "higher order demand propagation semantics" to the standard semantics is explained and it is used to define a backward strictness analysis. The strictness information deduced by this analysis is very accurate, because demands can actually be constructed during the analysis. These demands conform better to the analysed functions than abstract values, which are constructed alone with respect to types like in other existing strictness analyses. The richness of the semantic domains of higher order demand propagation makes it possible to express generalised strictness information for higher order functions even across module boundaries.

1 Introduction

Strictness analysis is one of the major techniques used in optimising compilers for lazy functional programs [15]. If a function is identified to be strict in some arguments, these arguments can safely (without changing the lazy semantics) be calculated prior to the function call, saving the effort of building a suspension and later entering it. Strictness information can also be used to identify concurrent tasks in a parallel implementation, since referential transparency guarantees, that function arguments can be reduced independently. *Generalised* strictness analysis can in addition derive an amount of evaluation, which is safe for a larger data structure (e.g. evaluating the spine of a list argument). Such information can be used to find larger tasks in a parallel implementation [2,7], hence reducing granularity. Though it is not always recommended to use generalised strictness information for a sequential implementation – because of the danger of introducing space leaks – it can in general improve simple strictness analysis results even in the sequential setting.

In this paper a new approach to generalised strictness analysis is proposed. The analysis is called demand propagation because evaluation demands are propagated from composed expressions to its components (*backward* w.r.t. function application). In contrast to other backward analyses like projection analysis [19,3] or abstract demand propagation [17] this analysis is applicable for a higher order *and* polymorphic language and works with infinite domains in the non-standard semantics.

In Sect. 2 a simple but realistic functional language based on the polymorphically typed lambda calculus is introduced together with its standard semantics.

K. Hammond, T. Davie, and C. Clack (Eds.): IFL '98, LNCS 1595, pp. 153-168, 1999.
© Springer-Verlag Berlin Heidelberg 1999

Demands, demand propagators and the demand propagation semantics are defined in Sect. 3. The utilisation of demand propagators for generalised strictness analysis is explained in Sect. 4. The soundness proof for the semantics can be read in [13].

Higher order demand propagation departs from other strictness analyses: its abstract values are higher order functions, which calculate the generalised strictness information via backward propagation of demands. A serious implication of this is that the abstract domains are in general infinite. Because of this, more accurate strictness information of a function can be expressed and made available to functions which use it in their definition, even across module boundaries. This can be seen by looking at the examples in the appendix and in [12]. How the analysis can deal with those infinite domains is briefly sketched in Sect. 5 and more thoroughly in [12]. As a bonus it is possible to trade accuracy against speed, making the analysis applicable for different stages of program development.

Further research topics and related work are discussed in Sects. 6 and 7.

2   Core Language Syntax and Semantics

The simple but realistic functional language defined in this section is based on the polymorphically typed lambda calculus. The language is higher order and provides user definable algebraic data types. It is a module language and the standard semantics of a module is a transformation of environments. The module's semantics transforms a given *import* environment into an *export* environment by adding to it the semantics of the functions, which are defined in the module.

2.1   Syntax of the Core Language

The syntax of the core language and its associated type language is given by:

$type := [\ \forall\ \{\ \textbf{tvar}\ \}\ .\ ]\ monotype$

$monotype := \textbf{tvar}\ |\ \textbf{INT}\ |\ monotype \rightarrow monotype\ |\ \textbf{tcons}\ \{\ monotype\ \}$

$usertype := [\ \forall\ \{\ \textbf{tvar}\ \}\ .\ ]\ algebraic$

$algebraic := [\ algebraic\ +\ ]\ \textbf{cons}\ \{\ monotype\ \}$

$expr := \textbf{var}\ |\ \textbf{cons}\ |\ expr\ expr\ |\ \lambda\ \textbf{var}\ .\ expression\ |\ \textbf{let}\ module\ \textbf{in}\ expr$

$\qquad |\ \textbf{case}\ expr\ \textbf{of}\ \{\ \textbf{cons}\ \{\ \textbf{var}\ \}\ \Rightarrow\ expr\ \}\ \textbf{var}\ \Rightarrow\ expr$

$module := \{\ \textbf{tcons} = usertype\ \}\ \{\ \textbf{var} = expr\ \}$

It consists of user type declarations and function declarations. Expressions can be built of variables, constructors, function applications, lambda abstractions, case- and let-expressions. All expressions are assumed to be typed, but for simplicity all type annotations are omitted in this paper. In a real implementation the principal types can be inferred by Hindley-Milner type inference. Nevertheless we define a type language which is used to index the semantic domains.

Polymorphic types are defined by universal quantification of all free type variables at the outermost level of the type, hence an expression's type must not contain a free type variable. The same holds for the user defined types. This is a common approach, that is e.g. followed in the definition of the functional language Haskell [14]. Constructors of an algebraic data type are assumed to be unique over all types.

The usual constants $0, 1, -1, \ldots, +, *, \ldots$ appear in the language as variables with their semantics assigned to them in a prelude environment. Integer numbers also represent constructors, which identify the components of the infinite sum $Z_\perp \cong (\{0\} \oplus \{1\} \oplus \{-1\} \oplus \ldots)_\perp$ and which can be used in a pattern of a case-alternative.

A case-expression must always contain a default alternative, to eliminate the necessity to handle pattern match errors in the semantics. An ordinary case-expression without a default alternative can easily be transformed by adding one with the expression bot, where bot is defined for all types and has the semantics $\perp$.

2.2 Standard Semantics of Core Language Modules

The definition of the standard semantics is given in Fig. 1 and consists of four parts:

1. **The Type Semantics $\mathcal{D}$:** The semantic domains associated to the types of the type language are complete partial ordered sets (cpos). They are constructed out of the flat domain for INT by sum-of-products construction for algebraic data types and continuous function space construction for functional types. These constructions yield again cpos as shown e.g. in [5]. Function domains are lifted here to contain a least element $\perp$ for functional expressions, which do not have a weak head normal form. A domain for a polymorphic type is defined as a type indexed family of domains. User type declarations can be polymorphic and mutual recursive. User defined types are represented by type constructors, which can be applied to the appropriate number of types yielding the domains for recursive data types, which themselves are defined as fixpoints of domain equations in the usual way [5]. Because we focus on the expression semantics here, we handle the type constructors as if they are predefined in the type environment for the type semantics.

2. **The Expression Semantics $\mathcal{E}$:** Syntactic expressions of a type τ are mapped to functions from an environment – describing the bindings of free variables to semantic values – into the domain belonging to τ. The semantics of polymorphic expressions are families of values for all instances of the polymorphic type.

3. **The User Type Declaration Semantics $\mathcal{U}$:** The sum-of-products domains for user defined data types come together with unique continuous injection functions in_c into the sum and with continuous projection functions $proj_{c,i}$ to the i-th factor of the summand corresponding to C. The user type definition semantics implicitly defines a constructor function for each constructor with the corresponding injection function as its semantics. For notational convenience we also define a function tag, which maps any non-bottom value of a sum to the constructor of the summand it belongs to. For $v \neq \perp$ it holds $v \in Image(in_{tag(v)})$.

4. **The Module Semantics $\mathcal{M}$:** The semantics of a core language module is a transformation of environments. Declarations in a core language module can refer to the semantics defined in the import environment. The semantics of the set of mutually recursive declarations in a module for a given import environment is the (always existing) minimal fixpoint of an equation describing the environment enrichment.

Fig. 1. Standard Semantics of the Core Language (cont.)

$\mathcal{E}: \forall \tau{:}\text{Type. Expr}^\tau \to \text{Env} \to \mathcal{D}[[\tau]]$ where $\text{Env} = \forall \tau. \text{Var}^\tau \oplus \text{Const}^\tau \to \mathcal{D}[[\tau]]$

$\mathcal{E}[[x]] \rho = \rho\ x$ þþþand $\rho\rho\rho\mathcal{E}[[C]] \rho = \rho\ C$

$\mathcal{E}[[e_1\ e_2]] \rho = \mathcal{E}[[e_1]] \rho\ (\mathcal{E}[[e_2]] \rho);$ resp. $\perp$, if $\mathcal{E}[[e_1]] \rho = \perp$

$\mathcal{E}[[\lambda x.\ e]] \rho = \lambda v.\ \mathcal{E}[[e]] \rho[v/x]$

$\mathcal{E}[[\textbf{case } e \textbf{ of } C_1\ v_{11}...v_{1a1} \Rightarrow e_1; ...; C_n\ v_{n1}...v_{nan} \Rightarrow e_n; v \Rightarrow e_{def}]] \rho$

$\quad = \perp$, if $e = \perp$

$\quad = \mathcal{E}[[e_i]] \rho[proj_{C_i,1} (e)/v_{i1}, ..., proj_{C_i,ai} (e)/v_{iai}],$ if $tag(e) = C_i$

$\quad = \mathcal{E}[[e_{def}]] \rho[e/v],$ otherwise

$\quad$ where $e = \mathcal{E}[[e]] \rho$

$\mathcal{E}[[\textbf{let } m \textbf{ in } e]] \rho = \mathcal{E}[[e]] (\mathcal{M}[[m]] \rho)$

$\mathcal{U}: \text{Usertype} \to \text{Env} \to \text{Env}$

$\mathcal{U}[[\forall \alpha_1...\alpha_m.\ C_1\ \tau_{11}...\tau_{1a1} + ... + C_n\ \tau_{n1}...\tau_{nan}]] = [c_1/C_1, ..., c_n/C_n]$

$\quad$ where $c_i = \lambda v_1...v_{ai}.\ in_{C_i} (v_1,...,v_{ai})$

$\mathcal{M}: \text{Module} \to \text{Env} \to \text{Env}$

$\mathcal{M}[[T_1 = \mathcal{U}_1; ...; T_m = \mathcal{U}_m;\ fdefs]] \rho = \mathcal{A}[[fdefs]] (\rho\mathord{+}\mathord{+}\mathcal{U}[[\mathcal{U}_1]]\mathord{+}\mathord{+}...\mathord{+}\mathord{+}\mathcal{U}[[\mathcal{U}_n]])$

$\quad$ where $\mathcal{A}[[v_1 = e_1; ...; v_n = e_n]] \rho = \mu P.\ \rho[\mathcal{E}[[e_1]] P/v_1, ..., \mathcal{E}[[e_n]] P/v_n]$

$f = \mathcal{M}[[m]] \rho\ f$ is the semantics of a variable f in a module m with import env. ρ

Prelude semantics are provided for integer numbers, + and bot

3 Higher Order Demand Propagation Semantics

The aim of higher order demand propagation semantics is to express how evaluation demands on a given function application propagate to evaluation demands on the function arguments (lazy evaluation is presumed). The definition follows the structure of the definition of the standard semantics but maps the syntactical function definitions to so called demand propagators, which are defined below.

3.1 The Abstract Semantic Domains for Higher Order Demand Propagation

We now define the notions of demand and demand propagator. Note that demands and demand propagators are polymorphically typed. This is the reason why higher order demand propagation works for a polymorphic language.

Definition 1 (Demand). A *demand* Δ of type τ is a continuous function from the standard semantic domain $\mathcal{D}[[\tau]]$ to the two-point-cpos $2 = \{1\}_\perp$ with $\perp < 1$. The continuous function space of demands is again a cpos with $\Delta_1 < \Delta_2$, iff $\Delta_1 v < \Delta_2 v$ for all $v \in \mathcal{D}[[\tau]]$.

The continuity of Δ implies the closedness of the set $\Delta^{-1}(\{\bot\})$ with respect to the Scott-topology of the cpos. And the characteristic function Δ_C on a Scott-closed set C with $\Delta_C(C) = \bot$ and $\Delta_C(C) = 1$ is continuous, which shows that the functional notion is equivalent to the usual notion of demands as Scott-closed subsets of the value domain. We prefer the functional notion because it provides an easy way to define demands on polymorphic domains namely by polymorphic characteristic functions.

Operationally, demands represent evaluation strategies like evaluators in [2]. A semantic value is mapped to $\bot$, if and only if the related evaluation strategy fails for that value.

We introduce three basic demands, which are fully polymorphic and can be applied to all values and which are defined by[1]:

NO $v = 1$, for all v (no evaluation)
WHNF $v = \bot$, iff $v = \bot$ (evaluation to weak head normal form)
  FAIL $v = \bot$, for all v (non terminating evaluation).

Algebraic demands (e.g. for lists) can be constructed out of component demands:

$(C\ \Delta_1...\Delta_n)\ v = \inf\{\Delta_1\ v_1, ..., \Delta_n\ v_n\}$, if $tag(v)=C$, hence $v=in_c(v_1,...,v_n)$; $=\bot$, otherwise.

Note that the evaluation strategy for a constructor demand – e.g. CONS WHNF NO – forces evaluation to a Cons-node and the evaluation of the head of that node to weak head normal form. If applied to an empty list Nil, it fails. Such constructor demands arise from the analysis of a case-alternative.

Definition 2 (Demand Operations). Demands can be combined by the operators I and &, which are defined as pointwise supremum resp. infimum. Algebraic demands can be *projected* to a component ($\downarrow$) or *restricted* to some summands of the sum (\\). The projected demand is the demand induced on a specific factor of the sum-of-products. It arises from analysing constructor applications. The restricted demand is modified to be $\bot$ on all elements of a specified set of summands. Restriction is used to describe the propagation in a default alternative of a case-expression.

$(\Delta_1\ _{\&\ \Delta_2})\ v = \inf\{\Delta_1\ v, \Delta_2\ v\}$ and $(\Delta_{1|\Delta_2})\ v = \sup\{\Delta_1\ v, \Delta_2\ v\}$
$\Delta\downarrow_{C,i}\ v = \bot$, iff for all $v_1...v_n$: $\Delta\ (in_c\ (v_1,...,v,...,v_n)) = \bot$ (v at i-th position)
$\Delta\backslash CS\ v = \bot$, if $tag(v)\in CS$; $= \Delta\ v$, otherwise

Recursive demands can be defined as minimal fixpoints on the function space of demands, for example:

SPINE $= \mu\Delta.$ NIL I CONS NO Δ (we also write: SPINE = NIL I CONS NO SPINE)

(EVEN,ODD) $= \mu(\Delta_1,\Delta_2).$ (NIL I CONS NO Δ_2 , NIL I CONS WHNF Δ_1)

Remark 1. The general demands NO, WHNF and FAIL are also defined for function types. But demand propagation semantics is not interested in more complex functional

---

[1]Our thanks to one referee who remarked that the definition of WHNF is not parametric polymorphic. We consider WHNF as an overloaded name for instances in every type domain.

demands which can be imagined, since only non-functional context demands (which do not have "→" as the outermost type constructor) are propagated through the demand propagators. The demand, which will be propagated by a demand propagator, is always interpreted as a demand on the non-functional result type of the function, which can be deduced from the function's type.

This corresponds to the common operational semantics of lazy functional languages, which do not evaluate function applications until they are satisfied, meaning they are provided with the number of arguments stated in their definition. Paradoxically the lack of functional demands seems to be crucial to make the demand propagation semantics higher order.

Definition 3 (More-Effective Relation). The induced cpo on the function space of demands, has FAIL as its bottom element and NO as a universal greatest element. Since it is counter-intuitive to say, that NO is the greatest demand, we define a new partial order on demands: A demand Δ is called *more effective* than Δ', noted $\Delta \gg \Delta$', if and only if $\Delta < \Delta$' with respect to the induced cpo. Δ is called *effective*, if and only if $\Delta \gg$ NO.

Hence WHNF is the least effective demand. All demands are comparable with NO and WHNF. And they are comparable with FAIL, the most effective demand.

Example 1 (Motivation of Demand Propagators). The definition of a demand propagator has to reflect that context demands are always meant as demands on the non-functional result type of an expression (see Remark 1), hence the type of the context demand is the same for all partial applications of a function. In general the demand which is propagated to an argument will depend on *all* arguments of the function in at least two senses:

1. It depends on the existence of arguments, since a function application will only be evaluated if it has a sufficient number of arguments.
2. If one argument is itself a function – which is a common case in higher order functional languages – and if this function is applied to the argument, to which the demand is to be propagated, the propagation may depend on the propagation of some demand through this argument function. This is e.g. the case if the strictness of the higher order function map in its second argument is analysed for a strict or for a non-strict function as the first argument (cf. Example 5 in the appendix).

To deal with this situation, the demand propagator of a function only describes the dependence of the propagation from the existence and the values of argument demand propagators. A simple example illustrates, how demand propagation works and introduces a simple notation for parameterised demands, the λ-abstraction.

Let cond be the conditional function defined by

> cond = λb.λx.λy. case b of True $\Rightarrow$ x; False $\Rightarrow$ y

cond has the type $\forall \alpha.$ Bool$\to\alpha\to\alpha\to\alpha$, where Bool = True + False is defined as a user type. TRUE and FALSE are the corresponding algebraic constructor demands. The demand propagator COND for cond is noted by the following equation:

$$\underline{\text{COND}}\ \Delta = \underline{\lambda}\text{B}.\ \underline{\lambda}\text{X}.\ \underline{\lambda}\text{Y}.\ \underline{\text{B}}\ \text{WHNF}\ \&\ (\underline{\text{B}}\ \text{TRUE}\ \&\ \underline{\text{X}}\ \Delta\ |\ \underline{\text{B}}\ \text{FALSE}\ \&\ \underline{\text{Y}}\ \Delta)\ . \tag{1}$$

COND is a function which takes a demand Δ as the first argument and yields a so called parameterised demand, noted by $\underline{\lambda}$-abstractions. A $\underline{\lambda}$-abstraction can be interpreted as follows: if it is applied to an argument demand propagator, then it is an ordinary lambda abstraction for a demand propagator, which may be free in the body. If it is *not* applied it can be read as the propagated demand NO, stating that no demand is propagated, because the function is not provided with a sufficient number of arguments. To achieve this dual semantics the $\underline{\lambda}$-abstraction will later be defined as a pair of a propagated demand and an ordinary abstraction.

In our backward generalised strictness analysis we provide a context demand for a function application and aim to infer demands, which can be applied to the function's arguments without changing the lazy semantics. A demand propagator which does this job is called *safe* for this function (cf. Definition 6). It is obvious that a safe propagator can always propagate FAIL to FAIL and must propagate NO to NO, regardless of its argument propagators. Hence from now on we assume that all further demand propagator equations include these two cases and only note the case for effective non-failure demands. Thus with all these explanations in mind (1) can be unfolded to:

COND NO = (NO , $\underline{\lambda}\underline{B}$. (NO , $\underline{\lambda}\underline{X}$. (NO , $\underline{\lambda}\underline{Y}$. NO)))
COND FAIL = (FAIL , $\underline{\lambda}\underline{B}$. (FAIL , $\underline{\lambda}\underline{X}$. (FAIL , $\underline{\lambda}\underline{Y}$. FAIL)))
COND Δ = (NO , $\underline{\lambda}\underline{B}$.(NO , $\underline{\lambda}\underline{X}$.(NO , $\underline{\lambda}\underline{Y}.\underline{B}$ WHNF & ($\underline{B}$ TRUE & $\underline{X}$ Δ | $\underline{B}$ FALSE & $\underline{Y}$ Δ)))) , otherwise.

If COND is applied to an effective non-failure demand Δ and further to three argument demand propagators $\underline{B}$ and $\underline{X}$ and $\underline{Y}$, the body $\underline{B}$ WHNF & ($\underline{B}$ TRUE & $\underline{X}$ Δ | $\underline{B}$ FALSE & $\underline{Y}$ Δ) of the abstraction states, that in any case a WHNF demand is propagated to the first argument, and either TRUE is propagated to the first argument and Δ to the second or FALSE to the first and Δ to the third argument.

The propagated demand now depends on the values provided for the arguments of the parameterised demand. When testing for generalised strictness COND Δ is applied to a combination of the special demand propagators NO and ID, specifying propagation by arbitrary arguments (propagating every context safely to NO) or by an argument being tested (reproducing the context demand). The following can be deduced:

COND Δ ID NO NO = ID WHNF & (ID TRUE & NO Δ | ID FALSE & NO Δ) = WHNF
COND Δ NO ID NO = NO WHNF & (NO TRUE & ID Δ | NO FALSE & NO Δ) = NO
COND Δ NO NO ID = NO WHNF & (NO TRUE & NO Δ | NO FALSE & ID Δ) = NO .

Hence cond is found to be strict in the first argument. If an application of cond to some statically known arguments is analysed in another function definition using cond, the argument propagators are statically known and may express the propagation to a shared subexpression (cf. Examples 2 and 3 in the appendix).

From these motivation we collect the following formal definitions:

Definition 4 (Demand Propagator, Parameterised Demand). A *demand propagator* for a function of type $\tau=\tau_1\to\ldots\to\tau_n\to\tau'$ (τ' non-functional), is a continuous function, which maps a demand of type τ' (the *context demand*) to a parameterised demand. A *parameterised demand* is a pair of the *propagated demand* and a continuous function, which maps an argument demand propagator to a new parameterised demand.

The domains are defined by the following mutual recursive equations:

$\text{PDemand}^\tau = \forall\alpha.\ \text{Demand}^\alpha$

$\text{PDemand}^\tau = \forall\alpha.\ \text{Demand}^\alpha \times [\text{Propagator}^{\tau 1}\ \alpha \rightarrow \text{PDemand}^{\tau 2 \rightarrow \dots \rightarrow \tau n \rightarrow \tau'}\ \alpha]$

$\text{Propagator}^\tau = \forall\alpha.\ [\text{Demand}^\tau \rightarrow \text{PDemand}^\tau\ \alpha]$.

A demand Δ can be lifted into a parameterised demand of any type τ by the functions $\textit{lift}^\tau$ with $\textit{lift}^\tau(\Delta) = \Delta$, if τ is not functional, and $\textit{lift}^{\tau \rightarrow \tau'}(\Delta) = (\Delta, \textit{lift}^{\tau'}(\Delta))$.

Definition 5 (λ-Abstraction). Let $\pi = \pi(\underline{P})$ be a parameterised demand, which can depend on a demand propagator $\underline{P}$. Then $\underline{\lambda P}.\ \pi$ denotes the parameterised demand $(\text{NO}, \underline{\lambda P}.\ \pi)$.

The following demand propagators are essential for general strictness analysis:

$\underline{\text{NO}}^\tau\ \Delta = \textit{lift}^\tau(\text{NO})$, $\underline{\text{STRICT}}^\tau\ \Delta = \textit{lift}^\tau(\text{WHNF})$ and

$\underline{\text{ID}}^\tau\ \Delta = \Delta$, if τ is non-functional, and $\underline{\text{ID}}^{\tau \rightarrow \tau'}\ \Delta = \underline{\text{STRICT}}^{\tau \rightarrow \tau'}\ \Delta$

Remark 2. The definition of a parameterised demand for a function type as a pair reflects the fact that there are two things we want to do with it. The first purpose is to apply it to a known demand propagator for an argument of the function. This means that we want to apply its second component. On the other hand we want to see the parameterised demand as a propagated demand, for instance to propagate it further. In this case we refer to its first component. It would be a mess of notation, if we always wanted to write the projection to the correct component in a given utilisation of a parameterised demand. Fortunately from the context it is always clear which component is used. So the notation can be shortened in both cases. For example:

"$\underline{P}\ \Delta\ \underline{P_1}\ \underline{P_2}$" is the short form for "snd (snd ($\underline{P}\ \Delta$) $\underline{P_1}$) $\underline{P_2}$"

"$\underline{P}\ (\underline{P_1}\ \Delta)\ \underline{P_2}$" is the short form for "snd ($\underline{P}$ (fst ($\underline{P_1}\ \Delta$))) $\underline{P_2}$"

Only with this meaning it makes sense to say, a parameterised demand is applied to an argument demand propagator or is propagated by a demand propagator.

Remark 3. The operations on demands, which were introduced in Definition 2, generalise in a natural way to parameterised demands by applying them to the first component and recursively to the second (cf. [13]).

3.2   Definition of the Demand Propagation Semantics

We are now able to define the denotational higher order demand propagation semantics as an interpretation of the core language, taking the domains of demand propagators as the non-standard semantic domains. The formal definition is listed in Fig. 2.

Most defining rules of the expression semantics are straightforward parallel to the definitions of the standard semantics. Two notes about case-expressions and user type definitions will emphasize the peculiarities:

Fig. 2. Demand Propagation Semantics (cont.)

$\mathcal{E}$: $\forall\tau$. $\mathrm{Expr}^\tau \to \underline{\mathrm{Env}} \to \mathrm{Propagator}^\tau$ where $\underline{\mathrm{Env}} = \forall\tau$. $\mathrm{Var}^\tau \oplus \mathrm{Const}^\tau \to \mathrm{Propagator}^\tau$

$\mathcal{E}[[x]]\ \rho\ \Delta = \rho\ x\ \Delta \flat\flat\flat\flat\text{and}\flat\flat\flat\flat\ \mathcal{E}[[C]]\ \rho\ \Delta = \rho\ C\ \Delta$

$\mathcal{E}[[e_1\ e_2]]\ \rho\ \Delta = \mathcal{E}[[e_1]]\ \rho\ \Delta\ (\mathcal{E}[[e_2]]\ \rho)$

$\mathcal{E}[[\lambda x.\ e]]\ \rho\ \Delta = \lambda \underline{x}.\ \mathcal{E}[[e]]\ \rho[\underline{x}/x]\ \Delta$

$\mathcal{E}[[\mathbf{case}\ e\ \mathbf{of}\ C_1\ v_{11}...v_{1a1} \Rightarrow e_1;\ ...;\ C_n\ v_{n1}...v_{nan} \Rightarrow e_n;\ v \Rightarrow e_{def}]]\ \rho\ \Delta$

$\quad = \mathcal{E}[[e]]\ \rho\ \mathrm{WHNF}\ \&\ (\pi_1\ |\ ...\ |\ \pi_n\ |\ \pi_{def})$

$\quad\quad$ where $\quad \pi_i = \textit{lift}^\tau(\mathcal{E}[[e]]\ \rho\ (C_i\ \mathrm{NO}...\mathrm{NO}))\ \&\ \mathcal{E}[[e_i]]\ \rho[\underline{v_{i1}}/v_{i1}, ..., \underline{v_{iai}}/v_{iai}]\ \Delta$

$\quad\quad\quad\quad \underline{v}_{ij} = \lambda\Delta.\ \mathcal{E}[[e]]\ \rho\ (C_i\ \mathrm{NO}...\Delta...\mathrm{NO})$, with Δ at j-th position

$\quad\quad\quad\quad \pi_{def} = \mathcal{E}[[e_{def}]]\ \rho[(\lambda\Delta.\ \mathcal{E}[[e]]\ \rho\ \Delta\backslash\{C_1, ..., C_n\})/v]\ \Delta$

$\mathcal{E}[[\mathbf{let}\ m\ \mathbf{in}\ e]]\ \rho\ \Delta = \mathcal{E}[[e]]\ (\mathcal{M}[[m]]\ \rho)\ \Delta$

$\mathcal{U}$: $\mathrm{Usertype} \to \underline{\mathrm{Env}} \to \underline{\mathrm{Env}}$

$\mathcal{U}[[\forall\alpha_1...\alpha_m.\ C_1\ \tau_{11}...\tau_{1a1} + ... + C_n\ \tau_{n1}...\tau_{nan}]] = [\underline{C_1}/C_1, ..., \underline{C_n}/C_n]$

$\quad\quad$ where $\quad \underline{C}_i\ \Delta = \textit{lift}(\mathrm{FAIL})$, if $\Delta\ v = \perp$ for all v with $tag(v) = C_i$

$\quad\quad\quad\quad \underline{C}_i\ \Delta = \lambda\underline{v}_1.\ ...\ \lambda\underline{v}_{ai}.\ (\underline{v}_1\ \Delta\!\downarrow_{C_i,1}\ \&\ ...\ \&\ \underline{v}_{ai}\ \Delta\!\downarrow_{C_i,ai})$, otherwise

$\mathcal{M}$: $\mathrm{Module} \to \underline{\mathrm{Env}} \to \underline{\mathrm{Env}}$

$\mathcal{M}[[T_1 = \upsilon_1;\ ...;\ T_m = \upsilon_m;\ \mathrm{fdefs}]] = \mathcal{E}[[\mathrm{fdefs}]]\ (\rho ++ \mathcal{U}[[\upsilon_1]] ++ ... ++ \mathcal{U}[[\upsilon_n]])$

$\quad\quad$ where $\mathcal{E}[[v_1 = e_1;\ ...;\ v_n = e_n]]\ \rho = \mu P.\ \rho[\mathcal{E}[[e_1]]\ P/v_1, ..., \mathcal{E}[[e_n]]\ P/v_n]$

$\underline{F} = \mathcal{M}[[m]]\ \rho\ f$ is the semantics of a variable f in a module m with import env. ρ

The semantics of the prelude definitions are given by

$\underline{\mathrm{NUM}}_n\ \Delta = \mathrm{FAIL}$, if $\Delta\ n = \perp$; $= \mathrm{NO}$, otherwise (cf. also $\underline{C}_i$ in the definition of $\mathcal{U}$ above)

$\underline{\pm}\ \Delta = \lambda\underline{x}.\ \lambda\underline{y}.\ \underline{x}\ \mathrm{WHNF}\ \&\ \underline{y}\ \mathrm{WHNF}\flat\flat\flat\flat\text{and}\flat\flat\flat\flat\underline{\mathrm{BOT}}^\tau\ \Delta = \textit{lift}^\tau(\mathrm{FAIL})$

1. The propagator for a case-expression propagates a **WHNF** demand to the expression to be scrutinised and propagates the context demand to all alternatives of the case-expression to build the union of all propagated demands. The propagation to an alternative constrains the scrutinised value to match the pattern of the alternative and must take care of binding it components to the pattern variables.

2. The user type semantics $\mathcal{U}$ introduces a demand propagator for each constructor, which propagates the accordant projections of the context demand to the factors.

The main justification of the definition of higher order demand propagation semantics is its relation to generalised strictness, which is stated in the following section.

4 The Safety of Higher Order Demand Propagation

We have already motivated the notion of *safety* for demand propagators in Example 1 by roughly saying that a safe demand propagator calculates correct generalised strictness information of a function. To formulate and prove the Safety Theorem (Sect. 4.2) a formal definition of safety is provided now.

4.1 Demand Propagators and Generalised Strictness

In Example 1 we motivated how we deduce generalised strictness information of a function, namely by applying the demand propagator of the function to a context demand and to a combination of the NO and ID propagators, where NO stands for arbitrary arguments and ID for the tested argument. We could call a demand propagator *safe* for a function, if – applied in this way – it delivers correct generalised strictness information for every context demand. Definition 6 is stronger than this, and Corollary 1 shows that it implies the property stated above.

Definition 6 (Safety of a Demand Propagator).. Let $F : D \to \mathcal{D}[[\tau_1 \to \ldots \to \tau_n \to \tau]]$ (τ a non-functional type) be a function from some domain D into a domain of a type. And let $\underline{F} \in \text{Propagator}^{\tau_1 \to \ldots \to \tau_n \to \tau}$ be a demand propagator of this type. Then $\underline{F}$ is called *safe* for F, if for all m (0ðmðn) holds:

if for all i (1ðiðm) $\underline{A}_i$ is safe for $A_i : D \to \mathcal{D}[[\tau_i]]$ then for all $v \in D$: $\qquad$ (2)

$$(\underline{F} \Delta \underline{A}_1 \ldots \underline{A}_m) \, v = \bot \text{ implies } \Delta \, ((F \, v) \, (A_1 \, v) \ldots (A_m \, v)) = \bot \, .$$

This recursive definition of safety is well-founded by the same definition reading for non-functional types, where m may only be zero and hence the definition does not depend on the safety of argument propagators.

$\underline{F}$ is defined to be *safe* for a semantic value $f \in \mathcal{D}[[\tau_1 \to \ldots \to \tau_n \to \tau]]$, if it is safe for any function $F = const \, f$, which yields f, ignoring its argument.

Definition 7 (Safety of an Environment). Let $\rho : \text{Env}$ be an environment of semantic values and let $\underline{\rho} : \underline{\text{Env}}$ be an environment of demand propagators. Then $\underline{\rho}$ is defined to be *safe* for ρ, if for all $x \in \text{Vars} \oplus \text{Constructors}$ holds: $\underline{\rho} \, x$ is safe for $\rho \, x$.

Corollary 1 (Deducing Generalised Strictness). Let $\underline{F} \in \text{Propagator}^{\tau_1 \to \ldots \to \tau_n \to \tau}$ be safe for $f \in \mathcal{D}[[\tau_1 \to \ldots \to \tau_n \to \tau]]$. For a context demand Δ, $\Delta_i := \underline{F} \Delta \text{ NO} \ldots \text{NO ID NO} \ldots \text{NO}$ (ID at the i-th position of n arguments) is the demand propagated to f's i-th argument. Then f is Δ_i-strict in its i-th argument in a Δ-strict context, meaning:

$$\Delta_i \, v_i = \bot \text{ implies } \Delta \, (f \, v_1 \ldots v_n) = \bot, \text{ for arbitrary } v_j, \, 1ðjðn, \, j \neq i \, .$$

Proof. The proposition follows directly from (2), since NO is safe for all functions and ID is safe for $V_i = \lambda v. \, v$.

4.2 Safety Theorem for the Higher Order Demand Propagation Semantics

Let m be a core language module, ρ an import environment and $\underline{\rho}$ an environment of demand propagators, which is safe for ρ. Then $\underline{\mathcal{M}}[[m]] \, \underline{\rho}$ is safe for $\mathcal{M}[[m]] \, \rho$.

Proof. The proof of this theorem works by proving a slightly stronger proposition by induction on the structure of the declarations in m and carrying the proposition to the fixpoint environment. It is expatiated in [13].

5 Putting Theory into Practice: The Demand Propagation Analysis

The practical strictness analysis using this higher order demand propagation semantics is not yet finished. But a design for the analysis is explained in [12]. The goal of demand propagation analysis is to deduce *safe* demand propagators for syntactic expressions. The propagated demands resulting from an application os a demand propagator to a context demand shall be *as effective as possible*, with the constraints of being still safe and computable. Termination (and also efficiency) of the analysis is obligatory, because its information will be used in the compilation process. It is well known that strictness is not generally decidable, hence one cannot hope to compute the most effective propagated demand for each application of a demand propagator. In fact it is not certain whether such a most-effective safe demand always exists. See [3] for a discussion of this question for projection analysis.

We now give a brief overview of how demand propagation analysis can be made practical (see [12] for a more detailed explanation):

1. From the Safety Theorem we know that higher order demand propagation assigns safe demand propagators to each function in a core language module. Demand propagators are higher order functions. Fortunately there is a known efficient way to calculate higher order functions, namely executing functional programs. Hence we represent the demand propagators in a simple specially suited higher order functional language, the semantics of which is given by the semantics of demand propagators and of the operations on demands and parameterised demands.
2. An operational semantics for this language can then be introduced, which is sound with respect to the denotational demand propagation semantics. And an abstract machine can be defined, which calculates applications of demand propagators to demands and argument propagators, yielding generalised strictness information.
3. The operational semantics is augmented by loop-detection – in a similar way to that described by Hughes and Ferguson [8] – and by approximation to guarantee its termination. This also permits us to adjust the level where approximation takes place, hence trading accuracy of the analysis against its speed.

6 Conclusions and Further Work

A new approach to strictness analysis has been defined. The analysis is capable of deducing generalised strictness for a realistic functional programming language. This is achieved by mapping function definitions to demand propagators by means of a non-standard interpretation. Demand propagators are higher order functions, which propagate context demands to the arguments of the function. Generalised strictness information can be deduced by applying a demand propagator to a context demand and to special arguments. The Safety Theorem guarantees the correctness of this strictness information. The actual computation of demand propagator applications is achieved by generating functional declarations for the demand propagators in a new functional language. Demand propagation can now take place by running programs on a – yet to be formally defined – abstract machine which supports loop-detection and approximation. A prototype implementation of the analysis in Haskell is in development.

As far as we know, higher order demand propagation analysis is the first backward strictness analysis, which can analyse polymorphic *and* higher order functions. This is possible because the new demand propagation language itself is polymorphically typed and higher order. The infinite semantic domains for higher order demand propagation allow very accurate generalised strictness information to be expressed and propagated even across module boundaries, which is difficult in existing strictness analyses, where the information is compiled into annotations to the function's type.

This paper gives just a first introduction to higher order demand propagation. To make it applicable in a real implementation, further work has to be done:

1. The operational semantics of the language used in demand propagation analysis has to be defined. This task is mainly completed and will be published soon together with a proof for the soundness of the operational semantics with respect to the denotational semantics of demand propagators given in this paper.

2. We plan to integrate a prototype of the analysis into a state-of-the-art compiler for a lazy functional language, proving that the analysis is also usable for realistic software engineering. At this stage it will be necessary to identify and attack complexity and efficiency issues of the analysis which has been unattended so far.

3. The examples in the appendix and in [12] show that higher order demand propagation can be more accurate than other existing strictness analyses. A methodical comparison of the power and the complexity of different strictness analyses would be very interesting but also seems to be very difficult.

7   Related Work

The most widely used framework for strictness analysis for lazy functional languages is an *abstract interpretation* introduced by Mycroft [10] and later enhanced for algebraic data types and higher order functions [18,2] and for polymorphism [1]. Evaluators for a type are defined there as special subsets of the standard semantics domain, which is isomorphic to the notion given here. Strictness analysis by abstract interpretation is a forward analysis using finite abstract domains. The strictness information for functions are represented by annotations on the function's type yielding in general poor propagation of strictness information of higher order functions to other modules.

Abstract reduction [11] is a method, which can handle infinite domains and uses a loop-detecting abstract reduction machine. The analysis again is a forward one and transportation of strictness information across module boundaries is also done by type annotations.

Projection analysis was first formulated in [19] for a first order monomorphic language. It was generalised to a higher order (but monomorphic) language [3] and to a polymorphic (but first order) language [1]. Projection analysis works with projections – namely idempotent functions, which approximate the identity. This concept has been proven to be more powerful than the concept of evaluators. For instance it can express general head strictness, which cannot be expressed with demands or evaluators. However the definition of demand propagators given here seems to be independent from the chosen concept of demands. And whether demand propagation can be also based on projections will be examined in further work. Projection analysis uses finite domains for all data types.

Backward analyses using infinite domains have been proposed by Dybjer (*Inverse Image Analysis* [4]), by Hall and Wise [6] and by Tremblay (*Abstract Demand Propagation* [17]). All these analyses are restricted to first order functions.

Another interesting relation of this work is to the proposal of evaluation strategies for parallel programming in [16]. An evaluation strategy is the operational equivalent to a demand defined here. However the intention of the proposal is to allow the programmer to specify evaluation strategies for calculations in a program, and the focus is not on the safety of these strategies. It would be interesting to examine how demand propagation analysis can be used to transform functional programs automatically to programs decorated with safe evaluation strategies and how this implicit parallelisation affects execution time.

References

1. G. Baraki. *Abstract Interpretation of Polymorphic Higher-Order Functions*. Ph.D. Thesis, University of Glasgow, 1993.
2. G. Burn. *Lazy Functional Languages: Abstract Interpretation and Compilation*. Pitman, 1991.
3. M.K. Davis. *Projection-Based Program Analysis*. Ph.D. Thesis, University of Glasgow, 1994.
4. P. Dybjer. Inverse Image Analysis. In Th. Ottman, editor, *Automata, Languages and Programming*. LNCS 267, pages 21-30, Springer-Verlag, 1987.
5. E. Fehr. *Semantik von Programmiersprachen*. Springer-Verlag, Heidelberg, 1989.
6. C.V. Hall and D.S. Wise. Compiling Strictness into Streams. In *Proceedings - 14th Annual ACM Symposium on Principles of Programming Languages*, pages 132-142, Munich, 1987.
7. M. Horn. *Improving Parallel Implementations of Lazy Functional Languages Using Evaluation Transformers*. Technical Report B 95-15, Dept. of Comp. Science, FU Berlin, 1995.
8. J. Hughes and A. Ferguson. A Loop-Detecting Interpreter for Lazy, Higher-Order Programs. In J. Launchbury and P.M. Sansom, editors, *Functional Programming, Workshops in Computing*, Springer-Verlag, 1992.
9. S. Kamin. Head Strictness Is Not a Monotonic Abstract Property. In *Information Processing Letters*, North Holland, 1992.
10. A. Mycroft. *Abstract Interpretation and Optimising Transformations for Applicative Programs*. Ph.D. Thesis, University of Edinburgh, 1981.
11. E. Nöcker. *Strictness Analysis Using Abstract Reduction*. Technical Report, University of Nijmegen, 1993.
12. D. Pape. *Higher Order Demand Propagation*. Technical Report B 98-15, Dept. of Comp. Science, FU Berlin, 1998.
13. D. Pape. *The Safety of Higher Order Demand Propagation*. Technical Report B 98-16, Dept. of Comp. Science, FU Berlin, 1998.
    Available at http://www.inf.fu-berlin.de/~pape/papers/
14. J. Peterson, K. Hammond, editors, and many authors. *Report of the Programming Language Haskell – A Non-Strict, Purely Functional Language – Version 1.4*.
    Available at http://www.haskell.org/onlinereport/
15. S.L. Peyton Jones. *The Implementation of Functional Programming Languages*. Prentice-Hall, 1987.
16. P. W. Trinder, K. Hammond, et. al. Algorithm + Strategy = Parallelism. In *Journal of Functional Programming*, 8(1), 1998.

17. G. Tremblay. *Parallel Implementation of Lazy Functional Languages Using Abstract Demand Propagation*. Ph.D. Thesis, McGill University Montréal, 1994.
18. P. Wadler. Strictness Analysis on Non-Flat Domains by Abstract Interpretation. In S. Abramsky and C. Hankin, editors, *Abstract Interpretation of Declarative Languages*, Ellis-Horwood, 1987.
19. P. Wadler and R.J.M. Hughes. Projections for Strictness Analysis. In *Proceedings of the 1987 Conference on Functional Programming Languages and Computer Architecture*, Portland, Oregon, LNCS 274, Springer-Verlag, 1987.

Appendix: Example Analyses

The relation $\Downarrow$ on parameterised demands defines an operational (reduction-) semantics for demand propagation, which is not formally defined in this paper, but introduced in [12]. The reduction follows algebraic rules, which can easily be proven for the operators on demands and parameterised demands. Some reductions for the recursive examples given here follow from loop-detection and are indicated as such.

Example 2 (Joint Strictness). Imagine that cond from Example 1 is used to define the function
```
> uncond = λb.λx. cond b x x
```

In this context of use the second and the third argument of cond are always identical. Thus in the application of the demand propagator for cond in the demand propagator for uncond the context demand is propagated to x in both alternatives of the conditional, hence always, implying that uncond is strict in both arguments. More: if the context demand is more effective than WHNF, so is the propagated demand (they are identical). The reduction goes as follows

UNCOND Δ = $\underline{\lambda B.\lambda X.}$ COND Δ $\underline{B}$ $\underline{X}$ $\underline{X}$ $\Downarrow$ $\underline{\lambda B.\lambda X.}$ $\underline{B}$ WHNF & ($\underline{B}$ TRUE & $\underline{X}$ Δ | $\underline{B}$ FALSE & $\underline{X}$ Δ) ,

hence: UNCOND Δ $\underline{NO}$ $\underline{ID}$ $\Downarrow$ $\underline{NO}$ WHNF & ($\underline{NO}$ TRUE & $\underline{ID}$ Δ | $\underline{NO}$ FALSE & $\underline{ID}$ Δ)$\Downarrow$NO&(Δ|Δ) $\Downarrow\Delta$.

This example shows that so called *joint strictness* can be analysed. But demand propagation is even able to find strictness, which other analyses cannot detect:

Example 3 (Forcing Summands of a Sum). Imagine cond to be used in the function
```
> strange = λz.λx.λy. cond e x y

>        where e = case z of 0⇒(case x of 0⇒False;
x⇒True); z⇒True
```

The demand propagator of cond states that e is demanded with TRUE and x is demanded, or it is demanded with FALSE and y is demanded. The demand propagator of e now states, that demanding e with FALSE, demands x with WHNF, because the only alternative, in which e evaluates to False is, if z is zero, and in this case x will be demanded. The reduction goes as follows:

STRANGE Δ = $\underline{\lambda Z.}$ $\underline{\lambda X.}$ $\underline{\lambda Y.}$ COND Δ $\underline{E}$ $\underline{X}$ $\underline{Y}$

        where $\underline{E}$ Δ = $\underline{Z}$ WHNF & ($\underline{X}$ WHNF & ($\underline{FALSE}$ Δ | $\underline{TRUE}$ Δ) | $\underline{TRUE}$ Δ)

$\Downarrow$ $\underline{\lambda Z.}$ $\underline{\lambda X.}$ $\underline{\lambda Y.}$ $\underline{E}$ WHNF & ($\underline{E}$ TRUE & $\underline{X}$ Δ | $\underline{E}$ FALSE & $\underline{Y}$ Δ)

$\Downarrow \underline{\lambda z}.\ \underline{\lambda x}.\ \underline{\lambda y}.\ \underline{z}$ WHNF & ($\underline{z}$ WHNF & $\underline{x}$ Δ I $\underline{z}$ WHNF & $\underline{x}$ WHNF & $\underline{y}$ Δ)

$\Downarrow \underline{\lambda z}.\ \underline{\lambda x}.\ \underline{\lambda y}.\ \underline{z}$ WHNF & $\underline{z}$ WHNF & ($\underline{x}$ Δ I $\underline{y}$ Δ) ,

since $\underline{E}$ WHNF $\Downarrow \underline{z}$ WHNF & ($\underline{x}$ WHNF & ($\underline{\text{FALSE}}$ WHNF I $\underline{\text{TRUE}}$ WHNF) I $\underline{\text{TRUE}}$ WHNF) $\Downarrow \underline{z}$ WHNF

$\underline{E}$ TRUE $\Downarrow \underline{z}$ WHNF & ($\underline{x}$ WHNF & ($\underline{\text{FALSE}}$ TRUE I $\underline{\text{TRUE}}$ TRUE) I $\underline{\text{TRUE}}$ TRUE) $\Downarrow \underline{z}$ WHNF

$\underline{E}$ FALSE $\Downarrow \underline{z}$ WHNF & ($\underline{x}$ WHNF & ($\underline{\text{FALSE}}$ FALSE I $\underline{\text{TRUE}}$ FALSE) I $\underline{\text{TRUE}}$ FALSE)

$\Downarrow \underline{z}$ WHNF & ($\underline{x}$ WHNF & (NO I FAIL) I FAIL) $\Downarrow \underline{z}$ WHNF & $\underline{x}$ WHNF .

It follows: $\underline{\text{STRANGE}}$ Δ $\underline{\text{ID}}$ $\underline{\text{NO}}$ $\underline{\text{NO}}$ $\Downarrow \underline{\text{ID}}$ WHNF & $\underline{\text{NO}}$ WHNF & ($\underline{\text{NO}}$ Δ I $\underline{\text{NO}}$ Δ) $\Downarrow$ WHNF

$\underline{\text{STRANGE}}$ Δ $\underline{\text{NO}}$ $\underline{\text{ID}}$ $\underline{\text{NO}}$ $\Downarrow \underline{\text{NO}}$ WHNF & $\underline{\text{ID}}$ WHNF & ($\underline{\text{ID}}$ Δ I $\underline{\text{NO}}$ Δ) $\Downarrow$ WHNF

$\underline{\text{STRANGE}}$ Δ $\underline{\text{NO}}$ $\underline{\text{NO}}$ $\underline{\text{ID}}$ $\Downarrow \underline{\text{NO}}$ WHNF & $\underline{\text{NO}}$ WHNF & ($\underline{\text{NO}}$ Δ I $\underline{\text{ID}}$ Δ) $\Downarrow$ NO .

Hence demand propagation analysis can infer, that `strange` is strict in its first *and in its second* argument. No other strictness analysis we know would have found the strictness in the second argument.

Note that the demand propagators $\underline{\text{TRUE}}$ and $\underline{\text{FALSE}}$ are not special but are defined implicitly by the semantics $\underline{\mathcal{U}}$ for the user defined data type Bool = False + True. Hence similar examples can be constructed for arbitrary user defined data types.

Example 4 (Construction of Conforming Demands). This example shows, how demands are constructed by the demand propagation analysis, yielding demands, which are not in the abstract domains for existing strictness analyses. Let the function `sum2` be defined by

```
> sum2 = λxs. case xs of  Nil ⇒ 0
>     Cons a t ⇒ case t of   Nil ⇒ 0
>                 Cons b t ⇒ a+b
```

The demand propagator for `sum2` is given by the following equation:

$\underline{\text{SUM2}}$ Δ = $\underline{\lambda xs}.\ \underline{xs}$ WHNF &

($\underline{xs}$ NIL I $\underline{xs}$ (CONS NO NO) & ($\underline{T}$ NIL I $\underline{T}$ (CONS NO NO) & $\underline{A}$ WHNF & $\underline{B}$ WHNF))

where $\underline{T}$ Δ = $\underline{xs}$ (CONS NO Δ), $\underline{A}$ Δ = $\underline{xs}$ (CONS Δ NO) and $\underline{B}$ Δ = $\underline{T}$ (CONS Δ NO)

$\Downarrow \underline{\lambda xs}.\ (\underline{xs}$ NIL I $\underline{xs}$ (CONS NO NIL) I $\underline{xs}$ (CONS WHNF (CONS WHNF NO)) ,

hence: $\underline{\text{SUM2}}$ Δ $\underline{\text{ID}}$ $\Downarrow$ NIL I (CONS NO NIL) I (CONS WHNF (CONS WHNF NO)) .

An effective demand on `sum2` propagates to the demand "evaluate the first and the second list-element to weak head normal form", which is neither an element of the 4-point-list-domain used in [18] or [2], nor of the finite domain of projections for lists used in [3]. Though it could be defined in those frameworks, there is no general approach to identify the evaluators, which are well suited for a given program. Those analyses can only detect simple strictness for `sum2`, which turns out to be a loose of information, if for instance the function `plus` should be analysed:

```
> plus = λa.λb. sum2 (Cons a (Cons b Nil))
```

The demand propagator for `plus` is:

$\underline{\text{PLUS}}$ Δ = $\underline{\lambda A}.\ \underline{\lambda B}.\ \underline{\text{SUM2}}$ Δ $\underline{c}$

where c Δ = CONS ($\underline{A}$ Δ$\downarrow_{\text{cons},1}$) (CONS ($\underline{B}$ Δ$\downarrow_{\text{cons},2}\downarrow_{\text{cons},1}$) NIL)

$\Downarrow \underline{\lambda A}.\ \underline{\lambda B}.\ (\underline{c}$ NIL I $\underline{c}$ (CONS NO NIL) I $\underline{c}$ (CONS WHNF (CONS WHNF NO)))

⇓ $\underline{\lambda A}$. $\underline{\lambda B}$. $\underline{A}$ WHNF & $\underline{B}$ WHNF

since $\underline{C}$ NIL ⇓ FAIL and $\underline{C}$ (CONS NO NIL) ⇓ FAIL

and $\underline{C}$ (CONS WHNF (CONS WHNF NO)) ⇓ $\underline{A}$ WHNF & $\underline{B}$ WHNF .

Hence: PLUS Δ ID NO ⇓ WHNF

  PLUS Δ NO ID ⇓ WHNF .

Demand propagation analysis finds correctly, that plus is strict in both arguments. If only the simple strictness information of sum2 had been used, the strictness of plus had not been detected, hence plus had been compiled without taking the advantage of optimisation.

Example 5 (Higher Order, Polymorphic Analysis). Define the higher order and polymorphic function map by:

```
> map = λf.λxs. case xs of   Nil ⇒ Nil
>     Cons h t ⇒ Cons (f h) (map f t)
```

The demand propagator for map is given by the following equation:

MAP Δ = $\underline{\lambda F}$. $\underline{\lambda XS}$. $\underline{XS}$ NIL I $\underline{XS}$ (CONS NO NO) & $\underline{F}$ $\Delta\downarrow_{Cons,1}$ $\underline{H}$ & MAP $\Delta\downarrow_{Cons,2}$ $\underline{F}$ $\underline{T}$

  where $\underline{H}$ Δ = $\underline{XS}$ (CONS Δ NO) and $\underline{T}$ Δ = $\underline{XS}$ (CONS NO Δ) .

In the following reduction we infer the amount of strictness in the second argument in the context of a SPINEELEM demand (SPINEELEM = CONS WHNF SPINEELEM). For illustration, $\underline{F}$ remains a variable in this reduction:

MAP SPINEELEM $\underline{F}$ ID   ⇓ NIL I (CONS NO NO) & $\underline{F}$ WHNF $\underline{H}$ & MAP SPINEELEM $\underline{F}$ $\underline{T}$

  ⇓ NIL I CONS ($\underline{F}$ WHNF ID) (MAP SPINEELEM $\underline{F}$ ID) .

In the general case, when nothing is known about f, we set $\underline{F}$ = NO and find:

MAP SPINEELEM NO ID ⇓ NIL I CONS NO (MAP SPINEELEM NO ID) ⇓ SPINE .

The last reduction is done by loop-detection and identifying the recursive pattern of SPINE = CONS NO SPINE. The same is done in the following reductions.

If strictness of f is known ($\underline{F}$ WHNF ID ⇓ WHNF), we can infer:

MAP SPINEELEM $\underline{F}$ ID ⇓ NIL I CONS WHNF (MAP SPINEELEM $\underline{F}$ ID) ⇓ SPINEELEM .

And finally, if even more strictness of f is known (e.g. for f = length with LENGTH WHNF ID ⇓ SPINE), then the propagated demand is again more informative:

MAP SPINEELEM LENGTH ID ⇓ NIL I CONS SPINE (MAP SPINEELEM LENGTH ID) ⇓ SPINESPINE .

All this information is captured in the demand propagator MAP for map, and since this demand propagator is represented as a function in the language of demand propagation analysis, this information can be used for any special use of map in the program, even in another module. The latter were not possible, if strictness is a flat annotation to the type signature of the function, as usually.

Dynamic Types and Type Dependent Functions

Marco Pil

Computing Science Institute, University of Nijmegen
Postbus 9010, 6500 GL Nijmegen, The Netherlands
marcop@cs.kun.nl

Abstract. When programs communicate with other programs, flexibility is demanded. Programs do not necessarily have information about each other. When assigning types to these communications a certain amount of dynamic typing is unavoidable. But we do not want our entire language to become dynamically typed, and consequently an interface between the statically and dynamically typed parts of the program has to be defined. Such an interface, using *dynamics*, has been introduced by Abadi et al. Leroy and Mauni extended the system of dynamics to allow the inclusion of polymorphic objects in dynamics. In this paper we extend the system even further with a restricted form of type dependent functions, which allow us to abstract over the types of the dynamics on functional level. In CLEAN, these type dependent functions will be implemented by overloading.

1 Introduction

When programs communicate with other programs, or possibly with other incarnations of themselves, flexibility is demanded. Programs do not necessarily know about each other's existence and may have been terminated before others are launched. Well-known examples of such communication are asynchronous message passing and file I/O.

Typing file I/O differs from typing ordinary expressions because at compile-time there is no knowledge about the contents of a file at run-time. In general, there is no static link between the name of a file and the type of its contents. Thus, types of the parts of a program that perform file I/O can only be checked at run-time, when reading or writing. Therefore a certain amount of dynamic typing is unavoidable.

But we do not want our entire language to become dynamically typed. Statically typed programming languages allow earlier error checking, and generation of more efficient object code than languages where all type consistency checks have to be performed at run-time. An interface between the statically and dynamically typed parts of the program has to be defined.

The concept of *objects with dynamic types*, or *dynamics* for short, as introduced by Abadi et al. [1], can provide such an interface. Values of this Dynamic type are, roughly speaking, pairs of a value and a type, such that the value component can be typed with the type component.

H. Hammond, T. Davie, and C. Clack (Eds.): IFL'98, LNCS 1595, pp. 169–185, 1999.

In Leroy and Mauni [7] the system of dynamics has been extended to be able to include polymorphic objects in dynamics. In this paper we extend the system with a restricted form of type dependent functions. These functions enable us to abstract over the types that are used in dynamic type patterns and in the construction of dynamic objects.

This paper has the following structure. First we will introduce dynamics in CLEAN, then we define a simple language with dynamic types. Thereafter we specify a type system for this language in which we work out the details: we will define an operational semantics, and prove decidability of type assignment.

2   Dynamics

This section introduces dynamics as they will be implemented in Dynamic [6], using the syntax as introduced in Pil [8].

For typing communication between independent programs, we would like to perform run-time type checks, but we do not want every object in the program to be tagged with its type. That is why we distinguish between objects with only a static type and objects with a dynamic type.

A dynamic consists of a normal object that has been paired with an encoding of its type to enable run-time type checks.

From a statical point of view all dynamics belong to same static type — the type Dynamic. Values of type dynamic are self-described as far as types are concerned. They contain enough type information to be type checked at run-time.

A dynamic is created by pairing an object with an encoding of its type, using the dynamic construct:

> dynamic expr :: type

where it can be checked statically that the expression expr is indeed of the static type type.

Example 1. Examples of dynamics are:

> dynamic True :: Bool
> dynamic fib :: Int → Int
> dynamic reverse :: [a] → [a]

The access to objects of type Dynamic is limited. The value can only be accessed if its type matches a specific statically determined type. For this purpose the pattern match mechanism of CLEAN has been extended to describe matching on types.

It is guaranteed at compile-time that if the type contained in the dynamic matches the statically specified type described in the patterns, then the value contained in the dynamic can safely be used in the right hand side expression, since it is known to be of the appropriate type.

Example 2. An example of a dynamic pattern match is:

```
f :: Dynamic → Int
f (x :: Int)        = x
f (g :: Int → Int) = g 5
f  else            = 0
```

The type patterns need not fully specify the demanded type: they may include *type pattern variables*, which match any subexpression of the dynamic's type. The type pattern has scope over the whole alternative, that is, over both the type pattern(s) and the right hand side expression.

Example 3. The use of type pattern variables allow the specification of powerful functions that are polymorphic in the types of the dynamics:

```
dynamicApply :: Dynamic → Dynamic → Dynamic
dynamicApply (f :: a → b) (x :: a) = dynamic (f x) :: b
dynamicApply  df              dx    = dynamic "Error" :: String
```

The new feature presented in this paper is that the type pattern variables do not need to have a binding occurrence in a type pattern. It can also be bound by the function type. In this case they scope over the whole function, i.e., the function type and all function alternatives (both left-hand side and right-hand side).

If a function type binds a type pattern variable a, this is indicated by adding a type context TC a and annotating the variables with a caret ($\hat{\ }$). The type class TC stands for *Type Code*, since the function has been overloaded in the representation of the type of a.

Example 4. A type context to bind type pattern variable a:

```
f :: Dynamic → a → Dynamic | TC a
f (g :: a^ → b) x = dynamic (g x) :: b
f  dg            x = dynamic "Error" :: String
```

At run-time it will be checked whether the dynamic argument of f is a function from some a to some b, and that this a matches the type for x that has been determined by the context in which f has been applied.

The type variables that are bound by a type context do not necessarily have to occur in dynamic type patterns. They can also appear in the dynamic type expressions on the right-hand side:

Example 5. The function wrap wraps a value into a dynamic:

```
wrap :: a → Dynamic | TC a
wrap x = dynamic x :: a^
```

The mechanism of overloading takes care that a correct type code is deduced from the context in which wrap has been used.

So type dependent functions allow us to abstract over types of dynamics beyond the scope of a function, just as type pattern variables let us abstract over the these types within one function alternative. This more powerful form of abstraction is often desired. For illustration, consider the function lookup that searches through a list of dynamics until it finds an integer and returns it, or fails to come up with such element and aborts.

```
lookup :: [Dynamic] → Int
lookup [ ]         = abort "No integer in the list"
lookup [x::Int : xs] = x
lookup [ dy   : xs] = lookup xs
```

Note that instead of allowing the program to abort, one can write a function lookup :: [Dynamic] → (Maybe Int) that yields No if the list contains no integer.

The lookup function can easily be altered to search the list for the first Real or Bool, but it cannot be generalised to a polymorphic function:

```
lookup :: [Dynamic] → a        (Wrong)
lookup [ ]         = abort "No element of the correct type in the list"
lookup [x::a : xs] = x
lookup [ dy  : xs] = lookup xs
```

This version of lookup is incorrect: because it is parametric in the representation of the type it is looking for, it is not actually polymorphic.

With the new mechanism of type dependent functions we are now able to write such general lookup function:

```
lookup :: [Dynamic] → a   | TC a
lookup [ ]         = abort "No element of the correct type in the list"
lookup [x::a^ : xs] = x
lookup [ dy   : xs] = lookup xs
```

where the actual type of a is determined by the context in which lookup has been used, for example (let dynlist be a list of dynamics):

(lookup dynlist) + 5

sin (lookup dynlist)

In the first example the first integer is picked from the dynlist and added to 5. The latter example applies the *sin* function to the first Real in the dynlist.

2.1 Implementation Issues

It is undesirable for the compiler to generate an specialised instantiation for all different types. Rather than ad-hoc polymorphism one would like parametric polymorphism; the same implementation for every instance.

To accomplish this, the CLEAN compiler will transform the type dependent functions, giving them extra arguments. The type (expressions) on which the function depends are passed in these arguments.

Example 6. The transformed version for the lookup function will be:

```
lookup :: (TypeCode a) → [Dynamic] → a
lookup tc [ ]        = abort "No element of the correct type in the list"
lookup tc [x::tc : xs] = x
lookup tc [ dy   : xs] = lookup tc xs
```

And the applications of lookup will be transformed by the compiler to:

```
(lookup TypeCode_Int dynlist) + 5
```

```
sin (lookup TypeCode_Real dynlist)
```

The formal language in the next chapter is based on this idea; the fact that a function depends on a certain type is reflected by using an extra argument in which the type code can be passed.

3   A Formal System for Expressions with Dynamic Types

This section describes a formal system that formalizes the notion of objects with dynamic types. It is based on the formal system for term graph rewriting as introduced by Barendsen and Smetsers [3]. The formal system allows reasoning about decidability of typing and provides a handle for the presentation of the operational semantics.

First the syntax of the formal language will be given in full, and then the new constructs (w.r.t. the language introduced by Barendsen and Smetsers [3]) will be discussed individually. Finally typing rules will be given for the new constructs.

3.1   Syntax

Definition 1. *Types are built up from type variables, and type constructors:*

$$\sigma ::= \alpha \mid a \mid \mathsf{T}\,\vec{\sigma} \mid \sigma_1 \to \sigma_2$$

where T *ranges over the type constructors. The function type can be seen as a special binary type constructor.*

Note that there are two kinds of variables: generic variables $\alpha, \beta, \ldots$ that are used in type schemes, and type pattern variables $a, b, \ldots$ that are used for the construction and pattern matching of dynamics. Intuitively the generic variables α may be seen as universally quantified, while the type pattern variables a have the properties of existentially quantified variables.

Definition 2. *Expressions are generated by:*

$$E ::= x \mid C(E_1, \ldots, E_k) \mid \text{let } x = E \text{ in } E' \mid \text{letrec } \vec{x} = \vec{E} \text{ in } E$$
$$\mid \text{case } E \text{ of } \vec{P} = \vec{E} \mid E \, E' \mid \mathbf{F}(\sigma_1, \ldots, \sigma_j, E_1, \ldots, E_k)$$
$$\mid \langle \sigma, E \rangle$$
$$\mid \underline{\text{open }} E \text{ } \underline{\text{as}} \text{ } \langle a, x \rangle \text{ } \underline{\text{in}} \text{ } E'$$
$$\mid \underline{\text{typecase }} a \text{ } \underline{\text{of}} \vec{P}_t = \vec{E} \text{ } \underline{\text{fail}} = E'$$
$$\mid \underline{\text{equal }} a \text{ } a' \text{ } \underline{\text{success}} = E \text{ } \underline{\text{fail}} = E'$$
$$\mid \underline{\text{coerce }} a \text{ } a' \text{ } \underline{\text{success}} = E \text{ } \underline{\text{fail}} = E'$$
$$P ::= C(x_1, \ldots, x_k)$$
$$P_t ::= T \, a_1, \ldots, a_k$$

where C ranges over data constructors, $\mathbf{F}$ over function symbols and T over the type constructors.

Definition 3. *The notion of* symbol type *has been redefined[1] to incorporate abstractions over type variables. A symbol type of arity k and type arity j is a quantified $k + 1$ tuple $\Pi a_1 \ldots a_j.(\sigma_1, \ldots, \sigma_k, \tau)$. This will be denoted as:*

$$\Pi a_1 \ldots a_j. \, (\sigma_1, \ldots, \sigma_k) \, \triangleright \, \tau$$

The types $\vec{a}$ are called type arguments, *whereas the types $\vec{\sigma}$ are called* argument types. *The type τ is the* result type.

3.2 Introduction of New Constructs

Dynamics can be constructed by pairing a type and an expression:

$$\langle \sigma, E \rangle$$

where the type σ may include both type variables, to express polymorphism, and type pattern variables, which have been bound by an **open** or a **typecase** construct.

A dynamic can be unpaired using an **open** construct. Its value component is bound to a term variable (x) and its type component to a type pattern variable (a):

$$\underline{\text{open }} DynamicExpr \text{ } \underline{\text{as}} \text{ } \langle a, x \rangle \text{ } \underline{\text{in}} \text{ } Expr$$

Now the actual type component should unify with a statically specifed type (or with another actual type component). For this there are three constructs: the **typecase**, the **equal**, and the **coerce** constructs.

The **typecase**-construct enables matching on type constructors.

$$\underline{\text{typecase }} a \text{ } \underline{\text{of}} \, T_1 \, \vec{a_1} = E_1$$
$$\vdots$$
$$T_n \, \vec{a_n} = E_n$$
$$\underline{\text{fail}} \quad = E_{fail}$$

---

[1] as compared to the definition in Barendsen and Smetsers [3]

The intended meaning is that the selector type-expression a is matched against the type patterns T_i $\vec{a_i}$. The first pattern T_j $\vec{a_j}$ that matches, will cause the branch E_j to be taken. If none of the patterns match, the branch E_{fail} will be taken.

The type pattern variables $\vec{a_i}$ are bound by the **typecase**, and may be used in E_i in the same way as variables that have been introduced by an **open**-construct.

As with the normal case-construct, we only consider *left-linear* functions: no type variable may occur more than once in the same pattern. Moreover, these type pattern variables are 'local': they only occur in T_i $\vec{a_i} = E_i$.

The **equal**-construct is used to compare two types at run-time.

$$\underline{\text{equal}}\ a\ b\ \underline{\text{success}} = E_{succ}$$
$$\underline{\text{fail}}\quad = E_{fail}$$

The intended meaning is that if a is unifiable b then the expression E_{succ} will be evaluated, otherwise E_{succ}.

However, it is not always desirable to unify types. The comparison can also consist of a coercion, to check whether one type is an instance of the other.

$$\underline{\text{coerce}}\ a\ b\ \underline{\text{success}} = E_{succ}$$
$$\underline{\text{fail}}\quad = E_{fail}$$

With the intended meaning that if a coercible to b, i.e. if b is a instance of a, then the expression E_{succ} will be evaluated, otherwise E_{fail}.

Note that the constructs **typecase**, **equal**, and **coerce** match on type pattern variables instead of full types. This is done to make the proof of decidability of type checking easier (see Sect. 3.4), since more complex types are not required when CLEAN expressions are translated to this formal language.

The **type dependent functions** are represented on the level of function definitions by the fact that the first j arguments of a function are type pattern variables, and that the symbol type of such function quantifies over those j variables: $\Pi a_1 \ldots a_j.\ \vec{\sigma} \rhd \tau$ (where the $\vec{a}$'s may occur in both $\vec{\sigma}$ and τ).

$$F\ a_1 \ldots a_j\ x_1 \ldots x_k = E$$

The syntax of the **function application** has been adapted to allow the type arguments to the function to be specified:

$$\mathbf{F}(\sigma_1, \ldots, \sigma_j, E_1, \ldots, E_k)$$

where $\mathbf{F}$ has arity k and type arity j.

3.3 Rules for Type Assignment

In this section, after a few auxiliary definitions, the typing rules for the new language constructs will be given. The typing rules for the existing parts can be found in Barendsen and Smetsers [3].

Auxiliaries In addition to the standard basis (**B**), we need a *type basis* (**T**) that keeps track of which type pattern variables have been declared in surrounding expressions, and an *equation basis* (**E**) that holds equations (of the form $\sigma \sim \tau$) of types that may be assumed to be equal but are syntactically different.

Definition 4. *(i) A term basis **B** is finite set of term variable declarations of the form $x : \sigma$, where x is term variable and σ is a type.*

*(ii) A type basis **T** is finite set of type variable declarations of the form $\alpha : \star$, where α is a type (pattern) variable.*

*(iii) An equation basis **E** is a finite set of type equations of the form $\sigma \sim \tau$, where σ and τ are types.*

*(iv) We write Γ as an abbreviation of **B**, **T**, **E**.*

Definition 5. *(i) The set of type variables $\mathsf{TV}(\sigma)$ of a type σ is defined inductively by:*

$$\mathsf{TV}(\alpha) = \{\alpha\} \qquad \mathsf{TV}(\mathsf{T}\,\vec{\sigma}\,) \quad = \bigcup_i \mathsf{TV}(\sigma_i)$$
$$\mathsf{TV}(a) = \{a\} \qquad \mathsf{TV}(\sigma_1 \to \sigma_2) = \mathsf{TV}(\sigma_1) \cup \mathsf{TV}(\sigma_2)$$

*(ii) The set of type variables $\mathsf{TV}(\mathbf{B})$ of a basis **B** is defined by naturally extending the definition:*

$$\mathsf{TV}(\mathbf{B}) = \bigcup \{\mathsf{TV}(\sigma) \mid x : \sigma \in \mathbf{B}\}$$

Definition 6. *A type σ is* well-formed *w.r.t. a type basis **T***

$$\mathbf{T} \vdash \sigma : \star$$

*iff it only contains variables that have been declared in **T**, i.e. iff it can be constructed using the following rules:*

$$\mathbf{T} \vdash \alpha : \star \qquad \mathbf{T}, a{:}\star \vdash a : \star \qquad \frac{\mathbf{T} \vdash \sigma_1 : \star \quad \cdots \quad \mathbf{T} \vdash \sigma_k : \star}{\mathbf{T} \vdash \mathsf{T}\sigma_1 \ldots \sigma_k : \star}, \quad arity(T) = k$$

Note that the star ($\star$) does not play the same role as the star ($*$) in Barendregt's λ-cube. The intuition behind the $\star$ is that all types that may be used as terms are inhabitants of $\star$. Thus saying: "This type is well-formed" is equivalent to "This type may be used as a term".

Type variables may always be used as terms, type pattern variables only when they are introduced by the surrounding expression, and composite types only when each of their components may be used.

Definition 7. *Two types are* equivalent in **E** *(notation $\sigma \sim \tau$) iff $\mathbf{E} \vdash \sigma \sim \tau$ can be derived using the following rules:*

$$\mathbf{E}, \sigma \sim \tau \vdash \sigma \sim \tau \qquad \frac{\mathbf{E} \vdash \sigma \sim \tau}{\mathbf{E} \vdash \tau \sim \sigma} \qquad \frac{\mathbf{E} \vdash \sigma \sim \rho \quad \mathbf{E} \vdash \rho \sim \tau}{\mathbf{E} \vdash \sigma \sim \tau}$$

$$\frac{\mathbf{E} \vdash \mathsf{T}\,\vec{\sigma} \sim \mathsf{T}\,\vec{\tau}}{\mathbf{E} \vdash \sigma_i \sim \tau_i} \qquad \frac{\mathbf{E} \vdash \sigma \sim \tau}{\mathbf{E} \vdash \rho[\alpha := \sigma] \sim \rho[\alpha := \tau]}$$

Typing Rules for the Constructs **Dynamic construction:** Values of type Dynamic can be constructed by pairing an expression and a type. Constraints on this pairing are that the expression is typable with the type $(E : \sigma)$ and that the type is well-formed $(\sigma : \star)$:

$$\frac{\mathbf{T} \vdash \sigma : \star \quad \mathbf{B}, \mathbf{T}, \mathbb{E} \vdash E : \sigma}{\mathbf{B}, \mathbf{T}, \mathbb{E} \vdash \langle \sigma, E \rangle : D} \ , \quad \mathsf{TV}(\sigma) \cap \mathsf{TV}(\mathbf{B}) = \emptyset \quad \text{(Dynamic construction)}$$

where D represents the type of dynamic expressions (Dynamic).

Note that the constraint is only about variables in $\mathbf{B}$. Due to the introduction of type dependent functions, this constraint is not needed for type pattern variables in $\mathbf{T}$.

open construct: A *dynamic* can unpaired using the **open**-construct, where the value component is bound to a term variable and the type component to a type pattern variable.

When typing the expression (E_2) one may assume that the term variable is typable with the type pattern variable $(x : a)$, which is represented by adding this to $\mathbf{B}$, and that a may be used (restrictively) as a term in *Expr*, which is represented by adding $a : \star$ to $\mathbf{T}$.

As with existentially quantified types, neither x nor a may be used outside the scope of the **open**-expression. In particular, is it not allowed that the type of an **open**-expression depends on a.

This amounts to the following type rule for **open**-expressions (Dynamic destruction):

$$\frac{\mathbf{B}, \mathbf{T}, \mathbb{E} \vdash E_1 : D \qquad \mathbf{B}, x{:}a, \mathbf{T}, a{:}\star \vdash E_2 : \tau}{\mathbf{B}, \mathbf{T}, \mathbb{E} \vdash \underline{\text{open}} \ E_1 \ \underline{\text{as}} \ \langle a, x \rangle \ \underline{\text{in}} \ E_2 : \tau} \ , \quad a \notin \mathsf{TV}(\tau)$$

typecase construct: The **typecase**-construct enables matching on typeconstructors. It requires that the type a that is matched upon is well-formed $(a : \star)$. And in the branch E_i it may be assumed that the type pattern variables $\vec{a_i}$ are well-formed $(\vec{a_i}{:}\star)$.

When typing the branch E_i, the selector type-expression a may be freely substituted for the type pattern $T_i \ \vec{a_i}$ and vice versa, which is reflected by adding $a \sim T_i \ \vec{a_i}$ to the equivalence basis $\mathbb{E}$.

An auxiliary type rule states that if two types are equivalent, the one may be substituted for the other:

$$\frac{\mathbf{B}, \mathbf{T}, \mathbb{E} \vdash E : \sigma \quad \mathbb{E} \vdash \sigma \sim \tau}{\mathbf{B}, \mathbf{T}, \mathbb{E} \vdash E : \tau} \qquad \text{(substitution rule)}$$

Now the typing rule for the **typecase**-construct can be formulated $(\forall_{1 \leq i \leq n})$:

$$\frac{\mathbf{T} \vdash a : \star \quad \mathbf{B}, \mathbf{T}, \vec{a_i}{:}\vec{\star}, \mathbb{E}, a{\sim}T_i \ \vec{a_i} \vdash E_i : \tau \quad \mathbf{B}, \mathbf{T}, \mathbb{E} \vdash E_{fail} : \tau}{\mathbf{B}, \mathbf{T}, \mathbb{E} \vdash \left(\begin{array}{l} \underline{\text{typecase}} \ a \ \underline{\text{of}} \ \dots \\ \qquad T_i \ \vec{a_i} = E_i \ \dots \\ \qquad \underline{\text{fail}} \ = E_{fail} \end{array} \right) : \tau} \ , \quad \vec{a_i} \notin \mathsf{FV}(\tau)$$

As with the open-construct, the variables $\vec{a}_i$, which are bound by the typecase may not occur in the result type τ.

equal construct: Types can be compared (even unified) using the **equal** construct. It is required that both types that are to be compared are well-formed $(a : \star, \quad b : \star)$. Furthermore when typing E_{succ} the types a and b can be used interchangeable.

This results in the following type rule for an equal-expression (type equality):

$$\frac{\mathbf{T} \vdash a : \star \quad \mathbf{T} \vdash b : \star \quad \mathbf{B}, \mathbf{T}, \mathbb{E}, a \sim b \vdash E_{succ} : \rho \quad \mathbf{B}, \mathbf{T}, \mathbb{E} \vdash E_{fail} : \rho}{\mathbf{B}, \mathbf{T}, \mathbb{E} \vdash \begin{array}{l} \mathrm{equal}\ a\ b\ \underline{\mathrm{success}} = E_{succ} \\ \phantom{\mathrm{equal}\ a\ b\ }\underline{\mathrm{fail}} = E_{fail} \end{array} : \rho}$$

coerce construct: The type rule for the **coerce** construct is analogous to that of the **equal** construct (type coercion):

$$\frac{\mathbf{T} \vdash a : \star \quad \mathbf{T} \vdash b : \star \quad \mathbf{B}, \mathbf{T}, \mathbb{E}, a \sim b \vdash E_{succ} : \rho \quad \mathbf{B}, \mathbf{T}, \mathbb{E} \vdash E_{fail} : \rho}{\mathbf{B}, \mathbf{T}, \mathbb{E} \vdash \begin{array}{l} \mathrm{coerce}\ a\ b\ \underline{\mathrm{success}} = E_{succ} \\ \phantom{\mathrm{coerce}\ a\ b\ }\underline{\mathrm{fail}} = E_{fail} \end{array} : \rho}$$

function definition: A function definition $\mathbf{F}\ \vec{a}\ \vec{x} = E$ with standard type $\Pi\ \vec{a}\ .\ \vec{\sigma} \rhd \tau$ is called *type correct* if

$$\vec{a} : \vec{\star},\ \vec{x} : \vec{\sigma} \vdash E : \tau$$

Note that the type variables $\vec{a}$ may occur in $\vec{\sigma}$ as well as in τ.

function application:

$$\frac{\mathcal{F} \vdash \mathbf{F} : \Pi\ \vec{a}\ .\ \vec{\sigma} \rhd \tau \quad \mathbf{T} \vdash \vec{\rho} : \vec{\star} \quad \mathbf{B}, \mathbf{T}, \mathbb{E} \vdash \vec{E} : \vec{\sigma}\ [\vec{a} := \vec{\rho}]}{\mathbf{B}, \mathbf{T}, \mathbb{E} \vdash \mathbf{F}(\rho_1, \ldots, \rho_j, E_1, \ldots, E_k) : \tau[\vec{a} := \vec{\rho}]}$$

where $\mathbf{F}$ has arity k and type arity j.

In appendix A the type rules of all syntactical constructs are summarised, including those that are defined in Barendsen and Smetsers [3].

3.4   Decidability of Type Checking

This section shows the decidability of type checking by presenting an algorithm.

Definition 8. *(i) A type equation $\sigma \sim \tau$ is distributed* over a type ρ *(notation $\rho^{[\sigma \sim \tau]}$) using the following inductive definition:*

$$\rho^{[a \sim \sigma]} = \rho[a := \sigma]$$
$$\rho^{[\sigma \sim a]} = \rho^{[a \sim \sigma]}$$
$$\rho^{[T\vec{\sigma} \sim T\vec{\tau}]} = \rho^{[\sigma_1 \sim \tau_1] \cdots [\sigma_k \sim \tau_k]}$$
$$\rho^{[\sigma_1 \to \sigma_2 \sim \tau_1 \to \tau_2]} = \rho^{[\sigma_1 \sim \tau_1][\sigma_2 \sim \tau_2]}$$
$$\rho^{[\sigma \sim \tau]} = \rho \quad , \quad \text{for all other type equations } \sigma \sim \tau$$

(ii) The distribution extends naturally to bases and expressions that contain types.

Let E be the expression that is to be typed with σ, $\mathbf{B} = \{x : \alpha, ...\}$ a term basis in which all free term variables in the expression have been assigned a fresh type, and $Tenv = \{a : \star ...\}$ a type basis that contains all free type pattern variables, then we look for a type checking algorithm that complies with the following specification:

$$\mathsf{check}(\mathbf{B}, \mathbf{T}, E, \sigma) = \begin{cases} \ast & \text{, if } \ast \text{ is the most general substitution such that} \\ & \quad \mathbf{B}^\ast, \mathbf{T} \vdash E^\ast : \sigma^\ast \\ \mathsf{fail} & \text{, if } E \text{ is not typable} \end{cases}$$

The implementation is given in appendix B, where the following auxiliary functions have been used:

- A unify function. This function, applied two types σ and τ, yields a most general substitution $\ast$ such that $\sigma^\ast = \tau^\ast$ if the types are unifiable and yields fail if they are not (see Robinson [9]).
- The operator $\oplus$ concatenates two substitutions and applies the second substitution to the arguments of the first. (Note that although this is intuitively clear, it is not a formal specification.)

3.5   Operational Semantics for the New Constructs

This section presents the evaluation rules of the new constructs of the formal language. They are given in the same notation as was used in Abadi et al. [1].

Definition 9. *An expression E is in* canonical form *if either*

$$\begin{aligned} &E \equiv \mathbf{C}\ (E_1, ..., E_k) && \text{and } E_1, ..., E_k \text{ are in canonical form, or} \\ &E \equiv \mathbf{F}\ E_1 ... E_i && \text{and } i < \mathsf{arity}_{\mathbf{F}} \text{ and } E_1, ..., E_i \text{ are in canonical form, or} \\ &E \equiv \langle \sigma, E \rangle && \text{and } \sigma \text{ and } E \text{ are in canonical form, or} \\ &E \equiv \mathsf{wrong} \end{aligned}$$

A type σ is in canonical form *if either*

$$\begin{aligned} &\sigma \equiv \alpha && \text{, or} \\ &\sigma \equiv \mathsf{T}\ \sigma_1 ... \sigma_j && \text{and } \sigma_1, ..., \sigma_j \text{ are in canonical form, or} \\ &\sigma \equiv \sigma_1 \to \sigma_2 && \text{and } \sigma_1 \text{ and } \sigma_2 \text{ are in canonical form, or} \\ &\sigma \equiv \mathsf{wrong} \end{aligned}$$

where wrong is the value of erroneous computations such as the application of one integer to another. This value is different from $\perp$ (nondetermination), which allows us to distinguish between programs that loop forever and programs that crash.

Below, we define the judgments *"expression E reduces to canonical expression v"* and *"type σ reduces to canonical type t"*, written as *"$E \Longrightarrow v$" and "$\sigma \Longrightarrow t$"*, for each new syntactical construct of the formal language. These judgments are presented in the same way as the rules for type assignment.

The evaluation of a **dynamic construct** involves the evaluation of both the expression and the type. If either the type or the expression reduces to wrong, then the whole dynamic reduces to **wrong**.

$$\frac{\vdash \sigma \Longrightarrow t \qquad \vdash E \Longrightarrow v}{\vdash \langle \sigma, E \rangle \Longrightarrow \langle t, v \rangle}$$

$$\frac{\vdash \sigma \Longrightarrow \text{wrong}}{\vdash \langle \sigma, E \rangle \Longrightarrow \text{wrong}} \qquad \frac{\vdash E \Longrightarrow \text{wrong}}{\vdash \langle \sigma, E \rangle \Longrightarrow \text{wrong}}$$

The evaluation of an **open construct** consists of the evaluation of its dynamic expression, the binding of the resulting canonical forms to the variables a and x, and the evaluation of the body expression, in which a and x have been substituted for their canonical forms. If the dynamic expression does not reduce to a canonical dynamic, or the body expression reduces to wrong, then the whole open expression reduces to **wrong**.

$$\frac{\vdash E \Longrightarrow \langle t, v \rangle \qquad \vdash E'[a := t, x := v] \Longrightarrow v'}{\vdash \underline{\text{open }} E \underline{\text{ as }} \langle a, x \rangle \underline{\text{ in }} E' \Longrightarrow v'}$$

$$\frac{\vdash E \Longrightarrow t' \quad (\ t' \text{ not of the form } \langle t, v \rangle\ )}{\vdash \underline{\text{open }} E \underline{\text{ as }} \langle a, x \rangle \underline{\text{ in }} E' \Longrightarrow \text{wrong}}$$

For the evaluation of a **typecase construct**, an auxiliary function is needed that unifies two canonical types. If unification is successful, this it yields a substitution ∗ for all type (pattern) variables that occur in both canonical types, and otherwise fail is returned.

A typecase expression is evaluated by evaluating its selector type and matching this against all patterns. The result of the evaluation is the canonical form of the expression that goes with the first pattern for which the unification with the evaluated selector expression succeeds. If no unification succeeds, then the fail expression is evaluated.

$$\frac{\vdash a \Longrightarrow t \quad \forall j < i.\text{unify}(t, T_j\ \vec{a_j}) = \text{fail} \quad \text{unify}(t, T_i\ \vec{a_i}) = * \quad \vdash E_i^* \Longrightarrow v}{\vdash \underline{\text{typecase }} a \underline{\text{ of }} \dots T_i\ \vec{a_i} = E_i\ \dots \atop \underline{\text{fail}} = E_{fail}} \Longrightarrow v$$

$$\frac{\vdash a \Longrightarrow t \quad \forall i\ .\ \text{unify}(t, T_i\ \vec{a_i}) = \text{fail} \quad \vdash E_{fail} \Longrightarrow v}{\vdash \underline{\text{typecase }} a \underline{\text{ of }} \dots T_i\ \vec{a_i} = E_i\ \dots \atop \underline{\text{fail}} = E_{fail}} \Longrightarrow v$$

$$\frac{\vdash a \implies \text{wrong}}{\vdash \text{typecase } a \text{ } \underline{\text{of}} \text{ } \dots \text{T}_i \text{ } \vec{a_i} = E_i \dots \atop \underline{\text{fail}} \quad = E_{fail}} \implies \text{wrong}$$

An **equal expression** is evaluated by evaluating both argument types, which are then unified using the unify function. If successful, the expression reduces to the success branch (to which the substitution has been applied), otherwise the result will be the canonical form of the fail branch. If either of the argument types reduces to wrong, the whole expression yields wrong.

$$\frac{\vdash a \implies t \qquad \vdash b \implies t' \qquad \text{unify}(t, t') = * \qquad \vdash E^*_{succ} \implies v}{\vdash \text{equal } a \text{ } b \text{ } \underline{\text{success}} = E_{succ} \atop \underline{\text{fail}} \quad = E_{fail}} \implies v$$

$$\frac{\vdash a \implies t \qquad \vdash b \implies t' \qquad \text{unify}(t, t') = \text{fail} \qquad \vdash E_{fail} \implies v}{\vdash \text{equal } a \text{ } b \text{ } \underline{\text{success}} = E_{succ} \atop \underline{\text{fail}} \quad = E_{fail}} \implies v$$

$$\frac{\vdash a \implies \text{wrong}}{\vdash \text{equal } a \text{ } b \text{ } \underline{\text{success}} = E_{succ} \atop \underline{\text{fail}} \quad = E_{fail}} \implies \text{wrong}$$

$$\frac{\vdash b \implies \text{wrong}}{\vdash \text{equal } a \text{ } b \text{ } \underline{\text{success}} = E_{succ} \atop \underline{\text{fail}} \quad = E_{fail}} \implies \text{wrong}$$

The evaluation of a **coerce construct** differs from that of an **equal** construct only in the auxiliary function. Instead of unifying both argument types, it must be checked whether the first type can be coerced to the second, i.e. whether the second type is an instance of the first.

On successful coercion the success branch will be evaluated with substitutions applied to it. Otherwise the fail branch will be reduced.

$$\frac{\vdash a \implies t \qquad \vdash b \implies t' \qquad \text{coerce}(t, t') = * \qquad \vdash E^*_{succ} \implies v}{\vdash \text{coerce } a \text{ } b \text{ } \underline{\text{success}} = E_{succ} \atop \underline{\text{fail}} \quad = E_{fail}} \implies v$$

$$\frac{\vdash a \implies t \qquad \vdash b \implies t' \qquad \text{coerce}(t, t') = \text{fail} \qquad \vdash E_{fail} \implies v}{\vdash \text{coerce } a \text{ } b \text{ } \underline{\text{success}} = E_{succ} \atop \underline{\text{fail}} \quad = E_{fail}} \implies v$$

$$\frac{\vdash\ a\ \Longrightarrow\ \textbf{wrong}}{\vdash\ \underline{\text{coerce}}\ a\ b\ \underline{\text{success}} = E_{succ} \quad \Longrightarrow\ \textbf{wrong}}$$
$$\underline{\text{fail}}\quad = E_{fail}$$

$$\frac{\vdash\ b\ \Longrightarrow\ \textbf{wrong}}{\vdash\ \underline{\text{coerce}}\ a\ b\ \underline{\text{success}} = E_{succ} \quad \Longrightarrow\ \textbf{wrong}}$$
$$\underline{\text{fail}}\quad = E_{fail}$$

The operational semantics for **function application** have been chosen to be call-by-value.

$$\frac{\vdash \vec{\sigma} \Longrightarrow \vec{t} \qquad \vdash \vec{E} \Longrightarrow \vec{v} \qquad \vdash body_{\mathbf{F}}[\vec{a}:=\vec{t}, \vec{x}:=\vec{v}] \Longrightarrow v'}{\vdash \mathbf{F}(\sigma_1,\ldots,\sigma_j, E_1,\ldots,E_k) \Longrightarrow v'}$$

4   Related Work and Conclusions

Abadi et al. present in [1] a theoretical framework for Dynamic types, complete with an extensive review of the history of dynamic typing in statically typed languages. They also mention a large number of languages in which restricted use has been made of the dynamic concept. In [2] this theoretical framework is extended to cover polymorphism. Higher order pattern variables are introduced to be able to match against polymorphic types. We decided to deal with polymorphism differently and use ordinary type variables to accomplish this.

The latter approach has also been taken by Leroy and Mauny. They describe in [7] how a simple version of Dynamic is implemented in ML. They also specify a more complicated system of dynamics with universally and existentially quantified variables. This system uses the existentially qualified types to specify dynamic matches with incomplete type information. These are basically the same as our type pattern variables.

Neither of both systems allow abstraction over the types of dynamics beyond the scope of a function, though practice has shown that programmers using dynamics have a strong need for such a powerful tool. The type dependent functions that are described in this paper make such abstraction possible.

In Persistent Haskell [4] a similar, but more restricted form of dynamic typing and type dependent functions has been used. Two Haskell operations provide acces to persistent values:

```
get :: Persistent a ⇒ PSHandle → PSid → IO a
use :: Persistent a ⇒ PSHandle → PSid → a → IO a
```

The class Persistent is comparable with the class TC that is used in CLEAN. The PSid corresponds to a filename (Name) and the PSHandle and IO are comparable to the input and ouput of of the uniquely attributed **Files**. Using these similarities, the **get** and **use** operations can be implemented in CLEAN by using dynamics and type dependent functions.

```
get :: *Files → Name → (Error, a, *Files) | TC a
get files name = Read name files
where
      Read :: Name → *Files → (Error, a, *Files) | TC a
      Read filename files
        # (error, dyn, files) = ReadDynamic filename files
        = case dyn of
              (value :: a^) = (error, value, files)
              else          = (WrongType, bottom, files)
```

The difference between CLEAN and Persistent Haskell is that in the latter language the typecheck is implicit and has to be done on the moment of access to the persistent store, whereas in CLEAN the check be postponed.

The full system of dynamic types with type dependent functions will be implemented in CLEAN version 2.0.

Acknowledgements

I would like to thank Erik Barendsen, Sjaak Smetsers and Rinus Plasmeijer for their valuable remarks and discussions.

References

1. M. Abadi, L. Cardelli, B. Pierce, and G. Plotkin. Dynamic Typing in a Statically Typed Language. *ACM Transactions on Programming Languages and Systems*, 13(2):237–268, 1991.
2. M. Abadi, L. Cardelli, B. Pierce, and D. Rémy. Dynamic Typing in Polymorphic Languages. *Journal of Functional Programming*, 5(1):111–130, 1995.
3. E. Barendsen and J. Smetsers. Uniqueness Typing for Functional Languages with Graph Rewriting Semantics. *Mathematical Structures in Computer Science*, 6:579–612, 1996.
4. A.J.T. Davie, K. Hammond, and J.-J. Quintela. *Efficient Persistent Haskell*, In *Draft Proc. 10th International Workshop on the Implementation of Functional Languages (IFL '98)*, London, England, pages 183–194, 1998.
5. M.C.J.D. van Eekelen and M.J. Plasmeijer. *Functional Programming and Parallel Graph Rewriting*, Addison-Wesley, 1993.
6. M.J.C.D. van Eekelen and M.J. Plasmeijer. *Concurrent Clean 1.0 Language Report*, Computing Science Institute, University of Nijmegen, http://www.cs.kun.nl/~clean/Clean.Cleanbook.html.
7. X. Leroy and M. Mauny. Dynamics in ML. *Journal of Functional Programming*, 3(4):431–463, 1993.
8. M. Pil. First Class File I/O. In *Proc. 8th. International Workshop on the Implementation of Functional Languages (IFL '96)*, Bad Godesberg, Germany, September 1996, volume 1268 of *LNCS*, pages 233–246. Springer-Verlag, 1997.
9. J. Robinson. A Machine-Oriented Logic Based on the Resolution Principle. *Journal of the Association For Computing Machinery* 12:23–41, 1965.

A   Type Rules Summarised

$$\mathbf{B}, x:\sigma \vdash x:\sigma$$

$$\frac{\mathcal{A} \vdash \mathbf{C}:\vec{\sigma} \rhd \tau \qquad \mathbf{B},\mathbf{T},\mathbb{E} \vdash \vec{E}:\vec{\sigma}}{\mathbf{B},\mathbf{T},\mathbb{E} \vdash \mathbf{C}(E_1,\ldots,E_k):\tau}$$

$$\frac{\mathbf{B},\mathbf{T},\mathbb{E} \vdash E:\sigma \qquad \mathbf{B}, x:\sigma, \mathbf{T},\mathbb{E} \vdash E':\tau}{\mathbf{B},\mathbf{T},\mathbb{E} \vdash \mathsf{let}\ x=E\ \mathsf{in}\ E':\tau}$$

$$\frac{\mathbf{B},\vec{x}:\vec{\sigma}, \mathbf{T},\mathbb{E} \vdash E_i:\sigma_i \qquad \mathbf{B},\vec{x}:\vec{\sigma}, \mathbf{T},\mathbb{E} \vdash E':\tau}{\mathbf{B},\mathbf{T},\mathbb{E} \vdash \mathsf{letrec}\ \vec{x}=\vec{E}\ \mathsf{in}\ E':\tau}$$

$$\frac{\mathbf{B},\mathbf{T},\mathbb{E} \vdash E:\tau \quad \mathcal{A} \vdash \mathbf{C}_i:\vec{\sigma}_i \rhd \tau_i \quad \mathbf{B},\vec{x}_i:\vec{\sigma}_i, \mathbf{T},\mathbb{E} \vdash E_i:\rho}{\mathbf{B},\mathbf{T},\mathbb{E} \vdash \mathsf{case}\ E\ \mathsf{of}\ \vec{P}=\vec{E}:\rho}, \text{if}\ P_i = \mathbf{C}_i\ \vec{x}_i$$

$$\frac{\mathbf{T} \vdash \sigma:\star \qquad \mathbf{B},\mathbf{T},\mathbb{E} \vdash E:\sigma}{\mathbf{B},\mathbf{T},\mathbb{E} \vdash \langle\sigma,E\rangle:D}$$

$$\frac{\mathbf{B},\mathbf{T},\mathbb{E} \vdash E_1:D \qquad \mathbf{B}, x:a, \mathbf{T}, a:\star \vdash E_2:\tau}{\mathbf{B},\mathbf{T},\mathbb{E} \vdash \underline{\mathsf{open}}\ E_1\ \underline{\mathsf{as}}\ \langle a,x\rangle\ \underline{\mathsf{in}}\ E_2:\tau}, \quad a \notin \mathsf{TV}(\tau)$$

$$\frac{\mathbf{B},\mathbf{T},\mathbb{E} \vdash E:\sigma \qquad \mathbb{E} \vdash \sigma \sim \tau}{\mathbf{B},\mathbf{T},\mathbb{E} \vdash E:\tau}$$

$$\frac{\mathbf{T} \vdash a:\star \quad \mathbf{B}, \mathbf{T}, \vec{a_i}:\vec{\star}, \mathbb{E}, a\sim T_i\ \vec{a_i} \vdash E_i:\tau \quad \mathbf{B},\mathbf{T},\mathbb{E} \vdash E_{fail}:\tau}{\mathbf{B},\mathbf{T},\mathbb{E} \vdash \begin{array}{l} \underline{\mathsf{typecase}}\ a\ \underline{\mathsf{of}}\ \ldots \\ \qquad T_i\ \vec{a_i} = E_i\ \ldots :\tau \\ \qquad \underline{\mathsf{fail}}\ \ = E_{fail} \end{array}}, \quad \vec{a_i} \notin \mathsf{FV}(\tau)$$

$$\frac{\mathbf{T} \vdash a:\star \quad \mathbf{T} \vdash b:\star \quad \mathbf{B}, \mathbf{T}, \mathbb{E}, a\sim b \vdash E_{succ}:\rho \quad \mathbf{B},\mathbf{T},\mathbb{E} \vdash E_{fail}:\rho}{\mathbf{B},\mathbf{T},\mathbb{E} \vdash \begin{array}{l} \underline{\mathsf{equal}}\ a\ b\ \underline{\mathsf{success}} = E_{succ} \\ \qquad\quad\ \underline{\mathsf{fail}}\ \ \ = E_{fail} \end{array}:\rho}$$

$$\frac{\mathbf{T} \vdash a:\star \quad \mathbf{T} \vdash b:\star \quad \mathbf{B}, \mathbf{T}, \mathbb{E}, a\sim b \vdash E_{succ}:\rho \quad \mathbf{B},\mathbf{T},\mathbb{E} \vdash E_{fail}:\rho}{\mathbf{B},\mathbf{T},\mathbb{E} \vdash \begin{array}{l} \underline{\mathsf{coerce}}\ a\ b\ \underline{\mathsf{success}} = E_{succ} \\ \qquad\quad\ \underline{\mathsf{fail}}\ \ \ = E_{fail} \end{array}:\rho}$$

$$\frac{\mathcal{F} \vdash \mathbf{F}:\Pi\ \vec{a}\ .\ \vec{\sigma} \rhd \tau \quad \mathbf{T} \vdash \vec{\rho}:\vec{\star} \quad \mathbf{B},\mathbf{T},\mathbb{E} \vdash \vec{E}:\vec{\sigma}\ [\vec{a}:=\vec{\rho}]}{\mathbf{B},\mathbf{T},\mathbb{E} \vdash \mathbf{F}(\rho_1,\ldots,\rho_j,E_1,\ldots,E_k):\tau[\vec{a}:=\vec{\rho}]}$$

A function definition $\mathbf{F}\ \vec{a}\ \vec{x}= E$ with standard type $\Pi\ \vec{a}\ .\ \vec{\sigma} \rhd \tau$ is called *type correct* if

$$\vec{a}:\vec{\star},\ \vec{x}:\vec{\sigma} \vdash E:\tau$$

B   Type Checking Algorithm

(see also Section 3.4)

$$\text{check}(\mathbf{B}, \mathbb{T}, x, \sigma) = \text{unify}(\mathbf{B}(x), \sigma)$$

$$\text{check}(\mathbf{B}, \mathbb{T}, \mathbf{C}\,\vec{E}, \rho) = \text{check}(\mathbf{B}, \mathbb{T}, E_i, \sigma_i) \oplus$$
$$\text{unify}(\rho, \tau)$$
$$\text{where } \vec{\sigma} \triangleright \tau \text{ is the standard } \mathcal{A}\text{-type of } \mathbf{C}$$

$$\text{check}(\mathbf{B}, \mathbb{T}, \text{let } x = E \text{ in } E', \sigma) = \text{check}(\mathbf{B} \cup x{:}\alpha, \mathbb{T}, E', \sigma) \oplus$$
$$\text{check}(\mathbf{B}, \mathbb{T}, E, \alpha)$$
$$\alpha \text{ fresh}$$

$$\text{check}(\mathbf{B}, \mathbb{T}, \text{letrec } \vec{x}{=}\vec{E} \text{ in} E', \sigma) = \bigoplus_i \text{check}(\mathbf{B} \cup \vec{x}\vec{\alpha}, \mathbb{T}, E_i, \alpha_i) \oplus$$
$$\text{check}(\mathbf{B} \cup \vec{x}\vec{\alpha}, \mathbb{T}, E', \sigma)$$
$$\vec{\alpha} \text{ fresh}$$

$$\text{check}(\mathbf{B}, \mathbb{T}, \text{case } E \text{ of } \vec{P}{=}\vec{E}, \rho) = \bigoplus_i (\text{check}(\mathbf{B} \cup \vec{x}_i\vec{\sigma}_i, \mathbb{T}, E_i, \rho) \oplus \text{unify}(\tau_i, \alpha))$$
$$\oplus\ \text{check}(\mathbf{B}, \mathbb{T}, E, \alpha))$$
$$\text{where } P_i = \mathbf{C}_i\,\vec{x}_i \text{ and the standard } \mathcal{A}\text{-type}$$
$$\text{of } \mathbf{C}_i \text{ is } \vec{\sigma}_i \triangleright \tau_i$$
$$\alpha \text{ fresh}$$

$$\text{check}(\mathbf{B}, \mathbb{T}, \langle \sigma, E \rangle, \tau) = \text{if } \text{TPV}(\sigma) \in \mathbb{T} \text{ then}$$
$$\text{check}(\mathbf{B}, \mathbb{T}, E, \sigma) \oplus$$
$$\text{unify}(\tau, D)$$
$$\text{elsefail}$$

$$\text{check}(\mathbf{B}, \mathbb{T}, \underline{\text{open }} E \underline{\text{ as }} \langle a, x \rangle, \sigma) = \text{check}(\mathbf{B}, \mathbb{T}, E, D) \oplus$$
$$\underline{\text{in }} E'$$
$$\text{check}(\mathbf{B} \cup x{:}a, \mathbb{T} \cup a{:}{\star}, E', \sigma)$$

$$\text{check}(\mathbf{B}, \mathbb{T}, \underline{\text{typecase }} a \underline{\text{ of}} \ldots, \sigma) = \text{if } a \in \mathbb{T} \text{ then}$$
$$T_i\,\vec{b}_i = E_i \ \ldots \qquad \bigoplus_i (\text{check}(\ \mathbf{B}^{[a \sim T_i\,\vec{b}_i]},$$
$$\underline{\text{fail}} \ \ = E_{fail}$$
$$\mathbb{T} \cup \vec{b}_i{:}{\star},$$
$$E_i^{[a \sim T_i\,\vec{b}_i]}, \sigma^{[a \sim T_i\,\vec{b}_i]})$$
$$\oplus\ \text{check}(\mathbf{B}, \mathbb{T}, E_{fail}, \sigma)$$
$$\text{else fail}$$

$$\text{check}(\mathbf{B}, \mathbb{T}, \underline{\text{equal }} a\,b \qquad , \sigma) = \text{if } a \in \mathbb{T} \wedge b \in \mathbb{T} \text{ then}$$
$$\underline{\text{success}} = E_{succ} \qquad \text{check}(\mathbf{B}^{[a \sim b]}, \mathbb{T}, E_{succ}^{[a \sim b]}, \sigma^{[a \sim b]}) \oplus$$
$$\underline{\text{fail}} \ \ = E_{fail} \qquad \text{check}(\mathbf{B}, \mathbb{T}, E_{fail}, \sigma)$$
$$\text{else fail}$$

$$\text{check}(\mathbf{B}, \mathbb{T}, \underline{\text{coerce }} a\,b \qquad , \sigma) = \text{if } a \in \mathbb{T} \wedge b \in \mathbb{T} \text{ then}$$
$$\underline{\text{success}} = E_{succ} \qquad \text{check}(\mathbf{B}^{[a \sim b]}, \mathbb{T}, E_{succ}^{[a \sim b]}, \sigma^{[a \sim b]}) \oplus$$
$$\underline{\text{fail}} \ \ = E_{fail} \qquad \text{check}(\mathbf{B}, \mathbb{T}, E_{fail}, \sigma)$$
$$\text{else fail}$$

Putting the Spine Back in the Spineless Tagless G-Machine:
An Implementation of Resumable Black-Holes

Alastair Reid

Department of Computer Science, Yale University
New Haven CT 06520, USA
reid-alastair@cs.yale.edu

Abstract. Interrupt handling is a tricky business in lazy functional languages: we have to make sure that thunks that are being evaluated can be halted and later restarted if and when they are required. This is a particular problem for implementations which use black-holing. Black-Holing deliberately makes it impossible to revert such thunks to their original state to avoid a serious space leak. Interactive Haskell implementations such as Hugs and hbi catch interrupts and avoid the problem by omitting or disabling black-holing. Batch mode Haskell implementations such as HBC and the Glasgow Haskell Compiler (GHC) avoid this problem by disabling black-holing or by providing no way to catch interrupts. This paper describes a modification to GHC's abstract machine (the Spineless Tagless G-Machine) which simultaneously supports both interrupts and black-holing.

1 Introduction

Black-Holing [6] is an important technique for avoiding space leaks in lazy functional languages. When a program starts to evaluate an unevaluated thunk, it copies the contents of the thunk onto the stack (or into registers) and overwrites the thunk with an object known as a "black-hole." When the program completes evaluation of the unevaluated thunk, the thunk is overwritten a second time with the value of the thunk. If the program tries to evaluate a thunk which is already being evaluated, it reports an error. This is the correct behaviour in a sequential evaluator: it can only happen if the value of the original thunk depends on itself and would have caused an infinite loop in a system which did not support black-holes. (Concurrent evaluation requires different behaviour and is discussed in Sect. 5.4.) Black-Holing a thunk is important because it removes references to the free variables of the thunk; if one of these references is the last reference to the variable, the variable can be garbage collected immediately — reducing the heap usage of the program. Jones [6] shows that simple tail-recursive functions such as last can run in constant space with black-holing but require linear space without black-holing.

The problem with black-holing is that it assumes that evaluation of a thunk will not stop until the value of the thunk has been found. This is a problem if

H. Hammond, T. Davie, and C. Clack (Eds.): IFL'98, LNCS 1595, pp. 186–199, 1999.
© Springer-Verlag Berlin Heidelberg 1999

we wish to pause evaluation of a thunk to handle an interrupt or if we wish to speculatively evaluate a thunk while waiting for user input and pause evaluation when user input arrives. In both circumstances, black-holed thunks are left in the heap and incorrectly report errors if they are subsequently evaluated.

An obvious fix is to revert black-holes to their original form when an interrupt occurs. There are two problems with this:

1. To revert a black-hole to its original form, we have to preserve the contents of the original thunk until evaluation of that thunk completes (i.e., until we're certain it will not need to be reverted). Doing so retains references to the thunk's free variables restoring the space leak that black-holing is designed to fix.
2. Reverting the black-hole to its original form causes us to discard a lot of the work we performed in partially evaluating the object. This is contrary to one of the primary properties of lazy evaluation: every thunk is evaluated at most once.

Our solution to these problems is not to revert the black-hole to its original form but to revert the black-hole to (a representation of) its current partially evaluated state.

On the Spineless Tagless Graph-reduction Machine (STG machine) [8], the state of a partially evaluated thunk is stored on the stack; naïve implementations of graph reduction do not use the stack in this way: they store the entire state of a thunk on the "spine" of the thunk. We therefore dub our technique "Putting the Spine back in the Spineless Tagless G-Machine."

2   Updates in the STG Machine

The STG machine is described in detail by Simon Peyton-Jones [8]; here we provide an overview of the most important parts of the evaluation and update machinery.

On a naïve implementation of graph reduction, an update is performed on each reduction step. For example, in reducing

```
let x = compose id id 42 in x
```

to 42, a naïve implementation would update x three times with id (id 42) then with id 42 and finally with 42. This is inefficient because it requires the allocation of many intermediate values and because it requires a large number of writes into the heap.

The STG machine avoids these costs by delaying updates until an expression has been reduced to weak head normal form: each thunk is evaluated at most once.[1] To do this, the STG machine maintains a list of thunks which are in the

---

[1] The STG machine also allows thunks to be marked as being non-updatable if they are not shared. Black-Holing causes no problems for non-updatable thunks so they are ignored in this paper.

process of being evaluated. This list is threaded through the evaluation stack and is manipulated as follows:

- When an (updatable) thunk is "entered" (i.e., evaluation starts), the STG machine does four things:
  1. a pointer to the thunk is pushed onto the update list (this thunk is known as the "updatee");
  2. the contents of the thunk are pushed onto the stack;
  3. the thunk is overwritten with a black-hole;[2] and
  4. the thunk's code is executed. If the thunk is an application node, this enters the object on top of the stack.
- When evaluation of a thunk completes, the top of the stack contains one of two things:
  - A return address: the evaluator simply jumps to the return address.
  - An entry in the update list: the evaluator overwrites the updatee with the value of the thunk, removes the update frame from the list and tries to return the value again.

3   Reverting Black-Holes

As we noted in the introduction, black-holing causes problems if we interrupt execution because it is neither possible nor entirely desirable to revert a black-hole to its original form. The solution is simple and, with the aid of 20-20 hindsight, very obvious: instead of reverting the black-hole to its original form, we overwrite black-holes with that part of the stack required to complete evaluation of the thunk. That is, we revert each black-hole on the update list as follows:

1. The black-hole is overwritten with a "resumable black-hole" containing the contents of the stack above the update frame. If, as is usually the case, the black-hole is too small to hold the resumable black-hole, a fresh resumable black-hole is created and the black-hole is overwritten with an indirection to the resumable black-hole.
2. The update frame is removed from the head of the update list.
3. A pointer to the black-hole is pushed onto the stack.

When the update list is empty, the remainder of the stack is discarded.

When the STG machine enters a resumable black-hole, it does exactly the same as when it enters an updatable application node. That is:

1. a pointer to the resumable black-hole is pushed onto the update list;
2. the contents of the resumable black-hole are pushed onto the stack;
3. the resumable black-hole is overwritten with a black-hole; and
4. the object on top of the stack is entered.

---

[2] An optimisation known as "lazy black-holing" allows this step to be delayed until garbage collection time and is discussed in Sect. 5.1.

The only difference between resumable black-holes and application nodes lies in how they are garbage collected: since we create resumable black-holes by copying data off the stack, they have to be garbage collected like miniature stacks.

Fig. 1 shows how this works while evaluating this expression

```
let a = enumFromTo 1 100
    b = tail a
    c = head b
in c
```

Initially (Fig. 1.i), the heap contains three updatable application nodes a, b and c (representing the variables a, b and c respectively), the stack (shown with the "top" towards the bottom of the page) contains some data D and the top of the stack contains a pointer to c. (One of the strengths of our technique is that it oblivious to what data (if any) occurs between update frames. It is therefore sufficient to label the areas between update frames A ...D; we need not worry about the contents or sizes of these areas.)

Figs. 1.ii to 1.iv show how the spine of the graph is unwound during evaluation of c. As each application node is entered, an update frame is pushed onto the stack and added to the head of the update list, the contents of the node are copied onto the stack and the node is black-holed.

Let us suppose that an interrupt occurs just after a is entered. The next time a thunk is entered (i.e., when enumFromTo is entered), the evaluator detects that the thread is to be killed and start to revert all the black-holes on the update list.

Figs. 1.v to 1.viii show how the spine of the graph is reconstructed from the stack while reverting black-holes. As each black-hole is reverted, the black-hole is overwritten with a resumable black-hole containing the contents of the stack above the update frame, the update frame is removed from the head of the update list and a pointer to the black-hole is pushed onto the stack. When the update list is empty, the remainder of the stack is discarded.

Suppose now that we start evaluating something else and, in the course of that expression, we enter thunk c. The behaviour of the STG machine on entering a resumable black-hole reverses the sequence of steps from Fig. 1.viii to Fig. 1.v. That is:

1. Since c is a resumable black-hole, the evaluator adds an update frame to the list, pushes the data C on the stack, pushes b on the stack, black-holes c and enters b resulting in Fig. 1.vii.

2. On entering b, the evaluator adds an update frame to the list, pushes the data B on the stack, pushes a on the stack, black-holes b and enters a resulting in Fig. 1.vi.

3. On entering a, the evaluator adds an update frame to the list, pushes pointers to 100, 1 and enumFromTo on the stack, black-holes a and enters enumFromTo resulting in Fig. 1.v.

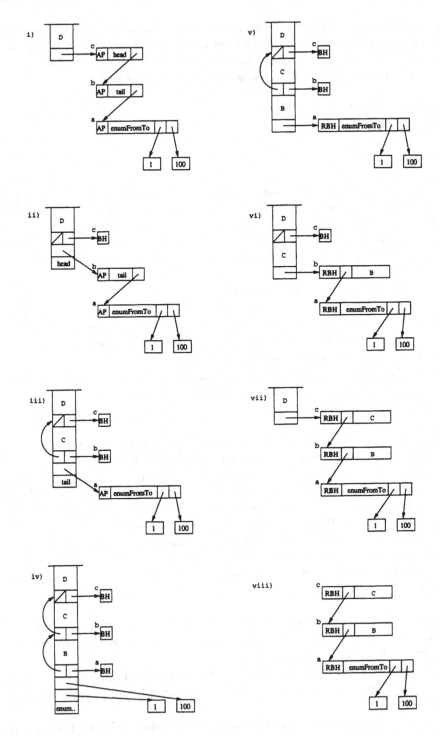

Fig. 1. Reverting Black-Holes

The stack has now been restored to its original state prior to the interrupt and execution continues as before. A similar sequence unfolds if the new evaluation enters a or b.

An obvious concern is that using this technique will somehow re-introduce the space leak that black-holing is supposed to remove. This clearly does not happen:

- Nothing is changed during normal evaluation. We use exactly the same representation and store exactly the same data as in the original STG machine with black-holing.
- The resumable black-holes generated when discarding a stack require almost exactly the same space as the original stack.
- After an interrupt occurs, every resumable black-hole contains exactly the data needed to evaluate it and so it doesn't leak space unless the original evaluation mechanism leaked space.

Despite this, we might still find that a resumable black-hole takes more space than the original updatable thunk (a thunk may take more space when evaluated). We might also find that a resumable black-hole takes *less* space than the original updatable thunk (a thunk may also take *less* space when evaluated). This is a fundamental property of lazy evaluation rather than a special property of black-holes or resumable black-holes: it also happens in naïve graph reducers which have neither.

Another concern is that the benefits of using this technique may come at a significant cost in performance or in complexity of the runtime system. Again, this does not happen:

- Since nothing is changed during normal evaluation, no overhead is imposed on programs that are not interrupted.
- When a program is interrupted, we copy stack segments into resumable black-hole objects on the heap; when a black-hole is resumed, we copy the stack segments back onto the stack. These costs are typically quite small (smaller than other runtime costs such garbage collection) and are only incurred when interrupts occur.
- The implementation is as simple as our description: it consists of a few hundred lines of C to implement the new object type and to copy stack segments into resumable black holes.

4   Catching Interrupts

The previous section describes how to pause evaluation without leaving blackholes in the heap but says nothing about what to do after evaluation has been paused. This section outlines how to catch interrupts in a programming environment (Hugs) and in the programming language itself. Only the first one has been implemented as yet.

Catching interrupts is absolutely essential in an interactive system such as Gofer [5] or Hugs: we have to be able to terminate long-running programs or programs that have entered infinite loops and continue. We have written a modified version of Hugs which uses the STG machine for evaluation. When the user interrupts an evaluation, the Hugs user interface sets a flag in the runtime system to indicate that an interrupt occurred. Every time the evaluator enters a node, it tests this flag to see whether it should terminate the current evaluation by reverting all black-holes on the update list.

To catch interrupts in (Sequential) Haskell we need to add a function like Haskell 1.3's catch function:

```
catchInterrupt :: IO a -> IO a -> IO a
```

The expression e 'catchInterrupt' h executes the expression e. If e terminates before an interrupt occurs, the result of e is returned; if an interrupt occurs before e terminates, the *handler* h is executed and the result of h is returned.

To implement this, we define a new type of frame which can be inserted in the update list. These *interrupt handler* frames contain a pointer to a handler thunk; they are added to the list when catchInterrupt is executed and removed from the list when catchInterrupt completes. When an interrupt occurs, the runtime reverts all black-holes down to the topmost interrupt handler frame, removes the interrupt handler frame and enters the handler thunk.

5   Variations

The STG machine is a very flexible architecture allowing a number of optimisations and extensions. This section describes how reverting black-holes interacts with five such optimisations and extensions.

5.1   Lazy Black-Holing

Sect. 9.3.3 of the STG paper [8] describes an optimisation of black-holing known as "lazy black-holing" which delays black-holing a thunk until the next garbage collection. When garbage collection occurs, it is a simple matter to run down the update list and black-hole any thunks which are not already black-holed. This does not affect the ability of black-holing to eliminate space leaks because the space leak does not manifest itself until the next garbage collection and so there is no harm in delaying black-holing until then. The benefit of lazy black-holing is that it avoids the extra effort required to black-hole a thunk whose evaluation completes before a garbage collection occurs.

The only thing that changes when reverting black-holes if we use lazy black-holing is that we may have to revert a thunk on the update list which hasn't been black-holed yet. Two questions arise: *should* we revert the thunk; and *can* we revert the thunk. The answer to both questions is "yes":

1. Nothing goes drastically wrong if we don't revert the thunk but we lose some laziness. That is, we discard the result of partially evaluating the thunk and have to repeat that effort if the thunk is re-entered. Worse still, we lose

an *unpredictable* amount of laziness depending on when we last black-holed thunks on the update list. To avoid these problems, we choose to revert all thunks on the update list even if they haven't been black-holed yet.

2. We might worry that a thunk on the update list could be smaller than a black-hole making it impossible to overwrite with either a resumable black-hole or an indirection to a resumable black-hole. Fortunately, this cannot happen: the system already requires that all updatable thunks are big enough to overwrite with a black-hole. This is required since we are able to black-hole all the thunks on the update list before reverting them.

5.2   The seq and strict Functions

Haskell 1.3 added the ability to force evaluation of a thunk using the (equivalent) functions **seq** and **strict** instead of by using a **case** expression. A **case** expression would have pushed a return address onto the stack but, because **seq** can be used on objects with any type (including functions), they require a different implementation. The **seq** function is implemented by pushing a "continuation" onto the stack, and adding a "SEQ frame" to the update list so that the evaluator enters the continuation correctly. If the evaluator finds a "SEQ frame" on the update list when it returns a value, it removes the frame, discards the value and enters the continuation on top of the stack.

This requires the following change to our revertible black-holing mechanism. When we encounter an exception handling frame on the stack, we create a thunk which will push a SEQ frame onto the stack, push the stack contents and resume evaluation. Since the STG machine doesn't have node types that do this already, we have to add **SEQ** nodes to the system. When a **SEQ** node is entered, the evaluator adds a SEQ frame to the update list, pushes the node's contents on the stack and enters the top node.

Fig. 2 shows how SEQ frames are reverted when executing the expression

```
let a = 1 + 2
    b = a 'seq' x
in b
```

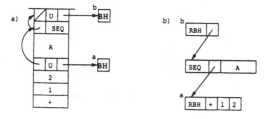

Fig. 2. Reverting SEQ Frames

Fig. 2a shows the state of the stack just before entering +. Thunks a and b have been black-holed and the update list consists of an update frame for a, a SEQ frame and an update frame for b. Frames on the update list are tagged with U for update frames and SEQ for SEQ frames.

Reverting the black-holes and SEQ frames in Fig. 2a yields Fig. 2b. The black-holes are reverted exactly as before and the SEQ frame has been turned into a SEQ node containing a pointer to a.

This isn't the only possible way of dealing with SEQ frames. An alternative is to allow resumable black-holes to contain lists of SEQ frames and fill in resumable black-holes with everything on the stack that occurs between two update frames: pending arguments, return addresses, environments, SEQ frames, etc. This avoids the cost of introducing SEQ nodes at the expense of making resumable black-holes more complex. This extra complexity is most keenly felt in the garbage collector — which is already quite complex enough!

5.3   Exception Handling

We recently extended the STG machine with an exception handling mechanism [10,11] which uses the update list to store exception handlers as well as updatees. When the evaluator finds an exception handler on the update list as it is trying to return a value, it removes the exception handler and tries again.

This requires the following change to our revertible black-holing mechanism. When we encounter an update frame on the update list, we (already) create a thunk to push an update frame onto the stack, push the stack contents and continue evaluation where it left off. Similarly, when we encounter an exception handling frame on the stack, we create a thunk to push an exception handling frame onto the stack, push the stack contents and resume evaluation. Since the STG machine doesn't have node types that do this already, we have to add CATCH nodes to the system. When a CATCH node is entered, the evaluator adds an exception handler frame to the update list, pushes the node's contents on the stack and enters the top node.

Fig. 3 shows how exception handlers are reverted when executing the expression[3]

```
let a = print 1
    b = a 'catchException' h
    c = b >> x
in y
```

Fig. 3a shows the state of the stack just before entering print. Thunks a, b and c have been black-holed and the update list consists of an update frame for a, an exception handler frame, an update frame for b and an update frame

---

[3] The expression a 'catchException' h evaluates a and returns its result; if an exception is thrown while evaluating a, then the handler h is invoked and the result of h is returned.

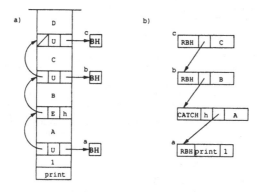

Fig. 3. Reverting Exception Handlers

for **c**. Frames on the update list are tagged with **U** for update frames and **E** for exception handler frames.

Reverting the black-holes and exception handlers in Fig. 3a, results in Fig. 3b. The black-holes are reverted exactly as before and the exception handling frame has been turned into a **CATCH** node containing the handler **h**, the application node **a** and the data **A**.

Again, we could have added support for exception handling by enriching the structure of resumable black-holes. The tradeoff here is exactly as it was with SEQ frames but since the choice is now between one complex object and three simple objects the decision to introduce a new node type isn't quite so clear.

5.4 Concurrent Haskell

The STG machine has been extended to support concurrent threads [9]. In a concurrent system, black-holing is modified as follows. We add a queue of threads to every black-hole — the "blocking queue" of the black-hole. The first time a thunk is entered, it is overwritten with a black-hole with an empty queue. If another thread tries to enter a black-hole that thread is suspended and added to the blocking queue. When evaluation of a thunk completes, its black-hole is overwritten with the value of the thunk and all threads in the blocking queue are added to the (global) queue of runnable threads.

This blocking behaviour requires the following change when reverting black-holes: when a black-hole is reverted, all threads in the blocking queue are added to the (global) queue of runnable threads. When these threads next try to execute, the first thread will enter the resumable black-hole and rebuild the stack exactly as it was when the thread was interrupted and all subsequent threads will be added to the blocking queue as before.

To catch interrupts in Concurrent Haskell [9] we need to add two things:[4]

---

[4] A full threads library might add further features, here we restrict ourselves to the minimum required to catch interrupts.

1. The ability to terminate a thread; and
2. The ability to wait for an interrupt to occur.

It is then straightforward to create threads which wait for interrupts and kill other threads when they occur. This can be combined with functions which wait for a given time period to provide timeouts as well.

To terminate a thread, we need to add thread identifiers and a function to kill a thread. The function `killThread` must revert all black-holes on the thread's update list before killing the thread.

```
data ThreadId  -- abstract
forkIO     :: IO a -> IO ThreadId
getThreadId :: IO ThreadId
killThread :: ThreadId -> IO ()
```

We also need a way of waiting for an interrupt. This requires a small change to the runtime system to maintain a list of threads waiting for interrupts and add the threads to the runnable queue when an interrupt occurs. This is a (simplified) form of how timers are currently handled.

```
waitForInterrupt :: IO ()
```

5.5 Parallel Haskell

The STG machine has been extended to run on parallel architectures [14]. Black-holes act in the same way as in Concurrent Haskell (i.e., threads block on thunks which are already being evaluated). The big change from Concurrent Haskell is that each processor only has access to a small part of the global heap; if a processor requires an object stored in another part of the graph, it must ask another processor to send it the object. If the object is already being evaluated by a processor, the request blocks until evaluation terminates.

We have not implemented resumable black-holes in Parallel Haskell but we believe that it should be straightforward since reverting the black-holes on a thread's stack is a local operation. When a thread is interrupted, all pending updates are reverted in the same way as in Concurrent Haskell. Just as threads blocked on a black-hole are moved to the queue of runnable threads in Concurrent Haskell, so blocked requests (to move an object to another processor) are moved to the queue of "runnable" requests. Note that it is very important that an object cannot be moved while it is being evaluated since we must be able to overwrite the original object with a resumable black-hole when a thread is interrupted.

Being able to interrupt a thread is particularly important in Parallel Haskell since it makes it possible to control speculative evaluation on idle processors [7]. When resources (CPU and memory) are abundant, speculative threads can be created; and when resources are scarce or poorly balanced between processors, speculative threads can be terminated. Using our revertible black-holes, terminating a thread has the effect of splitting its stack into many small parts allowing unwanted parts to be reclaimed and allowing parts required by other processors to move to the other processor.

6   Related Work

Lazy functional programs can suffer from a variety of space leaks. Whilst many of these problems can only be eliminated by modifying your program, some space leaks can be fixed in the evaluator or in the garbage collector.

One of the first such fixes was the "lazy tuple matching" space leak reported by Hughes [3]. The problem is that extracting a component of a data-structure (aka "tuple matching") is performed lazily and so the runtime system may hang onto a large data structure of which only a small component is required. Wadler showed how this could be fixed by modifying the garbage collector [15] and, more recently, Sparud showed how this could be solved by modifying the evaluator [13].

Another space leak which can be automatically plugged was accidentally introduced by "optimising" tail calls in the G-machine. This problem was identified and fixed by Jones with the introduction of black-holing [6].

Shortly after the introduction of black-holing, Runciman and Wakeling found a baffling space leak using their heap profiling tool [12]. They suspected a problem in their tool until they realised that the problem was the same one reported by Jones. Adding black-holing to their compiler removed this leak and resulted in a factor of four reduction in the cost of running a benchmark. The combination of black-holing, Wadler's fix for the "lazy tuple match" leak and fixing programming problems identified by their tool reduced the space-time cost of their program by two orders of magnitude.

Until now, the major problem with black-holing has been its incompatability with interrupts and with speculative evaluation. Mattson and Griswold [7] use "grey-holes" (a kind of revertible black-hole) to synchronize threads in a Parallel Haskell implementation but, unlike resumable black-holes, terminating a speculative thread reverts grey-holes to their original form. This suffers from the two problems listed in the introduction: it reintroduces the space leak; and it discards work. They suggest that discarding work is beneficial since the unevaluated form of the thunk is often smaller than the evaluated form but Hughes [4] suggests that the opposite is sometimes true.

Trinder et al.[14] use black-holes when moving objects from one processor to another. While the object is in transit, it is overwritten with a "revertible black-hole." If the object is rejected (perhaps because the receiver runs out of heap space), the black-hole is reverted to its original form; otherwise, the revertible black-hole acts like a normal black-hole and is updated with an indirection to the (as yeat still unevaluated) thunk on the remote processor. Like Mattson and Griswold, the black-hole may be reverted to its original form, but this doesn't cause the same problems since revertible black-holes only last long enough to successfully transfer an object from one processor to another. Their system has no need for resumable black-holes since it does not support interrupt catching and it provides task migration in preference to speculative evaluation.

More recently, Chakravarty uses a similar technique to cover communication latencies in his massively parallel STG machine [2]. Besides his different motivation (Chakravarty does not mention interrupts, killing threads or black-holing), there are some important technical differences:

- Chakravarty suspends closures (using objects like our resumable black-holes) while waiting for a value to be received from a remote processor and resumes the closure when the value arrives. Since each closure requires different sets of values from other processors, Chakravarty only suspends the topmost closure instead of reverting all closures currently under evaluation. If the program terminates successfully, all suspended closures will have been restarted.
- In contrast, we are concerned with interrupting normal sequential evaluation: closures are suspended when an interrupt is received and restarted only if and when they are needed by the interrupt handler. Since interrupts affect the entire execution, we suspend all closures which are currently under evaluation by walking down the update list. Most resumable black-holes are not required by the interrupt handler and are quickly garbage collected.

In short, Chakravarty suspends closures which are waiting to be sent input while we suspend closures which are waiting for their output to be (re)demanded.

Looking farther afield, similar problems and similar solutions are found whenever computer scientists want to cancel speculative evaluation or handle exceptions.

- The most important feature of exception and interrupt handling mechanisms is the ability to specify how to clean up shared state. In imperative languages, is necessary to write your own cleanup code since the language cannot be expected to know how to restore your program to a consistent state. This is not necessary in the pure subset of Haskell (i.e., the part of Haskell where black-holing is used) because the the lack of side-effects limits the problems to those introduced by the implementation. In the imperative subset of Haskell, the programmer must write their own cleanup code — we recently added exception-handling to Haskell for this purpose [10, 11].
- Multiscalar processors perform a considerable amount of speculative evaluation and must clean up their internal state when a speculative evaluation is terminated. For example, Breach et al. [1] describe an architecture which tracks dependencies between different stages of the processor. Terminating one stage automatically terminates those stages which have used values produced by the terminating stage. Like our technique, cleanup is performed automatically; unlike our approach work done by the stage is discarded to undo side-effects (and also to conserve resources).

7   Conclusions

The Spineless Tagless G-Machine is an efficient graph-reduction machine which stores the spine of the graph on the stack (rather than storing it on the heap) and which uses black-holing to avoid the resulting space leak. This optimisation comes at a cost: we can't resume interrupted evaluations because black-holing assumes that thunks are only entered once. We have shown that this problem can be resolved efficiently by restoring the spine of the graph to the heap and we have outlined how it interacts with a range of extensions to the language and to the implementation.

Acknowledgements We are grateful to Simon Peyton Jones, Simon Marlow and John Peterson for comments on our approach and on this paper and to Paul Hudak and Greg Hager whose interest in programming robots in Haskell helped motivate this work. We are also grateful to the anonymous referees for their interesting and useful feedback — we found the pointers to related work outside the Haskell community particularly intriguing.

References

1. S. Breach, T.N. Vijaykumar, and G.S. Sohi. The Anatomy of the Register File in a Multiscalar Processor. In *27th. Annual International Symposium on Microarchitecture (MICRO-27)*, pages 181–190. ACM press, 1994.
2. M. Chakravarty. Lazy Thread and Task Creation in Parallel Graph-Reduction. In C. Clack, A. Davie, and K. Hammond, editors, *Proc. 9th. International Workshop on the Implementation of Functional Languages (IFL'97), St Andrews, Scotland, September 1997*, volume 1467 of *LNCS*, pages 231–249. Springer-Verlag, 1998.
3. R.J.M. Hughes. *The Design and Implementation of Programming Languages*. PhD thesis, Oxford University, 1984.
4. R.J.M. Hughes. Parallel Functional Languages use Less Space. In *Symposium on Lisp and Functional Programming*, Austin, Texas, 1984.
5. M. Jones. The Implementation of the Gofer Functional Programming System. Research Report YALEU/DCS/RR-1030, Yale University, May 1994.
6. R.E. Jones. Tail Recursion Without Space Leaks. *Journal of Functional Programming*, 2(1):73–79, January 1992.
7. J.S. Mattson Jr. and W.G. Griswold. Speculative Evaluation for Parallel Graph Reduction. In *Parallel Architectures and Compilation Techniques (PACT'94)*, pages 331–334. North-Holland, August 1994.
8. S.L. Peyton Jones. Implementing Lazy Functional Languages on Stock Hardware: the Spineless Tagless G-Machine. *Journal of Functional Programming*, 2(2):127–202, April 1992.
9. S.L. Peyton Jones, A.D. Gordon, and S.O. Finne. Concurrent Haskell. In *Proc. 23rd. ACM Symposium on Principles of Programming Languages (POPL'96)*, pages 295–308, St Petersburg Beach, Florida, January 1996. ACM Press.
10. S.L. Peyton Jones, A. Reid, A. Hoare, S. Marlow, and F. Henderson. A Semantics for Imprecise Exceptions. In *Proc. 1999 ACM Conference on Programming Language Design and Implementation (PLDI'99)*, To Appear, May 1999.
11. A. Reid. Handling Exceptions in Haskell. Research Report YALEU/DCS/RR-1175, Yale University, Department of Computer Science, August 1998.
12. C. Runciman and D. Wakeling. Heap Profiling of Lazy Functional Programs. *Journal of Functional Programming*, 3(2):217–246, April 1993.
13. J. Sparud. Fixing Some Space Leaks Without a Garbage Collector. In *Proc. 1993 ACM Conference on Functional Programming Languages and Computer Architecture (FPLCA'93)*, 1993.
14. P.W. Trinder, K. Hammond, J.S. Mattson Jr., A.S. Partridge, and S.L. Peyton Jones. GUM: a Portable Parallel Implementation of Haskell. In *Proc. 1996 ACM Conference on Programming Language Design and Implementation (PLDI'96)*, Philadelphia, pages 78–88, May 1996.
15. P.L. Wadler. Fixing a Space Leak With a Garbage Collector. *Software — Practice and Experience*, 17(9):595–608, 1987.

Towards a Haskell/Java Connection*

Claus Reinke

Department of Computer Science
University of Nottingham
University Park
Nottingham NG7 2RD, UK
czr@cs.nott.ac.uk

Abstract. This paper reports on preliminary work on a connection between Haskell and Java, with the goal of making software components written in Java available to Haskell programmers. We discuss several approaches, but find the Java platform surprisingly closed against other languages. We decide to use an indirect approach, based on proposed native interfaces for Haskell and Java, and describe this in more detail. A side-by-side overview of Hugs and the Java Virtual Machine highlights some similarities of the implementation designs. Both systems also have similar problems and solutions with respect to foreign language interfaces. Finally, we relate the proposed connection between Haskell and Java to other recent work on component-based programming in Haskell.

1 Introduction

One of the major problems of functional languages is that most research projects and their budgets do not support the man-power necessary for the development and maintenance of the large collection of libraries that makes a language useful in practice. Connecting Haskell [12] to the popular Java platform [15] promises access not only to an increasing number of portable libraries, including graphical user interface components, but also to large scale components written in the Java language. In this paper, we investigate the options for such a connection and describe an approach based on the native interfaces of both languages. This approach has been used for a prototype implementation that uses Hugs and Sun's Java Development Kit, but employs proposed standards for the native interfaces to improve portability. The preliminary work described here can be seen as complementary to recent work on a Haskell/COM interface [9].

The work described in this paper was triggered by a discussion of the state of art in graphical user interface libraries for Haskell, specifically those available for use within our current project [19]. Despite the abundance of high-quality designs and implementations (for an overview, see Noble's thesis [23]), it seemed questionable whether industrial users of Haskell could be convinced to learn and use what to them must appear as highly non-standard and non-ported libraries.

---

* The work described in this paper is sponsored by an EPSRC grant GR/L34761 for the project on "First-class modules for component-based programming"

H. Hammond, T. Davie, and C. Clack (Eds.): IFL'98, LNCS 1595, pp. 200–215, 1999.
© Springer-Verlag Berlin Heidelberg 1999

Among the alternatives considered were the graphical user interface framework Haggis [8], Tk-based solutions derived from TkGofer [5, 7] and COM-based interfaces to existing user interface libraries [9, 20].

Haggis in its full glory was judged as rather heavy-weight, leading to a search for light-weight alternatives. A Tk-based approach would be portable while a COM-based approach would allow familiar GUI libraries to be used. Despite ongoing efforts to provide support for COM on non-Microsoft platforms, we are not aware of any portable, COM-based GUI libraries or even of platform-independent COM interfaces for GUI programming (many distributed COM applications delegate user interfaces to workstations running Microsoft Windows, running only server functionality on non-Microsoft platforms [21]).

In comparison, Java [15] provides a set of graphical user interface libraries that have already been ported to various platforms. While the libraries may still have some shortcomings, they are actively developed to match user requirements, and the Java language itself is currently so popular that knowledge of the language and its libraries seems to be imperative for software companies.

Our initial motivation for working on a connection between Haskell and Java was that we wanted to know whether Java's GUI libraries could be made available to Haskell programmers. However, closer investigation of the Java platform revealed that two of its most attractive features are its portability and a large, still growing collection of libraries. According to feature articles on the Java web site [15], the number of application programmer interfaces (APIs) in the Java developer kit (JDK) alone has grown from 200 in 1995 to 1600 today.

If we can make Java components available to Haskell programmers, we give them access to this growing collection of portable libraries on an increasing number of platforms. We can thus share the results of the enormous development efforts that go into those libraries, graphical user interfaces being just one example. A high-level connection between Haskell and Java would not only enable software reuse on a large scale, it would also fit in nicely with the major topic of our current project, component-based programming.

In this paper, we are mainly concerned with an investigation of the options for implementing such a connection. The choice of Haskell comes from the project context of our work, but much of the discussion should be useful for other functional languages, too. We outline some of the possible approaches towards a Haskell/Java connection in Sect. 2, describe our own approach in more detail in Sect. 3 and 4, and discuss the context of our work in Sect. 5. We summarise our preliminary conclusions in Sect. 6.

2   Overview and Options

For the rest of this text, we fix our Haskell implementation to be Hugs [14], commenting on portability issues where appropriate.

Fig. 1 gives side by side overviews of Hugs and a typical Java implementation, focusing on the abstraction levels that are layered on top of the implementation platform. Programs ($P_{Haskell}$, P_{Java}) are first translated from source code into

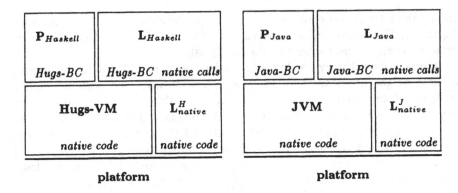

Fig. 1. Haskell/Hugs versus Java/JVM

bytecode (BC) for a virtual machine (VM), and then executed by an implementation of this machine. The virtual machine is implemented as a bytecode interpreter written in the native code of the implementation platform. Library code ($L_{Haskell}$, L_{Java}) is basically treated as other source code, but may include calls to native libraries (e.g., for input/output and graphics) – we assume here that all native calls are hidden in library code. Such native calls are identified in the compilation phase and the necessary native libraries are (dynamically) linked with the native code for the virtual machine.

Note that Hugs bytecode is an internal format, i.e., bytecode compiler and bytecode interpreter form an integrated system. In contrast, bytecode compiler and virtual machine are separated on the Java side, with a standard representation of the intermediate bytecode in Java class files (see Chapter 4 of the JVM specification [15]). On both sides, the intermediate interpretation level can be eliminated by compiling to native code.

Fig. 1 shows some similarities in the implementation designs, but more importantly, it provides us with a roadmap that suggests several possible approaches for a connection between Haskell and Java.

2.1 Bilingual Interprocess Communication

The obvious approach would be to establish both systems side by side on the same implementation platform and to let Haskell and Java programs communicate via some form of interprocess communication. In the given context, a Java process would have to act as a server to Haskell clients.

Communication with a Server Program Written in Java

In a first variant, the Java server program would be written from scratch, an approach that has been used successfully with various graphical user interface libraries for functional languages (e.g., TkGofer [5]).

There is no direct match of the communication capabilities of the languages in question: Java comes equipped with libraries for binary and Unicode input/output as well as for networking across sockets. In contrast, support for Unicode in Haskell is limited to the language report [12] and the Chalmers implementation [2]. Some Haskell implementations offer libraries for binary or socket input/output, but they are not yet part of the standard libraries [13].

Beyond these minor problems, the situation is not quite as simple as for a connection to Tcl/Tk [6] – Tcl is essentially an untyped language executed by an interpreter that provides direct access to its execution mechanism by means of an *eval* procedure. Therefore, a Tcl/Tk server program can consist of a simple loop that accepts Tcl/Tk commands from an input stream, passes them on to eval, and forwards the results to an output stream.

In contrast, it is rather difficult to reuse functionality of a Java implementation for a server program. Java is typed and separates program execution into compilation to bytecode and interpretation of this code – a Java compiler may not even be available in the Java runtime environment. As a consequence, the Java server would have to be a full blown interpreter for a yet to be defined communication protocol. This might still be practicable if we restrict our attention to Java's graphical user interface classes, but it becomes less so if the protocol should be expressive enough to give access to arbitrary Java components.

The task of writing a Java interpreter in Java could be simplified if at least parts of the Java runtime system could be reused for the server program. The Java core reflection API, introduced in version 1.1 of Java, partially addresses this problem [18], but its implementations have a reputation of not being very efficient.

Using Existing Protocols for Communication

Another possibility to reduce coding efforts on the Java side is to use communication protocols that are already supported by Java libraries.

If the Haskell clients would send Java bytecode (in the standard class file format), the Java server loop could be simple: receive the class file, load the class from memory at runtime, and call some start method in the newly created class. This approach would give access to the complete Java language, including all of its standard libraries. However, it would place on the Haskell side the burden of constructing standard-compliant Java class files to realise the requested calls to Java libraries, and it would not address the issue of receiving results.

A more symmetric approach could be built on top of Java's object serialisation [18], which enables the encoding of objects into streams of bytes and the reconstruction of objects from such streams. Based on object serialisation and communication via sockets, Java already supports a protocol for remote method invocation (RMI) [18], which would seem just the right tool to make calls to the Java side. However, Java's RMI support is (currently) explicitly restricted to intra-language communication. Both partners in the RMI protocol are assumed to be Java objects, which means that a client library written in Haskell would have to pretend to be a JVM making RMI requests.

RMI offers both a protocol and a data interchange format, but its disadvantages seem comparable to those of sending class files. A heavy burden is placed on the Haskell side: construction and interpretation of standard-compliant serialised objects and implementation of the RMI protocol. On the Java side, adapter code would have to be written to prepare Java library code for use via RMI.

At an even higher and language-independent level, the Java platform has been extended to support Object Request Brokers (ORBs) according to the Common Object Request Broker Architecture (CORBA) [11] standard (compare Java IDL [18]). Using the Internet Inter-ORB Protocol (IIOP), requests and replies can be exchanged between Java ORBs and ORBs supporting other languages. If a CORBA IDL binding for Haskell was available (a mapping between CORBA's Interface Definition Language and Haskell), a Haskell ORB could be implemented and used to relate requests from Haskell programs to Java objects via IIOP and a Java ORB.

2.2   Targeting the Java Platform

A second approach would be to build one the systems on top of the other. For instance, Java or the JVM could be used as an implementation platform for Haskell, by writing a Haskell interpreter in Java or by compiling Haskell source code to bytecode for the JVM. In both cases, access to Java libraries would be simplified, as either the interpreter running Haskell programs or the executables generated from them would themselves run on an instance of the JVM. In other words, Java or its bytecode would be the native code of such implementations.

The dual approach of implementing Java on top of Haskell would not help with our library problem. To begin with, calling a Java bytecode interpreter written in Haskell to get access to the Java libraries does not seem to be the most promising solution. Worse than that, the non-portable native parts of the Java libraries, the parts that need to be reimplemented for every new platform, would have to be implemented in Haskell!

To our knowledge, there is currently only one project investigating the compilation of Haskell to Java virtual machine code [26, 27]. This particular project focuses on "whether Java processors could be programmed with lazy functional languages in the context of embedded applications", trying to reuse the implementation platform instead of the Java libraries built on top of it. However, there are similar projects for Standard ML [3] and for Scheme [4] that explicitly address the issue of calling Java from the functional language.

This approach is, in principle, quite promising as it not only alleviates the inter-language calling problems but also allows functional programs, or at least the bytecode generated from them, to be executed wherever a Java virtual machine is available. Unfortunately, the experiences reported for the first Haskell to Java bytecode compiler hint at serious performance problems, some of which seem to be of a fundamental nature. In other words, the Java virtual machine is designed specifically for the needs of Java programs and shows certain deficiencies when used for bytecode generated from Haskell programs. Wakeling

[26, 27] lists difficulties with implementing tail-calls and high costs of memory allocation/reclamation as the main issues.

2.3   Accessing Parts of the Java Platform Directly

Finally, Fig. 1 shows some of the internal structure of the Java platform, suggesting that parts of it could be accessed directly.

Our original goal was to profit from the development efforts put into ports of the Java libraries to a variety of hardware platforms. The outcome of these efforts are the native parts of the Java libraries. Unfortunately, neither the division of labour nor the interface between the Java and native parts of the Java libraries is standardised. Therefore, any attempt to use the native parts of these libraries directly would be unreliable and vendor-specific at best, not to mention the need to recode the portable parts of the libraries in Haskell.

JavaSoft has tried to establish the Java native interface specification (JNI) [17] as a standard for the interaction of Java with native code and of native code with the JVM (for an overview of JNI, see Sect. 3.1). The purpose of JNI is to ease the task of porting Java code that uses native methods, and to simplify the development and maintenance of native libraries.

There is no requirement that JNI should be the only native interface supported by a given JVM, so the argument regarding the accessibility of the native parts of the Java libraries remains untouched. However, part of JNI provides us with a standard interface of native code to the JVM. This means that we can directly invoke and control an instance of the JVM without needing to write any server code in Java!

JNI offers almost the full functionality of a complete Java server, with a standard protocol and with the server functionality built in an increasing number of JVM implementations. Communication according to some protocol is replaced by direct calls to JNI functions, arbitrary Java components can be loaded and used using JNI, and efficiency was an explicit design goal for JNI, too.

2.4   Summary

The major problem with most of the approaches discussed in this section is that the Java platform was originally designed as a closed system, with connections only to other instances of the JVM, running other Java programs. The major reason for this was the intended platform independence of Java: any references to non-Java entities would potentially compromise the portability of Java.

Stressing portability in favour of interoperability might have been a valid strategy in a world in which all software was written in Java, but in practice it meant that cooperations between Java and non-Java software were less straightforward than necessary. Native interfaces were unofficial, non-portable and vendor-specific extensions of the Java platform, leaving programmers hardly any options but to establish some low-level communication protocol with non-Java software or to maintain various versions of their interface code.

Using the JVM as an implementation platform for Haskell is a promising medium-term approach, offering more than just an interface between Haskell and Java (once the efficiency problems are solved). In the context of our current project, we are tied to existing implementations, namely Hugs and GHC, but David Wakeling has already expressed interest in exploring the possibility of extending his implementations with an interface between Haskell and Java.

JNI and Java IDL are fairly recent additions to the Java platform. They were added in the development process from Java to Java 2 (formerly code-named JDK 1.2) in order to address the problems of integrating Java code with software written in other languages. Both technologies would allow us to make Java components available to Haskell programmers.

Using CORBA and its IIOP facility would not establish a direct connection between Haskell and Java (all Haskell- or Java-specifics would be masked out by the mapping to CORBA's IDL). With the extra translations and the indirect communications involved, it also seems to be a rather heavyweight approach if the main interest is in making Java libraries available to Haskell programmers. However, with the prospect of an industry-standard, language-independent interprocess communication facility in mind, an investigation of a CORBA IDL binding for Haskell would be a worthwhile project in its own right. The developers of HaskellDirect have given strong indications that they are interested in pursuing this idea as a natural complement to their COM IDL binding [9].

For our specific problem, we have chosen JNI as our entrypoint into the Java platform, as this approach promises the most direct route to a short-term solution. At the time of writing, the Haskell language still lacks a standard native interface, but support for native interfaces in Haskell implementations is quite advanced – various implementations exist and are tested, and there is at least one proposal for a standard foreign function interface for Haskell [25]. On top of the raw foreign function interfaces, there is even support for parameter and result marshalling [24, 9], providing a functioning, though not yet stable starting point for the Haskell side of the connection.

3   Native Interfaces

There are two major motivations for extending Java or Haskell with native interfaces: firstly, programmers sometimes need to call native code simply because it would be impracticable to recode the functionality provided by this code. Reasons include performance issues, access to platform-dependent services (e.g., hardware devices) or just the costs of porting existing code. The second motivation arises from the need to embed Java or Haskell in existing applications, so that each component of the complete product can be coded in the most suitable language. An extreme example are "Java-enabled" web-browsers where not individual Java programs, but complete implementations of the JVM form the components that need to be integrated into applications written in native code.

3.1   JNI – The Java Native Interface

JNI [17, 10] is an attempt to standardise the native interfaces that were already present in the major Java implementations. It defines how native code implementations are associated with Java method declarations that use the "native" keyword, it specifies an interface through which native methods can access JVM functionality, and it defines entrypoints into JVM libraries that can be used to create instances of JVMs from native code (the Invocation API).

For our present purposes, the last two parts are most relevant – basically, we want to turn Hugs (or the executable produced by a Haskell compiler) into a Java-enabled application. In other words, we need to be able to create an instance of the Java virtual machine and we need access to its functionality so that we may load and execute Java bytecode. Although not inherently interpreted, the JVM is specified as an abstract machine that loads its instructions in the form of class files containing bytecode at runtime (at startup or later). As a consequence, native code needs access to JVM functionality in order to link to dynamically loaded Java methods.

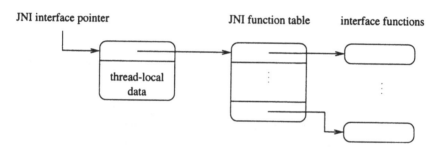

Fig. 2. JNI – interface pointer and function table

Fig. 2 depicts the basic organisation of the Java native interface. It is intensionally similar to a COM interface, but note again that it represents an interface to the JVM, not to individual Java objects. The interface functions enable programs to get JNI version information, to find and load class files, to throw or handle exceptions, to create and access objects, and to register native methods (see the JNI specification [17] for a complete list). All interface functions are called via a JNI interface pointer, which is passed as an additional parameter to native methods. In the case of native code calling Java, an interface pointer has to be obtained explicitly by creating an instance of the JVM.

The basic procedure to invoke a JVM and to call a static Java method named m with signature m_{sig} in a class named c is as follows (ignoring the error handling required at each step):

1. Construct the initialisation structure for a JVM.
2. Create an instance of the JVM, and obtain an interface pointer.
3. Find and load the Java class c, and obtain a pointer to the class object c_{obj}.

4. Get the method ID m_{id} for the method m with the type signature m_{sig} with respect to the class object c_{obj} (m_{sig} is used to resolve method overloading).
5. Call the static method, using the class object c_{obj} and the method ID m_{id}.
6. Destroy the JVM instance.

To access dynamically loaded or allocated Java objects, native code has to ask the JVM for object references or for method and field IDs (e.g., the method ID returned in step 4). Such IDs are valid until the corresponding (class) object is unloaded and allow the cost of dynamic lookup to be shared by several consecutive method calls or field accesses.

As Java is a language with implicit memory management, the JNI has to mediate between the JVM garbage collector and the native code on the validity of references to Java objects. In an attempt to keep this implicit, all object references passed to or returned from native methods are classified as *local references*, which means that they are valid until the native method returns. To modify this default behaviour, the native code can explicitly free local references or turn them into *global references*. Global and local references can be used interchangeably, but global references have to be freed explicitly in the native code.

3.2 GreenCard – A Foreign Function Interface Preprocessor for Haskell

The issues and solutions for foreign function interfaces are quite similar for Haskell in general, and readers familiar with the native interface for Hugs, especially with the Hugs server API (see the online documentation for Hugs [14]), will have noted even stronger similarities.

At the time of writing, Haskell does not have a standard foreign function interface, although draft proposals exist [25]. However, most Haskell implementations do allow calls to native code written in C, and a tool named Green Card [24] has been developed that allows the necessary non-standard Haskell code for several implementations to be generated from a single specification. Green Card also alleviates the task of converting data structures between Haskell and C (a process known as *marshalling*) and, via further Haskell extensions, addresses the issues of garbage collection in the presence of foreign functions and objects.

The input to Green Card is a Haskell module, extended with Green Card directives (lines prefixed with '%'). The basic directive is a procedure specification, consisting of four parts:

%fun   gives the name and Haskell type of the function
%call   specifies the translations of Haskell parameters into their
         C representations
%code   gives the procedure body in C
%result specifies the translations of C representations of results
         back into Haskell values

The full list of directives is described in the manual [24]. The most notable omission here are the data interface schemes (DISs), which describe the translations between Haskell objects and their C representations. These translations are needed for parameter and result marshalling.

From the annotated Haskell module, Green Card usually generates a plain Haskell module for one of the currently supported implementations (Hugs, GHC, and nhc13) as well as a C module. The generated Haskell code follows the implementation-specific convention for foreign function calls and takes care of parameter and result marshalling, using both the user code and a module of standard data interface schemes. In some cases, no separate C module is needed because the Haskell code can be linked with existing libraries.

A potential alternative to Green Card would be H/Direct [9], a development of Green Card that uses a standard interface definition language (IDL) instead of extended Haskell type signatures to specify foreign function interfaces. It also supports COM interfaces, and as we noted earlier, the JNI has been designed with the option of turning it into a COM interface in mind.

4   Connecting Haskell and Java

Based on the native interfaces of Haskell and Java, we can outline the implementation of a basic, low-level connection between the two languages. Actually, there are at least two ways to think about such a connection, as exemplified by the following basic scenarios:

Haskell-centric a Haskell programmer wants to make use of software components written in Java, e.g., in order to extend an application with a graphical user interface. In this case, the Haskell program would be in control, making occasional calls to the Java side.

Java-centric a Java programmer wants to write parts of an application in Haskell, e.g., in order to prototype the functionality behind a graphical user interface specified in Java. In this case, control over the combined application would be effected from the Java side, and certain events in the user interface would cause Haskell code to be called.

Both scenarios require essentially similar features, but the different emphasis may lead to different implementations. The Java-centric scenario, e.g., makes fewer requirements on the Java side, which would mainly use native methods to call out to some Haskell code. The Java-side invocation API would not be used, but the Haskell side would have to provide access to Haskell code from foreign languages. Basic means to call Haskell code from C exist (e.g., the Hugs Server API), and better support for this is under development [25], but at the time of writing, our own experiments have focussed on the Haskell-centric scenario, so we will only discuss this part here.

The basic idea is to use the invocation API in Java's native interface to access JVM functionality. In practice, the style of interaction is rather indirect (see Fig. 3): the Haskell code calls C code, which uses the JNI to invoke an instance of

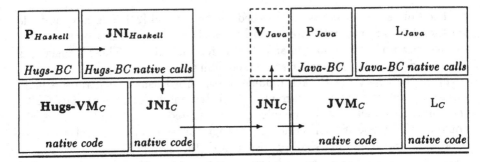

Fig. 3. Using JNI to call Java from Haskell

the JVM, which is then instructed to load and execute Java code. On the Java side, the effect of the JNI calls is to create a virtual Java program at runtime, which can then access the complete Java platform. On the Haskell side, a Haskell library hides some of the indirections and low-level details from the programmer, who can think almost directly in terms of using (virtual) Java code to access Java functionality. The Haskell and native libraries that provide access to the JNI are generated from a common source using Green Card to avoid dependencies on the language extensions of any particular Haskell implementation.

4.1 Preliminary Experience

Following the ideas outlined in this paper, a prototypical Green Card library has been developed that enables Haskell to call Java via JNI[1]. Although our initial idea was to provide Haskell programs with access to the GUI facilities of Java, the connection is fairly general. The mapping of JNI functionality to a Haskell library is not unique, but requires several design decisions. For instance, we have chosen to keep JNI interface pointers, and thus the whole indirection table for interface functions, implicit. Small wrapper functions provide static links for Green Card and make the indirect calls via the interface pointer.

Searching for classes and methods by name is expensive, and the JNI separates most operations into lookup and use to enable caching of the information gained by lookups. The wrappers for the corresponding JNI functions could try to handle this caching transparently, but we prefer to expose the full functionality to Haskell functions, similar to the situation with files and file handles.

Method and field IDs remain valid only as long as their respective (class) objects are loaded into the JVM. To avoid unloading of classes or disposal of objects for which IDs are still in use, references to the objects in question have to be kept. These references must be freed explicitly if they are no longer used directly or indirectly (via method or field IDs). Haskell extensions used by Green

---

[1] The Haskell/JNI prototype is available from http://www.cs.nott.ac.uk/~czr/JNI/

Card allow finalizer code to be attached to foreign objects, which enables us to hide the details of reference counting, but so far we are not counting method and field IDs as implicit references to their objects.

Our design decisions seem to offer an acceptable compromise between low-level control and code readability, and functional abstraction can be used to hide even more of the low-level details. Typically, this leads to a two-phase structure of Haskell programs that use the JNI: the first phase performs class loading and method lookup, whereas the second phase uses the methods as if the I/O monad had been replaced with a Java monad (Appendix A shows a fractal tree example from the Haskell/JNI web site). The main inconvenience of using JNI seems to be the inability to create subclasses on the client side, a feature heavily used in Java code. As a consequence, adapter code has to be written in Java to create such subclasses and to make them available to Haskell clients.

Apart from that, the basic connection turned out to be directly useful even without higher levels of abstraction built on top of it. For the small example programs we have tested so far, the subjective efficiency is reasonable on a SUN SPARCstation 5, and good on a 350 MHz Pentium II PC. Due to the caching of information gained by dynamic method lookup, even frequent calls to Java methods (as in the recursively computed tree graphic) seem to cause no problems. As expected, the same Java and Haskell code can be used on both platforms.

Although it would be possible to organise the execution of Java code at a low level of detail, e.g., to control the composition of a user interface step by step from the Haskell side, we advocate to organise the cooperation of Haskell and Java programs around larger components. The intention is to facilitate modularity and to keep the interface between Haskell and Java small. In our tree graphic example, the Haskell code is completely unaffected when a quit-button or a print-dialogue are added to the Java GUI. Similarly, the Java code (which mainly adds double-buffering to the Frame class in the abstract windowing toolkit AWT) can be reused to display two-dimensional line graphics from other Haskell programs.

Ideally, mixed applications would consist of separately reusable Haskell and Java components, with some additional glue code. It is too early to say whether such a separation will be possible for larger projects, or whether a tighter integration of Haskell and Java will be necessary. However, it is already obvious that most of the glue code should be generated from Java class files. We are experimenting with several possible mappings of Java packages, classes and objects to Haskell structures (such as modules, type classes and first-class structures).

Other complications include safe usage of JNI functionality in the presence of exceptions and overloading. Most calls to JNI functions have to be accompanied by checks for error conditions and exceptions, and errors and exceptions have to be represented and handled on the Haskell side. Moreover, C does not support overloading, which means that the JNI uses a mixture of type encoding in function names, union types for parameters, and method signatures expressed as strings. Type safe usage of this unsafe interface would be simplified by generating Haskell wrapper code for Java classes, but finding good encapsulations of JNI and Java functionality in Haskell libraries needs some further experimentation.

5   Related Work

Recently, work has been done on lifting the foreign language interface problem in Haskell from the low-level aspects of how to call a C function to the higher-level aspects of connecting software components. Most notably, Haskell programs have been used to script components in Microsoft's component object model COM [20], and the Green Card Haskell preprocessor is being developed into H/Direct, which is based on a proposed standard foreign function interface for Haskell [9, 25]. H/Direct still provides for a Haskell/C interface, but generates the necessary stub code from specifications in a standard, language-independent interface definition language (IDL). Using the same IDL which is used for the specification of COM components, H/Direct allows Haskell to call COM components independently of the language in which they were written, and it will make it possible to write COM components in Haskell.

Originally, COM was a language-independent but platform-specific standard. After some years of porting work at Software AG [1], Microsoft has recently announced increased efforts to support COM on non-Windows platforms (see press archive at [21]). Apart from increasing the usability of H/Direct, this move could, in the long run, open new options for a Haskell/Java connection. On Microsoft platforms, it should be possible to use the Haskell/COM interface for a Haskell/Java connection, since Microsoft provides a mapping from Java objects to COM components and back [22]. There were two reasons for not discussing this option in Sect. 2, each rendering it non-portable at the moment: missing support for COM on non-Windows platforms and missing support for a Java/COM interface in non-Microsoft JVMs. This issue is discussed briefly in the introduction of [17], and although there is no immediate sign of COM being adapted as an interface to Java objects, the JNI itself is designed so that it can become a COM interface to the Java virtual machine.

Oddly enough, the status of JNI as a standard native interface for Java is at the heart of an ongoing lawsuit between Sun Microsystems and Microsoft (both companies provide information about this lawsuit on their Java web pages [15, 16]). Following a preliminary injunction in the court case (November 17, 1998), Microsoft added support for JNI to its latest implementations of the JVM. In any case, other JVMs are available for Microsoft platforms that do support JNI, but this new development seems to strengthen the status of JNI.

In Sect. 2.1, we mentioned Java's language-specific remote method invocation protocol (RMI), and we noted that Java now offers support for the common object request broker architecture CORBA [11], which evolved from a language-independent remote method invocation protocol. RMI has traditionally been positioned as a Java-specific competitor to CORBA, but it is currently being extended so that it can be seen as a specialized Java ORB (see the RMI-IIOP documentation at the Java Developer Connection site [15]).

CORBA is currently the major alternative to COM, as far as software component architectures are concerned, and it would certainly be worthwhile to explore the possibility of CORBA support for Haskell. In a recent discussion on the Haskell mailing-list, the developers of H/Direct pointed out that their tool would be a suitable starting point, because CORBA interfaces are also described using an IDL, albeit not the same one as that used in COM. But then, CORBA support for Haskell would have to include object request brokers (ORBs) for Haskell objects, which raises the issue that CORBA is language- and platform-independent, but paradigm-specific: what exactly are the objects in Haskell programs?

6   Conclusions and Future Work

We have reported on our preliminary work towards a connection between Haskell and Java, with an emphasis on enabling Haskell programmers to use software components written in Java. As we describe work in progress, we have focussed on a discussion of options, issues, and solutions. Our prototype implementation allows us to load Java classes interactively and to call Java methods in a Hugs session. The implementation of the interface depends on a complex collection of software components, which led to an unexpected number of external issues, showing that some of the technologies are still under development.

Having established a low-level connection, the next steps should concern higher-level aspects, such as generating Haskell wrapper code from Java packages to automate the class loading and method lookup phase. This would also help to ensure type-safety of method calls across the JNI. Due to our initial goal to access the Java GUI libraries, the use of components written in Haskell from the Java side has also not yet received full attention, but the low-level part of this direction can be addressed by a combination of native Java methods (as supported by JNI) and the proposed foreign function interface for Haskell [25].

The proposed connection to Java fits in nicely with other recent work on foreign function interfaces for Haskell. In the long run, our work might be integrated into language-independent frameworks, such as Haskell/COM or Haskell/CORBA interfaces. However, the specifics of a connection between Haskell and Java help to demonstrate some unresolved issues in multilingual, component-based programming. This is a silent, but radical change in software development practice that has to be supported in language designs and in software development theory. It remains to be seen whether the old wars between programming paradigms will start again at the level of component architectures. Currently, the main competitors are object-oriented, and in an industry that largely ignores alternative paradigms, this biased view of language independence has gone unchallenged.

Component-based programming needs to be consolidated as a programming pattern within functional languages, using a definition of components that adequately describes both functional and external components. A core topic of our current project [19] is to investigate the idea of first-class modules as a basis for component-based programming, and although the work so far has focussed on functional components, we have good reason to believe that the language extensions needed for first-class modules could also provide an adequate representation of external components.

References

1. Software AG. EntireX DCOM Release. http://www.softwareag.com/corporat/solutions/entirex/, January 1999.
2. L. Augustsson. The HBC compiler. http://www.cs.chalmers.se/ augustss/hbc/hbc.html, January 1999.
3. N. Benton, A. Kennedy, and G. Russell. Compiling Standard ML to Java Bytecodes. In *Proc. 1998 International Conference on Functional Programming (ICFP '98)*, Baltimore, pages 129–140, September 1998.
4. P. Bothner. Kawa – Compiling Dynamic Languages to the Java VM. In *Proc. Usenix Conference in New Orleans*, June 1998.
5. K. Claessen, T. Vullinghs, and E. Meijer. Structuring Graphical Paradigms in TkGofer. In *Proc. 1997 International Conference on Functional Programming (ICFP '97)*, June 1997.
6. Tcl/Tk Consortium. Home Page. http://www.tclconsortium.org/, 1999.
7. C.B. Dornan. Tcl + Haskell = TclHaskell. In *Proc. 1998 Glasgow FP Group Workshop*, Pitlochry, Scotland, September 1998. see also http://www.dcs.gla.ac.uk/~nww/TkHaskell/TkHaskell.html.
8. S.O. Finne and S.L. Peyton Jones. Composing Haggis. In *Proc. 5th. Eurographics Workshop on Programming Paradigms for Computer Graphics*. Springer-Verlag, September 1995.
9. S.O. Finne, D. Leijen, E. Meijer, and S.L. Peyton Jones. H/Direct: A Binary Foreign Language Interface for Haskell. In *Proc. 1998 International Conference on Functional Programming, (ICFP '98)*, Baltimore, 1998.
10. R. Gordon. *Essential JNI: Java Native Interface.* Prentice Hall PTR, March 1998. ISBN 0-13-679895-0.
11. Object Management Group. OMG Home Page. http://www.omg.org/, 1999.
12. J. C. Peterson, K. Hammond, L. Augustsson, B. Boutel, F. W. Burton, J. Fasel, A. D. Gordon, R. J. M. Hughes, P. Hudak, T. Johnsson, M. P. Jones, E. Meijer, S. L. Peyton Jones, A. Reid, and P. L. Wadler. *Report on the Non-Strict Functional Language, Haskell, Version 1.4*, Yale University, 1997. Available at http://haskell.org.
13. K. Hammond, J. C. Peterson, L. Augustsson, B. Boutel, F. W. Burton, J. Fasel, A. D. Gordon, R. J. M. Hughes, P. Hudak, T. Johnsson, M. P. Jones, E. Meijer, S. L. Peyton Jones, A. Reid, and P. L. Wadler. *The Haskell Library Report, Version 1.4*, Yale University, 1997. Available at http://haskell.org.
14. Hugs Home Page. http://www.haskell.org/hugs/, January 1999.
15. Java Technology Home Page. http://java.sun.com/, January 1999.
16. Microsoft Technologies for Java Home Page. http://www.microsoft.com/java/, January 1999.
17. JavaSoft. Java Native Interface Specification, Release 1.1 (Revised May, 1997). ftp://ftp.javasoft.com/docs/jdk1.1/jni.ps, May 1997. For later modifications, see documentation of JDK1.2betaX.
18. JavaSoft. Java Development Kit, Version 1.2. http://java.sun.com/products/jdk/1.2/, January 1999. See the online documentation. JDK 1.2 was released in December 1998 as Java 2.
19. S.L. Peyton Jones and M.P. Jones. First-Class Modules for Component-Based Programming. http://research.microsoft.com/Users/simonpj/Papers/first-class-modules.ps.gz, April 1996.
20. S.L. Peyton Jones, E. Meijer, and D. Leijen. Scripting COM Components in Haskell. In *Proc. 5th. International Conference on Software Reuse*, Victoria, British Columbia, June 1998.

21. Microsoft. Component Object Model (COM). http://www.microsoft.com/com/default.asp, January 1999.
22. Microsoft. Integrating Java and COM. Follow links "Technical Information" and "Technical Articles" at [16], January 1999.
23. R. Noble. *Lazy Functional Components for Graphical User Interfaces*. PhD thesis, Department of Computer Science, University of York, November 1995.
24. The Green Card Team. The Green Card Manual (version 2.0). http://www.dcs.gla.ac.uk/fp/software/green-card/, January 1999.
25. The Haskell FFI Team. A primitive foreign function interface (draft specification). Follow the link to the "Primitive FFI design document" on http://www.dcs.gla.ac.uk/fp/software/hdirect/, June 1998.
26. D. Wakeling. A Haskell to Java Virtual Machine Code Compiler,. In C. Clack, A.J.T. Davie and K. Hammond, editors, *Proc. 9th. International Workshop on the Implementation of Functional Languages (IFL '97), St Andrews, Scotland, September 1997*, volume 1467 of *LNCS*, pages 39–52. Springer-Verlag, 1998.
27. D. Wakeling. Mobile Haskell: Compiling Lazy Functional Programs for the Java Virtual Machine. In *Proc. Principles of Declarative Programming (PLILP '98)*, Pisa, Italy, pages 335–352. Springer-Verlag, September 1998.

A   Simple Example of Using Haskell/JNI (Haskell Part)

```
import JNI

-- create an instance of the JVM, find our canvas class and its methods,
-- then start the real action; hide details using partial application
main =
 do createJVM ["-Djava.class.path=."]
    canvasClass <- findClass "MyCanvas"
    newCanvas <- getMethodID canvasClass "<init>" "(II)V"
    getGraphicsID <- getMethodID canvasClass "getGraphics"
                                            "()Ljava/awt/Graphics;"
    graphicsClass <- findClass "java/awt/Graphics"
    drawID <- getMethodID graphicsClass "drawLine" "(IIII)V"
    canvas <- newObjectA canvasClass newCanvas [jval width,jval height]
    offscreen <- callObjectMethodA canvas getGraphicsID []
    action (callVoidMethodA offscreen drawID) angle length (x0,y0)
 where
 { width  = 500; x0 = 250; angle  = 0;
   height = 500; y0 = 250; length = 100     }

-- the drawing routine; just a simple fractal tree
action draw angle length (x,y) | length < 1 = return ()
action draw angle length (x,y) =
  do
    draw [jval x, jval y, jval newx, jval newy]
    action draw (angle+pi/4) (length*0.6) (newx,newy)
    action draw (angle-pi/4) (length*0.6) (newx,newy)
  where
  { newx = x + length * (sin angle); newy = y - length * (cos angle) }

jval f = toJValue ((round f)::Int)
```

A Case Study: Effects of WITH-Loop-Folding on the NAS Benchmark MG in SAC

Sven-Bodo Scholz

Dept of Computer Science
University of Kiel
24105 Kiel, Germany
sbs@informatik.uni-kiel.de

Abstract. SAC is a functional C variant with efficient support for high-level array operations. This paper investigates the applicability of a SAC specific optimization technique called WITH-loop-folding to real world applications. As an example program which originates from the Numerical Aerodynamic Simulation (NAS) Program developed at NASA Ames Research Center, the so-called NAS benchmark MG is chosen. It comprises a kernel from the NAS Program which implements 3-dimensional multigrid relaxation.

Several run-time measurements exploit two different benefits of WITH-loop-folding: First, an overall speed-up of about 20% can be observed. Second, a comparison between the run-times of a hand-optimized specification and of APL-like specifications yields identical run-times, although a naive compilation that does not apply WITH-loop-folding leads to slow-downs of more than an order of magnitude. Furthermore, WITH-loop-folding makes a slight variation of the algorithm feasible which substantially simplifies the program specification and requires less memory during execution.

Finally, the optimized run-times are compared against run-times gained from the original FORTRAN program, which shows that for different problem sizes, the code generated from the SAC program does not only reach the execution times of the code generated from the FORTRAN program but even outperforms them by about 10%.

1 Introduction

SAC[21] is a functional programming language aimed at numerical applications. Basically, it can be considered a functional subset of C augmented with an array concept that allows for the specification of array operations that are applicable to arrays of any dimensionality. The central language construct for such high-level array operations is a dimension-invariant form of array comprehensions called WITH-loops. They allow for the definition of basic array operations similar to those available in array processing languages, such as APL[14], NIAL[15], or J[7], which subsequently can be combined to more sophisticated array operations [24]. Assuming a straightforward compilation scheme, this style of programming inherently leads to the creation of many superfluous intermediate array structures.

H. Hammond, T. Davie, and C. Clack (Eds.): IFL'98, LNCS 1595, pp. 216–228, 1999.

To avoid this overhead, a high-level optimization called WITH-loop-folding has been proposed in [23].

This paper investigates the effects of WITH-loop-folding on real world applications. For several reasons the NAS multigrid relaxation benchmark MG [3] is chosen as example: first of all, the benchmark is a suitable representative for many numerical applications. Furthermore, since the benchmark is designed for exploiting the capabilities of FORTRAN compilers a reasonable FORTRAN version is commonly available. This allows for an easy inter-language run-time comparison. Another motivation for the choice of the benchmark MG is the fact that the suitability of SAC for the dimension-invariant specification of multigrid relaxation algorithms in general is studied in [22]. Therefore, this paper can focus on the new aspects introduced by WITH-loop-folding.

In particular, the paper addresses the following questions:

- Does WITH-loop-folding yield an overall run-time improvement? How does that compare against implementation in other languages, such as FORTRAN?
- Does WITH-loop-folding allow for more specificational freedom without the loss of run-time efficiency? If so, does that have an impact on the programming style?

The paper is organized as follows: In the next section a brief overview on the NAS benchmark MG is given. Sect. 3 investigates the effect of WITH-loop-folding on the overall run-time of the benchmark and compares those figures against a FORTRAN77 and a SISAL implementation. Sect. 4 compares run-times obtained from different specifications on varying levels of abstraction for one part of the benchmark, the so-called relaxation kernel. After exploiting the effects of WITH-loop-folding for the given multigrid algorithm, Sect. 5 proposes a slight variant of the algorithm which allows for a far more elegant specification of the given approximation problem and furthermore improves the space consumption of the program. Sect. 6 puts the work presented in this paper into the context of other research done on the fusion of operations on large data structures. Finally, a conclusion is given in Sect. 7.

2   An Introduction to the NAS Benchmark MG

The NAS benchmark MG implements the V-cycle multigrid algorithm [4,5] to approximate a solution u of the discrete Poisson problem $\nabla^2 u = v$ on a 3-dimensional grid with periodic boundary conditions. The V-cycle algorithm consists of a recursive nesting of relaxation steps and smoothing steps on grids of different granularity as well as mappings between these grids. The upper part of Fig. 1 for a single V-cycle on a 64x64x64 grid depicts the order in which these transformations are applied (horizontal axis) and which grid sizes are involved (vertical axis).

This sequence of operations can easily be described by means of a recursive function v_cyc as specified in the lower part of Fig. 1. The function **mgrid** given

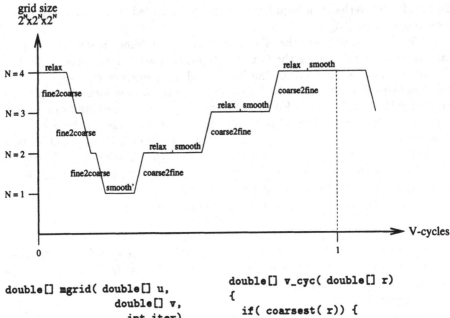

Fig. 1. An Outline of the V-cycle.

there as well, initiates `iter` V-cycles on a given 3-dimensional grid **v** and an initial approximation of the solution u.[1]

The functions `relax` and `smooth` merely re-compute the elements of an argument grid as weighted sums of their neighbor elements. Since the benchmark requires periodic boundary conditions the missing neighbors of border elements have to be taken from the "opposite side" of the grid. Fig. 2 depicts the situation in the 1-dimensional case. While all inner elements are re-computed using their direct neighbors, each of the two border elements has to be computed differently. Carrying over this principle to problems of higher dimensionalities, the sets of elements which require special treatment increase. In the 2-dimensional

---

[1] Note, that in real world applications the number of V-cycles applied depends on the convergence properties of the problem.

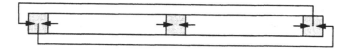

Fig. 2. Relaxation on 1-Dimensional Arrays.

case 9 different operations have to be performed, in case of three dimensions 27 operations are required.

To avoid such complicated specifications, the FORTRAN program given in the benchmark (see **http://www.nas.nasa.gov/NAS/NPB/**) represents the grids by arrays which have 2 more elements in each dimension. These hold copies of the values of the missing neighbor fields. Fig. 3 depicts a relaxation step for the 1-dimensional case using such extra elements. Since the border elements of

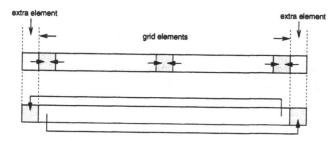

Fig. 3. Relaxation on 1-Dimensional Arrays Using Border Elements.

the arrays solely provide missing neighbor elements, the relaxation step itself becomes a unique operation for all inner elements of the array as shown in the upper part of Fig. 3. Subsequently, the border elements of the array have to be updated accordingly so that they hold the correct values from the "opposite side" of the grid (lower part of Fig. 3). For the 1-dimensional case as depicted here, this extended grid representation does not offer any benefits; still three different operations are required: the unique relaxation step, the updating of the leftmost element, and the updating of the rightmost element. However, for problems of higher dimensionalities this grid representation is advantageous since the number of different operations required does not grow exponentially but linearly, i.e., for the 2-dimensional case 5 operations and for the 3-dimensional case 7 operations are needed.

A dimension-invariant realization of **relax** and **smooth** based on such extended grids in SAC can be deduced straightforwardly. Let **A** and **S** be program constants that hold the arrays of weights needed for the computation of weighted sums of neighbor elements in **relax** and **smooth**, respectively. Then these functions can be specified as:

```
double[] relax( double[] u, double[] v)
{
  r = with( 0*shape(u)+1 <= x <= shape(u)-2)
      modarray( u, x, v[x] - weighted_sum( u, x, A));
  r = setup_periodic_border(r);
  return(r);
}


double[] smooth( double[] z, double[] r)
{
  z = with( 0*shape(r)+1 <= x <= shape(r)-2)
      modarray( r, x, z[x] + weighted_sum( r, x, S));
  z = setup_periodic_border( z);
  return( z);
}

inline double weighted_sum( double[] u, int[] x, double[] w)
{
  res = with( 0*shape(w) <= dx < shape(w) )
        fold( +, u[x+dx-1] * w[dx]);
  return(res);
}
```

where **setup_periodic_border** for each dimension copies those elements into the border elements that are needed for the next relaxation/smoothing step.

Re-using **weighted_sum** the mapping from fine grids to coarse grids can be specified in a similar way:

```
double[] fine2coarse( double[] r)
{
  rn = with( 0*shape(r)+1 <= x<= shape(r) / 2 -1)
       genarray( shape(r) / 2 + 1, weighted_sum( r, 2*x, P));
  rn = setup_periodic_border(rn);
  return(rn);
}
```

The specification of mappings from coarse to fine grids is more complicated. As explained in detail in [22], a dimension-invariant specification of that operation requires two consecutive WITH-loops:

```
double[] coarse2fine( double[] rn)
{
  r = with( 0*shape(rn) <= iv <= 2*shape(rn)-3 step 0*shape(rn)+2 )
      genarray( 2*shape(rn)-2, rn[iv/2] );

  r = with( 0*shape(r) < iv < shape(r)-1 ) {
        val = relaxkernel( r, iv, Q);
      } modarray( r, iv, val);

  r = setup_periodic_border(r);
  return(r);
}
```

This two-step process for 1-dimensional grids is depicted in Fig. 4. In the first step, the elements from the coarse grid are copied into every other position of a new array of double the size. The elements in between are initialized with zeros. Subsequently, a relaxation step is performed whose array of weights determines the interpolation of the values initialized with zero. For the 1-dimensional case, [0.5, 1, 0.5] serves as array of weights. Although in principle all elements are computed by the same scheme, the placement of zeros forces several values to be neglected as indicated by the dotted lines in Fig. 4. As a consequence, the elements of the resulting finer grid are computed from the elements of the coarser grid basically by two different operations: all elements with even indices (starting by index [0]) are simply copied from the coarser grid, whereas the other elements are averages of two adjacent elements of the coarser grid. Note here, that for problems of dimensionality n a choice of appropriate arrays of weights implicitly generates the required 2^n different operations.

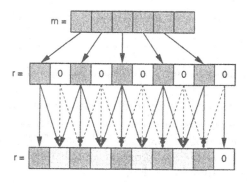

Fig. 4. Coarse-to-Fine-Mapping on 1-Dimensional Arrays.

3 Applying WITH-Loop-Folding to Mgrid

In this section the effect of WITH-loop-folding to the SAC specification of the benchmark outlined in the previous section is examined. Furthermore, the run-times are compared against those obtained from running compiled FORTRAN and SISAL solutions.

All those measurements are done in the same setting as in [22], i.e., a SUN ULTRASPARC-170 with 192MB of main memory serves as hardware platform. The FORTRAN program is compiled by the SUN FORTRAN compiler f77 version 4.2 which generates native code directly. The SISAL program is compiled by OSC version 13.0.2 which generates C code that subsequently is compiled into native code by GCC version 2.7.2.1. The optimization flags used are "-O4" for the FORTRAN compiler and "-O -nobounds -CC=gcc -cc=-O3 -seq" for the SISAL compiler.

The SAC program is compiled by the new SAC2C compiler version 0.7 which in comparison to the version used in [22] does not only include WITH-loop-folding but has an improved "back-end" for the generation of C code from WITH-loops. GCC version 2.7.2.1 with optimization level 3 is used again as the compiler for the C-code generated by SAC2c.

Fig. 5 shows the run-times relative to the time needed by the compiled FOR-TRAN program for three different problem sizes[2]. The problem-sizes investigated

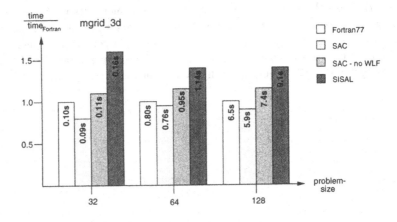

Fig. 5. Run-times for 3-Dimensional Multigrid Relaxation.

are 3-dimensional grids with 32, 64, and 128 elements per axis.

The SISAL implementation turns out to be the slowest solution. It runs about 40% slower than the FORTRAN program and about 50% slower than the optimized SAC version. While the SAC program compiled without WITH-loop-folding (SAC -noWLF) is about 10% slower than the FORTRAN solution, the version gen-

---

[2] The absolute run-times for one V-cycle are denoted inside the bars.

erated from the SAC program using WITH-loop-folding (SAC) is about 10% faster than the FORTRAN program.

The reason for the speed-up of about 20% gained by WITH-loop-folding can be attributed to the mapping from coarse to fine grids, `coarse2fine`. As explained in the previous section, it has to be specified as a two-step process in order to allow for a dimension-invariant program. Together with a specialization of `coarse2fine` to 3-dimensional arguments of specific shapes as done by the type inference system of SAC, WITH-loop-folding converts this operation into a direct computation of fine grids from coarse grids.

Fig. 6 depicts the effect of WITH-loop-folding for 1-dimensional grids. Whereas

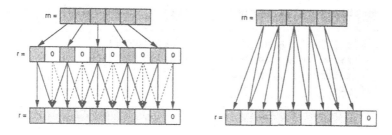

Fig. 6. Applying WITH-Loop-Folding to `coarse2fine`.

the version using two WITH-loops (left part of Fig. 6) subsequently applies two unique operations on the elements of the array representing the coarse grid, the version obtained by WITH-loop-folding (right part of Fig. 6) directly computes the resulting fine grid from the coarse grid by using two different operations: elements at odd index positions (marked in light grey in Fig. 6) are computed as the average of two adjacent elements of the coarse grid, and elements at even index positions (marked in dark grey) are simply copied from the coarse grid. As a consequence, the intermediate data structure as well as any superfluous computation (dotted lines in Fig. 6) can be avoided, resulting in a speed-up of about 20%.

4   WITH-Loop-Folding and Specificational Freedom

One of the aims of WITH-loop-folding is to provide a uniform optimization scheme which does not only allow for more modular specifications of array operations without substantial loss of run-time efficiency, but encourages the programmer to do so. This section investigates that effect in the context of the benchmark. Instead of re-coding the whole benchmark, only a part of it, namely the function `relax` (cf. Sect. 2), is examined more closely. This on the one side allows for a smaller scope during testing and on the other side carries over to the major part of the benchmark since most kernel routines of the benchmark (`smooth` and `fine2coarse`) are only slight variations of `relax`.

The similarity of these routines leads to the first variant of `relax` which allows for more code re-use. The central idea is to abstract the WITH-loop in the body of **relax** into a new function **relax_kernel**. As a consequence, the difference of **v** and a weighted sum of some elements in u can be specified as an array operation rather than element-wise:

```
double[] relax( double[] u, double[] v)
{
  res= v - relax_kernel( A, u);
  res = setup_periodic_border( res);
  return( res);
}


inline double[] relax_kernel( double[] w, double[] u)
{
  res = with( 0*shape(u)+1 <= x <= shape(u)-2) {
          val = weighted_sum( u, x, w));
        } modarray( u, x, val);
  return( res);
}
```

A more sophisticated variant of **relax** is based on the idea of replacing the element-wise specification of the re-computation of inner elements by operations on entire arrays. This turns the explicit selection and summation of neighbor elements in the body of **weighted_sum** into rotations and additions of entire arrays, respectively. Thus the function **weighted_sum** is not needed anymore and **relax_kernel** can be specified as:

```
inline double[] relax_kernel( double[] w, double[] u)
{
  res = with( 0*shape(w) <= dx < shape(w) )
        fold( +, rotate_vec( dx-1, u) * w[dx]);
  return(res);
}
```

where the function **rotate_vec** rotates the array u along all axes according to the rotation vector given by **dx-1**. In turn, **rotate_vec** can be defined in terms of **rotate** which is defined in the standard array library and rotates a given array a by **num** elements along a pre-specified axis **dimen**:

```
inline double[] rotate_vec( int[] rv, double[] a)
{
  for( i=0; i<shape(rv)[0]; i=i+1)
    a = rotate( i, rv[[i]], a);
  return(a);
}
```

```
inline double[] rotate( int dimen, int num, double[] a)
{
  max_rotate = shape(a)[[dimen]];
  num = num % max_rotate;
  if( num < 0) { num = num + max_rotate;}
  offset = modarray( 0*shape(a), [dimen], num);
  slice_shp = modarray( shape(a), [dimen], num);
  B = with ( offset <= i_vec < shape(a))
      modarray( a, i_vec, a[i_vec-offset]);
  B = with ( 0*slice_shp <= i_vec < slice_shp)
      modarray( B, i_vec, a[shape(a)-slice_shp+i_vec]);
  return(B);
}
```

Fig. 7 compares the run-times for the three different versions of **relax** introduced so far. The problem size examined here are 15 relaxation steps on a 2-dimensional array with 1000 elements per axis. All run-times are measured on the same architecture as the previous examples. Whereas the left column shows

	WLF	noWLF
Direct specification of **relax**	4.9s	4.9s
relax using **relax_kernel**	4.9s	5.5s
relax using **rotate**	4.9s	77.1s

Fig. 7. Run-times With and Without WITH-Loop-Folding.

the run-times of the three versions using WITH-loop-folding, the right column contains those obtained without. The direct solution as explained in Sect. 2 is not affected by WITH-loop-folding since that version does not contain any consecutive WITH-loops at all. In the second version, the subtraction operation without applying WITH-loop-folding leads to a single superfluous array which causes a slowdown of about 10%. In contrast, for the high-level specification which completely forgos any explicit indexing a non-folding compilation leads to a slowdown of about 1500%!

Despite these slowdowns introduced by a naive compilation, the run-times for the optimized versions are identical. Analyzing the generated C-code yields that the WITH-loops eventually generated by WITH-loop-folding in all three cases are almost identical.

5   A Variant Without Borders

The results of the previous section show that a specification based on the summation of rotated arrays does not lead to any performance losses in terms of run-time. The main difference of that solution in comparison to the others considered is that the border elements are re-computed as well. These computations are superfluous since `setup_periodic_border` copies these elements from inner elements of the array anyway. Having a closer look at the operations performed on the border elements yields that they are computed as weighted sums of their "neighbor elements" as well. Since `rotate` shifts the elements of an array cyclicly, missing neighbors implicitly are taken from the "opposite side" of the array. In fact, this algorithm performs an operation on the complete array that satisfies the original problem specification (cf. Fig. 2 in Sect. 2).

Therefore, the data layout for the arrays holding the grid elements can be simplified throughout the entire program by cutting off the border elements. As a result, the function `setup_periodic_border` becomes redundant and most other functions can be further simplified, for example, `relax` can be specified as:

```
double[] relax( double[] u, double[] v)
{
  return( v - relax_kernel( A, u));
}
```

This exactly resembles the mathematical specification given in [3]. Besides the specificational advantages of that solution it decreases the overall memory consumption and thus improves the overall performance.

6   Related Work

The effects of fusion techniques have been studied in various contexts.

In the area of functional programming, several variants of so-called *deforestation* have been proposed and examined [25, 9, 11, 19]. Since these techniques are tailor-made for the elimination of temporary lists, they implicitly assume that the length of the list(s) involved is statically unknown and that each function will be applied on all elements of the list(s).

Since these assumptions for array computations in general do not hold, other approaches in the context of functional programming have been proposed which are based on the idea of representing arrays as functions from indices to values [6, 13]. As a consequence, array operations can be folded by simply β-reducing them. Although this approach conceptually is very promising it still lacks a proof that an efficient implementation is possible [12].

Closer related to the work in this paper are the evaluations of fusion techniques in the context of high performance array languages, such as SISAL [18], FORTRAN90 [1], HPF [10], or ZPL [17]. Whereas earlier approaches in that field are based on traditional loop optimizations [27, 8, 2, 26] which are applied to scalarized versions of the high-level operations, more recent publications [20, 16] point out the importance of fusion operations that are applied to high-level operations. However, specificational benefits comparable to those presented in this paper are not possible in these languages, since they do not allow for the specification of dimension-invariant array operations, e.g. `rotate` or `rotate_vec` from Sect. 4.

7 Conclusion

This paper was to investigate, by means of a case study, the effects of WITH-loop-folding on a program kernel which originates from a real world application. The example chosen is the multigrid relaxation kernel from the NAS benchmarks. Applying WITH-loop-folding to a dimension-invariant SAC specification derived from the FORTRAN program given in the benchmark does not only yield the same run-times, it even outperforms them by about 10%. These improvements can be tracked down to some redundancies in the mapping from coarse to fine grids caused by the dimension-independent specification.

Besides these overall run-time benefits a gain in specificational freedom without any loss of run-time efficiency can be observed for a central part of the multigrid benchmark, the relaxation kernel. This allows for a variation of the algorithm based on rotations of entire arrays with a couple of advantages: the algorithm is more concise; it resembles the mathematical specification more directly; it is based entirely on standard array operations and thus encourages code re-use; and it requires less memory at run-time.

References

1. J.C. Adams, W.S. Brainerd, J.T. Martin, et al. *Fortran90 Handbook – Complete ANSI/ISO Reference.* McGraw-Hill, 1992. ISBN 0-07-000406-4.
2. D.F. Bacon, S.L. Graham, and O.J. Sharp. Compiler Transformations for High-Performance Computing. *ACM Computing Surveys,* 26(4):345–420, 1994.
3. D. Bailey, E. Barszcz, J. Barton, et al. The NAS Parallel Benchmarks. RNR 94-007, NASA Ames Research Center, 1994.
4. D. Braess. *Finite Elemente.* Springer, 1996. ISBN 3-540-61905-4.
5. A. Brandt. Multigrid Methods: 1984 Guide. Dept of applied mathematics, The Weizmann Institute of Science, Rehovot/Israel, 1984.
6. T. Budd. Composition and Compilation in Functional Programming Languages. Technical Report 88-60-14, Oregon State University, 1988.
7. C. Burke. *J and APL.* Iverson Software Inc., Toronto, Canada, 1996.
8. D.C. Cann. *The Optimizing SISAL Compiler: Version 12.0.* Lawrence Livermore National Laboratory, LLNL, Livermore California, 1993. part of the SISAL distribution.
9. W.-N. Chin. Safe Fusion of Functional Expressions II: Further Improvements. *Journal of Functional Programming,* 4(4):515–550, 1994.
10. High Performance Fortran Forum. *High Performance Fortran language specification V1.1,* 1994.
11. A. Gill. *Cheap Deforestation for Non-strict Functional Languages.* PhD thesis, Glasgow University, 1996.
12. J. Halen, P. Hammarlund, and B. Lisper. An Experimental Implementation of a Highly Abstract Model of Data Parallel Programming. TRITA-IT 97:2, Dept. of Teleinformatics, KTH, Stockholm, 1997.
13. P. Hammarlund and B. Lisper. On the Relation between Functional and Data Parallel Programming Languages. In *Proc. 1993 ACM Conference on Functional Programming Languages and Computer Architecture (FPLCA'93),* pages 210–222. ACM Press, 1993.
14. K.E. Iverson. *A Programming Language.* Wiley, New York, 1962.

15. M.A. Jenkins and W.H. Jenkins. *The Q'Nial Language and Reference Manuals.* Nial Systems Ltd., Ottawa, Canada, 1993.

16. E.C. Lewis, C. Lin, and L. Snyder. The Implementation and Evaluation of Fusion and Contraction in Array Languages. In *Proc. 1998 ACM SIGPLAN Conference on Programming Language Design and Implementation (PLDI '98).* 1998.

17. C. Lin. ZPL Language Reference Manual. UW-CSE-TR 94-10-06, University of Washington, 1996.

18. J.R. McGraw, S.K. Skedzielewski, S.J. Allan, R.R. Oldehoeft, et al. SISAL: Streams and Iteration in a Single Assignment Language: Reference Manual Version 1.2. M 146, Lawrence Livermore National Laboratory, LLNL, Livermore California, 1985.

19. L. Nemeth and S. Peyton Jones. A Design for Warm Fusion. In K. Hammond, A.J.T. Davie, and C. Clack, editors, *Draft Proc. 10th. International Workshop on Implementation of Functional Languages (IFL '98),* London, England, pages 381–393. University College, London, 1998.

20. G. Roth and K. Kennedy. Loop Fusion in High Performance Fortran. CRPC TR98745, Rice University, Houston, Texas, 1998.

21. S.-B. Scholz. *Single Assignment C - Entwurf und Implementierung einer funktionalen C-Variante mit spezieller Unterstützung shape-invarianter Array-Operationen.* PhD thesis, Institut für Informatik und Praktische Mathematik, Universität Kiel, 1996.

22. S.-B. Scholz. On Programming Scientific Applications in SAC - A Functional Language Extended by a Subsystem for High-Level Array Operations. In W. Kluge, editor, *Proc. 8th. International Workshop on the Implementation of Functional Languages (IFL'96), Bad Godesberg, Germany, September 1996,* volume 1268 of *LNCS,* pages 85–104. Springer-Verlag, 1997.

23. S.-B. Scholz. With-loop-folding in SAC–Condensing Consecutive Array Operations. In C. Clack, T. Davie, and K. Hammond, editors, *Proc. 9th. International Workshop on Implementation of Functional Languages, St Andrews, Scotland, September 1997,* volume 1467 of *LNCS,* pages 72–91. Springer-Verlag, 1998.

24. S.-B. Scholz. On Defining Application-Specific High-Level Operations by Means of Shape-Invariant Programming Facilities. In S. Picchi and M. Micocci, editors, *Proc. Array Processing Language Conference 98,* pages 40–45. ACM-SIGAPL, 1998.

25. P.L. Wadler. Deforestation: transforming programs to eliminate trees. *Theoretical Computer Science,* 73(2):231–248, 1990.

26. M.J. Wolfe. *High-Performance Compilers for Parallel Computing.* Addison-Wesley, 1995. ISBN 0-8053-2730-4.

27. H. Zima and B. Chapman. *Supercompilers for Parallel and Vector Computers.* Addison-Wesley, 1991.

Explicit Message Passing for Concurrent Clean

Pascal R. Serrarens and Rinus Plasmeijer

Computer Science Institute
University of Nijmegen, The Netherlands
{pascalrs,rinus}@cs.kun.nl

Abstract. In this paper, a message passing extension for Concurrent Clean is proposed which provides efficient and flexible communication. In contrast to other solutions in functional languages, we chose to have an asynchronous system. We discuss design decisions with respect to concurrent evaluation and communication of unique messages. Furthermore, we show some examples and implementation aspects.

1 Introduction

An important topic in computer science is concurrency. For many shared memory and distributed memory machines, concurrency is provided through a library which enables the programmer to create processes or threads and have communication between them. In that case, concurrency is outside the language, but for other languages, like Pict [20], concurrency is part of the language.

Functional languages designers have always shown a great interest in concurrency, especially with respect to to graphical user interfaces. Because of the absence of side-effects, functional languages are ideal for parallelism and concurrency. The problem is that concurrency often introduces non-determinism, which complicates reasoning. Several attempts have been made to introduce concurrency without non-determinism [7,8], but they are of limited use. It seems that non-determinism is really needed to describe systems like multi-user systems.

Concurrent Clean also provides threads and communication, through process annotations and lazy graph copying respectively. Although it has been shown that certain parallel algorithms can be described very elegantly and efficiently, Clean does not offer support for data-driven communication. This paper presents a way to add this to Concurrent Clean.

In Sect. 2 the concurrency constructs of Concurrent Clean are discussed and its shortcomings are summarised. After looking at some other solutions in Sect. 3, we present in Sect. 4 our new message passing primitives. Sect. 5 discusses some implementation issues, while Sect. 6 summarises what we did.

2 Clean and Concurrency

2.1 Process Annotations

Concurrent Clean [13] provides a number of process annotations, which can be used to create threads. These threads execute concurrently with all other threads,

H. Hammond, T. Davie, and C. Clack (Eds.): IFL'98, LNCS 1595, pp. 229–245, 1999.

in a way depending on the annotation: either parallel, on a different processor {| P |}, {| P at ... |}, or in an interleaved manner on the same processor {| I |}.

Inter-heap references are represented by channel nodes [9]. When an annotated expression is sent to another processor, a channel node is created in the local heap. When this channel node is evaluated, a request is sent to the processor holding the expression, which will then return the evaluated expression using a lazy copying mechanism as soon as it has been evaluated.

2.2 Shortcomings

Inter-process communication is available in the form of implicit lazy copying, which fits naturally with the lazy evaluation strategy of Clean. The disadvantage is that it can be rather slow: every graph has to be requested before it is sent, doubling the number of messages. A more efficient form of communication is data-driven communication, where data is sent as soon as it becomes available. Concurrent Clean does not provide a direct way to express this.

It is possible to provide data-driven communication with both Clean- and non-Clean programs, by creating an interface to, say, TCP/IP. But it would be better if we had one data-driven communication layer on a higher level of abstraction which can be used for communication between and within programs.

Concurrent Clean is aimed to be a general-purpose programming language, so it should be possible to implement various kinds of systems with it. However, it is not possible to write a multi-user system with it, as such a system is inherently non-deterministic and Clean does not provide a way to express this.

Dynamic types [16], which are currently being added to Clean, enable the type checking of objects which live longer than the program which uses them. An important use of dynamics is for file-I/O: this enables us to type check the contents of files. Dynamic tyoes can also be used for message passing between programs, enabling programs to communicate any data structure and any function in a type-safe manner.

Multicasting is getting more and more attention lately, especially for the internet. Broadcasting services, like audio and video on demand, send a lot of data to a large number of destinations. It is almost obligatory to use multicasting here. It is also very convenient when you can write your processes in such a way that you don't have to worry about the number of receivers.

3 Known Solutions

Object I/O Message Passing Clean's Object I/O system [2] already provides lightweight processes and message passing. The processes are built on top of Clean. Process creation, scheduling and message passing are done efficiently without the use of operating system support. Processes can send messages to receivers, which are special event handlers.

Although the Object I/O system's message passing has some of the properties we want, it does not have them all: it is deterministic and it does not provide inter-program communication or multicasting. Moreover, it depends on the object I/O processes and event handlers to work. This last property makes it unsuitable for a general message passing system in Concurrent Clean.

Concurrent Haskell Concurrent Haskell [15] does not have real message passing, but bases it on mutable locations, called MVar's. A value of type MVar t is a mutable location which can be empty or contain a single value of type t. Three operations are defined on MVar's: newMVar, for creating a new MVar, takeMVar, which reads out an MVar and blocks when it is empty, and putMVar which is used to fill an MVar. In the case of more than one process waiting for a value in an MVar, the process which will get the value will be chosen non-deterministically. A drawback of this approach is that the location of the MVar is not very clear and that communication may still be demand-driven. If the receiver and the MVar are not at the same location, a request will be sent to the MVar to obtain the message. This is always the case when we have multiple receivers at different locations, thus real multicasting is not possible.

Synchronous Message Passing Concurrent ML [17] and Facile [19] both provide synchronous communication primitives. In the former they are called **send** and **accept** and in the latter **send** and **receive**. Scholz [18] proposes a similar set of primitives for Haskell. In these systems, both the sender and receiver will block when the other party is not available. As this protocol is strictly one-to-one, multicasting is not possible. The matching of senders and receivers is non-deterministic, a sender cannot determine which process will receive the message. This kind of non-determinism makes reasoning hard, as it is difficult to ensure that a message will arrive at the right place. Jones and Hudak [8] propose a variant where two processors can only use the same channel when they are sender and receiver. This ensures that no non-deterministic effects can take place.

Totem, Isis, Transis Quite some work has been done on multicasting systems with total ordering: Totem [11], Isis [4], Horus [21], Transis [6]. In these systems all messages on the same channel are ordered, even when they were sent by different senders. This implies that every receiver receives all messages in the same order, which improves reasoning. It is achieved by putting the senders on a token ring. Senders are only allowed to send when they have the token. The token contains a sequence number, seq. Each time a sender gets the token it may send n messages, with message numbers seq to $seq + n - 1$. The token is then passed to the next sender with value $seq + n$. In this way all messages have an unique number, which is used to order the messages.

Eden Eden [10] also provides data-driven communication between processes in an implicit way. Processes can be defined used function-like process abstractions mapping input to output. The runtime system then ensures that the output is sent to the right processes which can then use it as their input values. It only provides one-to-one communication. Non-determinism is introduced using a predefined process abstraction **merge**.

Reliable Multicast Protocols Reliable multicast protocols have recently received much attention. One recent protocol is the Reliable Multicast Transport Protocol (RMTP) [14]. It provides one-to-many communication which is reliable over wide area networks. This rather low-level mechanism can be used to implement more complex many-to-many protocols, including the Clean message passing system we propose in this paper.

Broadcasting Sequential Processes N. Gehani describes a system of Broadcasting Sequential Processes (BSP) [12], which is based on CSP [5]. In this system processes can broadcast and multicast messages to other processes. Examples are given showing the usefulness of BSP. Furthermore, two broadcasting paradigms are discussed, unbuffered and buffered. The first is simpler to implement, but the second can solve critical problems like starvation. This system has most of the properties we look for.

4   Introducing Message Passing in Clean

Clean uses the world-as-value paradigm [1], based on the uniqueness type system [3], to make it possible to deal with side-effects in a pure functional way. An interactive Clean program is a function of type *World -> *World. The World is an abstract, specialised type which represents the complete environment of the program. The uniqueness type attribute * states that the environment type is unique, guaranteeing single threadedness which enables destructive updates of the environment. The message passing functions will initially use the World environment for doing I/O.

4.1   Communication between Programs

We decided to have a data-driven asynchronous message passing system in the spirit of Broadcasting Sequential Processes with buffered broadcasting. Our message passing system uses channels which are split into a sending and a receiving part: the send channel and the receive channel. They are offered to the programmer using abstract data structures:

```
:: SChannel a
:: RChannel a
```

Sending can only happen on a send channel, while receiving is only allowed on receive channels. This is very convenient: it is always clear in which direction the messages go. As send- and receive channels are first-class citizens, they can be shared and be sent on other channels, enabling flexible communication patterns.

A message sent on a send channel will be sent to all locations which possess the corresponding receive channels, where they will be queued until needed. A receive channel represents the list of messages in the order as they are sent using the send channels. The ordering between messages from two independent send channels is undetermined and depends on the environment in which the message is received.

We want to guarantee that all messages which are sent on a send channel can be received on a receive channel, so messages cannot be lost. This simplifies reasoning about these channels greatly, but has the consequence that setting up connections is a bit inconvenient.

Channels for inter-program use are maintained in a table for each local network. This table is basically a mapping from names to channels where no two channels can have the same name. Dynamic typing is needed for flexible, type-safe inter-program communication (see [16]), but for simplicity we assume that the messages between programs can be typed statically.

```
:: IPAddress :== String
:: ChName    :== String

:: Maybe a   = Just a | Nothing

createRChannel    :: ChName *World -> (Maybe (RChannel a), *World)

findSChannel      ::                ChName *World -> (SChannel a,*World)
lookupSChannel    :: IPAddress ChName *World -> (SChannel a,*World)

findSChannel_NB   ::                ChName *World ->
                                    (Maybe (SChannel a),*World)
lookupSChannel_NB :: IPAddress ChName *World ->
                                    (Maybe (SChannel a),*World)
```

Programs can create a new entry in the table using `createRChannel`: it tries to create a new channel with the given name and puts it in the table on the local network. If the name already exists, it will fail and return `Nothing`, otherwise it will give the receive side of the channel.

The send side of the channel can be retrieved from the table multiple times: the same send channel is returned. One way to obtain a send channel is using `findSChannel`. It will wait until a channel with the given name is available in the local table and return the send side when it is. We also have a non-blocking variant `findSChannel_NB` which returns `Nothing` when no channel with the given name is available at that moment.

It is also possible to wait for a channel on a certain machine. This is done using `lookupSChannel`, which checks whether the given machine has registered a channel with the given name. This machine may be located anywhere, the channel is always looked up in the table local to that machine. This function will wait until such a channel is available, while `lookupSChannel_NB` does not block.

Channels for local use can be created using `newChannel`. It returns both the send- and receive side of a new channel. As these channels are not registered on the network, it is not possible to add new send channels using, for example, findSChannel.

```
newChannel :: *World -> (SChannel a, RChannel a, *World)
```

We do not provide a function for closing channels. It is assumed that the garbage collector will close unused channels.

Sending and Receiving We have a number of functions on send- and receive channels:

```
send     :: (SChannel a) a *World -> *World
receive  :: (RChannel a)   *World -> (a, RChannel a, *World)
available :: (RChannel a)  *World -> (Bool, *World)
eom      :: (RChannel a)   *World -> (Bool, *World)
```

send sends the message argument to all locations of the receive sides of the channel. It will return immediately, as it is a asynchronous channel. The message is sent using the lazy normal form copying [9], which enables sending infinite structure. Strictness can be used to force the message to be in (root) normal form when it is sent.

The receive function retrieves one message from the buffer. The rest of the messages are returned as a new receive channel. This function is blocking, so when there are no messages available, it will wait until one arrives. This blocking behaviour can be avoided using the function available, which returns a boolean stating whether a message is available for receiving.

eom only works on channels created using newChannel. When, for such channels, all send channels have become garbage, no message can be sent on that channel anymore and we can decide that eom should return True. For receive channels created by createRChannel it is undecidable whether more messages will arrive, because it is always possible to create a new send channel using findSChannel or its siblings. For these channels, eom always returns False.

Example: Producer–Consumer In the next example, we have two programs: one being a producer, sending the numbers 1 to 10 on a send channel which it has found using the name "Consumer". The other program consumes 10 messages on the channel it created under the name "Consumer" and computes the sum of the received numbers:

(The keyword # indicates a let-expression which can be defined before a guard. It introduces a new lexical scope, while the right-hand-side identifiers can be re-used on the left-hand-side; they are internally tagged with a number)

Program 1, the producer

```
Start :: *World -> *World
Start w
   #  (sc, w) = findSChannel "Consumer" w
   = produce sc 10 1 w

produce :: (SChannel Int) Int Int *World -> *World
produce sc n i w
   | n == 0    = w
   | otherwise = produce sc (n - 1) (i + 1) (send sc i w)
```

Program 2, the consumer

```
Start :: *World -> (Int, *World)
Start w
   #  (maybe_rc, w) = createRChannel "Consumer" w
   = consumer maybe_rc w
where
   consumer Nothing   w = abort "channel already exists"
   consumer (Just rc) w = consume rc 10 0 w

consume :: (RChannel Int) Int Int *World -> (Int, *World)
consume rc n r w
   | n == 0    = (r, w)
   | otherwise =
      #   (i, rc, w) = receive rc w
      = consume rc (n - 1) (r + i) w
```

Communication between Threads

In the example above we have communication between two programs. We would also like to have the same system of producers and consumers inside one program, but this gives some troubles. As the producer and consumer are independent, we need independent sequences of computation inside one program. However, as all message passing functions use the world, this is not possible. Therefore we introduce threads. Threads behave like programs but use thread states and have type *TState -> *TState instead of *World -> *World.

Threads can be created using the new-thread functions, which can be used with another TState, the world environment or with (PState 1 p), for Object I/O programs.

```
class ThreadEnv env
where
  newIThread    ::             (*TState ->      *TState ) *env -> *env
  newPThread    ::             (*TState ->      *TState ) *env -> *env
  newPThreadAt  :: ProcId (*TState ->      *TState ) *env -> *env

  newIThread'   ::             (*TState -> (a,*TState)) *env -> (a,*env)
  newPThread'   ::             (*TState -> (a,*TState)) *env -> (a,*env)
  newPThreadAt' :: ProcId (*TState -> (a,*TState)) *env -> (a,*env)

instance ThreadEnv TState
instance ThreadEnv World
instance ThreadEnv (PState l p)
```

The new-thread functions come in two flavours: in one, the new thread only returns the final thread state; in the other, an additional result value is returned. In addition to this we have three evaluation strategies for threads, corresponding to the annotations provided by Concurrent Clean.

The functions are actually implemented using the annotations. As an example we give newIThread:

```
:: *TState = TState

newTState :: *env -> (*TState, *env) | ThreadEnv env
newTState e = (TState, e)

mergeTState :: *TState *env -> *env | ThreadEnv env
mergeTState ts e = e

newIThread :: (*TState -> *TState) *env -> *env | ThreadEnv env
newIThread f e
  #   (ts, e) = newTState e
      ts      = {| I |} f ts
  = mergeTState ts e
```

The function introduced in the previous section, like send, are overloaded in their environment argument, so they can be used in all three environments. However, for clarity we limit the environment usually to TState in this paper.

Example: Producer–Consumer Now we can write the producer-consumer program above using two threads instead of two programs. We use the same produce and consume functions: they are now overloaded in their environment.

```
Start :: *World -> (Int, *World)
Start w
    #   (sc, rc, w) = newChannel w
        w               = newPThread (produce sc 10 1) w
    = newPThread' (consume rc 10 0) w

produce :: (SChannel Int) Int Int *env -> *env | ThreadEnv env
produce sc n i e
    | n == 0    = e
    | otherwise = produce sc (n - 1) (i + 1) (send sc i e)

consume :: (RChannel Int) Int Int *env -> (Int, *env)
                                            | ThreadEnv env
consume rc n r e
    | n == 0    = (r, e)
    | otherwise =
        #   (i, rc, e) = receive rc e
        = consume rc (n - 1) (r + i) e
```

As send- and receive channels can be shared, we can easily create a channel
on which we have more than one producer and consumer. The program code for
the producer and consumer themselves do not have to be changed:

```
Start :: *World -> (Int, Int, *World)
Start w
    #   (sc, rc, w) = newChannel w
        w               = newPThread (produce sc 10 1) w
        w               = newPThread (produce sc 20 100) w

        (r1, w)         = newPThread (consume rc 5 0) w
        (r2, w)         = newPThread (consume rc 5 0) w
    = ( r1, r2, w )
```

Now we have two producers, one multicasting the numbers 1 to 10 and one
producing 100 to 119. The two receivers will both receive 5 numbers from the
channel, but as they use different environments, the result may be different, as
the ordering between messages coming from independent send channels depends
on the environment in which they are sent. So the first receiver may return (1
+ 2 + 100 + 101 + 102) = 306, while the second may give (100 + 1 + 101
+ 2 + 3) = 207.

Single Threaded Access to Channels

It is convenient to have unrestricted access to send- and receive channels, as we
have seen above. But there are cases where this is not desired. For example: if
you want to have a secure connection, where you are the only one who receives

the messages. Another possibility is that you want to ban non-determinism and forbid channels with more than one sender.

Fortunately, the uniqueness type system can help us to do exactly that. We provide a number of functions which guarantee single threaded access to channels by forcing them to be unique:

```
u_send      :: *(SChannel a) a *TState -> (*(SChannel a), *TState)

u_receive   :: *(RChannel a) *TState ->(a, *(RChannel a), *TState)
u_available :: *(RChannel a) *TState ->
                                  (Bool, *(RChannel a), *TState)
```

Communicating Unique Messages

If we want to receive unique graphs, we have to ensure that the message can be received only once. When a graph is copied to another heap using the graph copying algorithm, receiving more than once does not seem to be harmful: we can have two unique references, each to one copy of the graph. But it is generally undecidable whether a graph will be copied to another heap or be shared in the same heap.

Sending unique graphs can be useful: one could imagine two threads within one program running on the same processor. Both threads manipulate a data-structure in turn. When a thread has finished with the data structure it will send it to the other thread, which can then read the changes and update the data structure in place.

Another setting where sending unique graphs is useful is in token situations: a token is used by a number of threads to denote a privilege. A thread having the token is allowed to perform some action, like manipulating a data-structure or sending a message to a conference, where many other threads can see that message and threads may 'speak' in turn. When the token is made unique, ensuring that there is only one keeper of the token at all times is done by the type system and thus trivial. Of course the uniqueness property of the token should then be conserved while sending it over a channel.

Channels and Unicity If we have single-threaded access to receive channels, as in the previous section, then receiving unique messages would be fine: we cannot receive the same message more than once.

```
createRChannel :: ChName *TState ->
                     (Maybe v:(RChannel u:a), *TState), [v <= u]

newChannel :: *TState ->
                 (SChannel u:a, v:(RChannel u:a), *TState), [v <= u]
```

In the improved versions of createRChannel and newChannel above, the uniqueness type system guarantees that a receive channel has to be unique when unique messages are requested on it. This enables us to send unique messages.

Example: Token Ring Now it is possible to write a token-game function, where the uniqueness of the token is guaranteed by the type system. In the example below, the function `createRing` creates a ring of threads which are connected by channels. It takes a list of functions which operate on an unique token and will create a ring which a thread for every function in the list:

```
createRing :: [*T -> *T] *TState -> *TState
createRing fs ts
  # (sc, rc, ts)     = newChannel ts
  = buildRing fs rc sc ts
where
  buildRing :: [*T -> *T] *(RChannel *T) (SChannel *T) *TState
                                                -> *TState
  buildRing [f]     from_prev to_next ts
    = newPThread (tokenGame f from_prev to_next) ts
  buildRing [f:fs] from_prev to_next ts
    # (sc, rc, ts)     = newChannel ts
      ts               = newPThread (tokenGame f from_prev sc) ts
    = buildRing fs rc to_next ts
```

The function `tokenGame` demands the receive channel from the previous thread in the ring to be unique, because the token traveling on it should be unique. When the token is received from the previous thread, a function `f` is applied to it. Then the token is sent to the next thread in the ring and this function will recursively wait on the token again.

```
tokenGame :: (*T -> *T) *(RChannel *T) (SChannel *T) *TState ->
                                                *TState
tokenGame f from_prev to_next ts
  # (token, from_prev, ts) = receive from_prev ts
    token                  = f token
    ts                     = send to_next token ts
  = tokenGame f from_prev to_next ts
```

Example: Shared State

As a larger example we show an implementation for shared state, which can be updated and read by multiple threads independently. The shared state is implemented using a thread, called the state thread, which receives commands from other threads. The state thread is created using **newSharedState**, which takes an initial state, the receive side of the command channel and a location. **sharedState** is the main loop of the thread, receiving the commands and reacting to them: in the case of an **SS_Change** it applies the function argument to the state. The **SS_Get** command uses the fact that channels are first-class citizens and can be sent on other channels: it carries the send side of a reply channel on which the state will be sent.

```
:: SharedState a :== SChannel (SSMsg a)

:: SSMsg a
   = SS_Change (a -> a)
   | SS_Get    (SChannel a)

createSharedState :: ProcId a *TState -> (SharedState a, *TState)
createSharedState pid st ts
   # (comSc, comRc, ts) = newChannel ts
     ts                  = newSharedState st comRc pid ts
   = (comSc, ts)

newSharedState :: a (RChannel (SSMsg a)) ProcId *TState -> *TState
newSharedState st comRc pid ts
   = newPThreadAt pid (sharedState st comRc) ts
where
   sharedState st comRc ts
      # (m, comRc, ts)      = receive comRc ts
        (st, ts)            = handle m st ts
      = sharedState st comRc ts
   where
      handle (SS_Change f ) st ts = (f st, ts)
      handle (SS_Get rplSc) st ts = ( st, send rplSc st ts)
```

Implementing state manipulating functions is then relatively easy: it is basically a matter of sending the right messages on the command channel. In the case of changeSharedState the update function is sent as an SS_Change message. To obtain the shared state using getSharedState we first have to create the reply channel, which will be sent on the command channel in an SS_Get message. Then we wait the arrival of the state on the reply channel.

```
changeSharedState :: (a -> a) (SharedState a) *TState -> *TState
changeSharedState f sst ts = send sst (SS_Change f) ts

getSharedState :: (SharedState a) *TState -> (a, *TState)
getSharedState sst ts
   # (rplSc, rplRc, ts) = newChannel ts
     ts                 = send sst (SS_Get rplSc) ts
     (x, _, ts)         = receive rplRc ts
   = (x, ts)
```

We can also make a fault-tolerant version of the shared state. This is almost trivial, because we can easily create more threads receiving on the command channel. All shared state threads will receive all SS_Change functions and thus will keep the state up-to-date. In the case of a SS_Get message all shared state threads will send the (same) state on the reply channel, but only the first one is received. When `duplSharedState` is used, the shared state will be available, as long as at least one state thread is still running, making it more reliable.

```
duplSharedState :: [ProcId] a *TState -> (SharedState a, *TState)
duplSharedState pids st ts
    # (comSc, comRc, ts)     = newChannel ts
      ts                     = foldr (newSharedState st comRc) ts pids
    = (comSc, ts)
```

5 Implementation

For the implementation of the message passing system we assume to have an order-preserving, reliable communication protocol. The Clean send and receive channels are represented by reference and block nodes in the heap. Each channel has an unique global identification and reference nodes contain a destination list with the locations of corresponding block nodes:

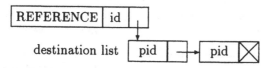

During a **send** action, the message will be sent to all locations in the destination list of the reference node, which enables multicasting. The messages are copied between heaps using the lazy normal form copying [9].

On the other side we have block nodes, which are similar to channel nodes:

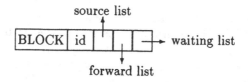

When a block node is evaluated by a reducer during a **receive**, the reducer will be suspended and placed in the waiting list of the block node. In contrast to channel nodes, no request message is sent. When a message arrives for the block node, the node is overwritten by a cons node with as arguments the arrived message and a reference to a copy of the old block node. Then, all threads in the waiting list are activated again. When the next message arrives, the new block node will be overwritten. So if two messages have been sent to the block node above, we will have to following graph in the heap:

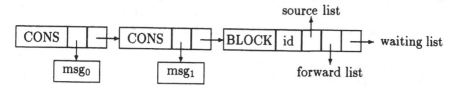

The function `available` simply looks at the message list, when it is a block node, it will return `False`, while it returns `True` for a cons node.

The block node's source list is used for two reasons: the runtime system needs it to send messages to the reference node when the block node becomes garbage, so that the location can be removed from the reference node's destination list. It is also used when copying a block node, to add the location of the new block node to the destination list. The destination list of a reference node is used in a similar way when copying and garbage collecting reference nodes.

When the destination list of a reference node is empty, no messages will be sent when `send` is used. What happens when the source list of a block node is empty depends on how the block node is created. When it is created using `createRChannel`, new reference nodes pointing to that block node can be created using, for example, `findSChannel`. Therefore such block nodes will operate normally, but when the receive channel has been created using `newChannel`, then it is not possible to create new reference nodes. In that case, no message will ever arrive at the block node. Threads which evaluate such a block node will therefore be suspended forever and will consequently become garbage. `available` will always return `False` and `eom` will return `True` on these receive channels.

When a reference node is copied from one heap to another, we have no special things to take into account, the node can simply be copied. However, when a block node is copied, we must guarantee that all messages will be received by the new copy of the block node in the correct order. This is done using the forward list in the block node. When a block node is copied, a STOP message with the new location is sent to the corresponding reference nodes, which will temporarily stop sending messages, put the location in their destination list and return an ACK message. The location of the new block node is then stored in the forward list of the block node. All messages still 'in the air' between the reference node and the old block node will be forwarded to the locations in the forward list between the time that the STOP message has been sent and all ACK's have been received. A location will be removed from the forward list when all corresponding ACK's have been received and a ENDFORWARD message is sent to the new location. After the new block node has received the ENDFORWARD message it has received all messages which were sent, up to the moment that the reference nodes have received their STOP message, in the correct order. Now it sends a START message to the reference nodes to notice them to start sending message again. As the reference nodes now also have the new destination in their destination list, they will send the messages directly to the new block node.

For the inter-program channels, we store in each heap all channels which are created there by `createRChannel`. When we want to create a new channel using `createRChannel`, the new channel name is broadcasted in a REQUEST message across the local network. A REJECT message will be returned if some heap already contains a channel with that name. A time-out expires when no REJECT message arrives. The new channel is then created and a CREATED message is broadcasted.

Table 1. The performance of message passing within (internal) and between (external) processors for various message sizes. Between braces are the number of messages sent.

message size	4 bytes	40 bytes	400 bytes	4000 bytes
internal	(10 k) 413 kb/s	(10 k) 4,444 kb/s	(100 k) 32 Mb/s	(100 k) 421 Mb/s
external	(10 k) 720 b/s	(10 k) 7,020 b/s	(2500) 64 kb/s	(250) 241 kb/s

findSChannel_NB broadcasts a LOOKUP message to all locations in the network, while lookupSChannel_NB sends it just to the given location. If a heap has a channel with the requested name in its heap, a CHANNEL message with the channel is returned. If no CHANNEL message is returned before the time-out expires, then Nothing is returned by the function. findSChannel and lookupSChannel first try to find the channel using the non-blocking version of the function. If that fails they will start listening to the CREATED messages. If the channel name in one of these messages matches the requested channel (and creator, for lookupSChannel), then the channel is returned.

Performance

A simple producer-consumer benchmark, transmitting a large number of integers, showed us that communication speed is good (Table 1). We measured the communication speed within one program, which was either running on one processor or distributed with the producer and consumer at different locations. We used a Power Macintosh 7600(PPC 604/132MHz) for the single-processor measurements and connected it with Ethernet to a Quadra 950(MC 68040/25MHz) for the two-processor measurements. For large messages, high speeds were achieved, but the table shows also that we have a rather high overhead for messages sent to other computers. The speed is low for messages which are only a few bytes. The sending and receiving of a message on the same processor always takes the same time, no matter the message size, because we can share the message between sender and receiver, removing the need to copy it. Note that the implementation is not yet optimised for speed.

6   Summary

We noticed that Concurrent Clean's implicit communication mechanism could be improved. Multicasting, data-driven communication, non-determinism and inter-program communication were not possible.

An extension for Concurrent Clean was proposed providing flexible message passing. The channels used for communication are split into a send channel and a receive channel, which clarifies the direction in which messages are sent. Non-determinism and multicasting are provided by channels with more than one sender or receiver respectively. By demanding send or receive channels to be unique we can ensure that no non-determinism will be introduced or more than one receiver gets the messages, while it enables us to safely send unique messages.

The channels can be used for communication between programs, but also within one program. For the latter we needed independent threads with their own state, which behave similar to programs operating on the world. The possibility to evaluate these threads interleaved or parallel gives us all we need to write many concurrent programs.

References

1. P.M. Achten. *Interactive Functional Programs - Models, Methods and Implementation*. PhD thesis, University of Nijmegen, February 1996.
2. P.M. Achten and M.J. Plasmeijer. Interactive Functional Objects in Clean. In C. Clack, T. Davie, and K. Hammond, editors, *Proc. 9th. International Workshop on Implementation of Functional Languages, St Andrews, Scotland, September 1997*, volume 1467 of *LNCS*, pages 305–322. Springer-Verlag, 1998.
3. E. Barendsen and J.E.W. Smetsers. Uniqueness Type Inference. In M. Hermenegildo and D. Swierstra, editors, *Proc. Programming Languages: Implementations, Logics and Programs (PLILP'95)*, volume 982 of *LNCS*, pages 189–207. Springer-Verlag, 1995.
4. K.P. Birman and R. van Renesse. *Reliable Distributed Computing with the Isis Toolkit*. IEEE Computer Society Press, Los Alamitos, CA, 1994.
5. Hoare C.A.R. Communicating Sequential Processes. *Communications of the ACM*, 21:666–671, Aug. 1978.
6. D. Dolev and D. Malki. The Transis Approach to High Availability Cluster Communication. *Communications of the ACM*, 39(4):64–70, April 1996.
7. I. Holyer and D. Carter. Deterministic Concurrency. In *Proc. 1993 Glasgow Workshop on Functional Programming*, pages 113–126. Springer-Verlag, July 1993.
8. M.P. Jones and P. Hudak. Implicit and Explicit Parallel Programming in Haskell. Technical Report YALEU/DCS/RR-982, Yale University, 1993.
9. M.H.G. Kesseler. Uniqueness and Lazy Graph Copying – Copyright for the Unique. In *Proc. 6th. International Workshop on the Implementation of Functional Languages (IFL'94)*, Norwich, UK, 1994. University of East Anglia.
10. U. Klusik, Y. Ortega, and R. Peña. Implementing Eden, or Dreams Become Reality. In *This Proceedings*.
11. L.E. Moser, P.M. Melliar-Smith, D.A. Agarwal, Budhia R.K., and C.C. Lingley-Papadopoulos. Totem: A Fault-Tolerant Multicast Group Communication System. *Communications of the ACM*, 39(4):54–63, April 1996.
12. Gehani N.H. Broadcasting Sequential Processes (BSP). *IEEE Transactions on Software Engineering*, 10(4), July 1984.
13. E.G.J.M.H. Nöcker, J.E.W. Smetsers, M.C.J.D. van Eekelen, and M.J. Plasmeijer. Concurrent Clean. In *Proc. PARLE'91 — Parallel Architectures and Languages Europe*, volume 506 of *LNCS*, pages 202–219, Eindhoven, The Netherlands, June 1991. Spinger-Verlag.
14. S. Paul, Sabnani K.K, J.C. Lin, and S. Bhattacharyya. Reliable Multicast Transport Protocol (RMTP). *IEEE Journal on Selected Areas in Communications*, 15(3):407–421, April 1997.

15. S.L. Peyton Jones, A.D. Gordon, and S.O. Finne. Concurrent Haskell. In *Proc. 23rd. ACM Symposium on Principles of Programming Languages (POPL'96)*, pages 295–308, St Petersburg Beach, Florida, January 1996. ACM Press.

16. M.R.C. Pil. First Class File I/O. In W. Kluge, editor, *Proc. 8th. International Workshop on the Implementation of Functional Languages (IFL'96), Bad Godesberg, Germany, September 1996*, volume 1268 of *LNCS*, pages 233–246. Springer-Verlag, 1997.

17. J. H. Reppy. Concurrent ML: Design, Application and Semantics. In P. E. Lauer, editor, *Functional Programming, Concurrency, Simulation and Automated Reasoning*, pages 165–198. Springer-Verlag, 1993.

18. E. Scholz. Four Concurrency Primitives for Haskell. In *ACM/IFIP Haskell Workshop*, La Jolla, Colifornia, 1995. Research Report YALEU/DCS/RR-1075.

19. B. Thomsen, L. Leth, S. Prasad, T-M. Kuo, A. Kramer, F. Knabe, and A. Giacalone. Facile Antigua Release Programming Guide. Technical Report ECRC-93-20, European Computer-Industry Research Centre, 1993.

20. D.N. Turner. *The Polymorphic Pi-Calculus: Theory and Implementation*. PhD thesis, Edinburgh University, 1995.

21. R. van Renesse, K.P. Birman, and S. Maffeis. Horus: A flexible Group Communications System. *Communications of the ACM*, 39(4), April 1996.

Author Index

Lecture Notes in Computer Science

For information about Vols. 1–1553
please contact your bookseller or Springer-Verlag

Vol. 1596: R. Poli, H.-M. Voigt, S. Cagnoni, D. Corne, G.D. Smith, T.C. Fogarty (Eds.), Evolutionary Image Analysis, Signal Processing and Telecommunications. Proceedings, 1999. X, 225 pages. 1999.

Vol. 1597: H. Zuidweg, M. Campolargo, J. Delgado, A. Mullery (Eds.), Intelligence in Services and Networks. Proceedings, 1999. XII, 552 pages. 1999.

Vol. 1598: R. Poli, P. Nordin, W.B. Langdon, T.C. Fogarty (Eds.), Genetic Programming. Proceedings, 1999. X, 283 pages. 1999.

Vol. 1599: T. Ishida (Ed.), Multiagent Platforms. Proceedings, 1998. VIII, 187 pages. 1999. (Subseries LNAI).

Vol. 1601: J.-P. Katoen (Ed.), Formal Methods for Real-Time and Probabilistic Systems. Proceedings, 1999. X, 355 pages. 1999.

Vol. 1602: A. Sivasubramaniam, M. Lauria (Eds.), Network-Based Parallel Computing. Proceedings, 1999. VIII, 225 pages. 1999.

Vol. 1603: J. Vitek, C.D. Jensen (Eds.), Secure Internet Programming. X, 501 pages. 1999.

Vol. 1605: J. Billington, M. Diaz, G. Rozenberg (Eds.), Application of Petri Nets to Communication Networks. IX, 303 pages. 1999.

Vol. 1606: J. Mira, J.V. Sánchez-Andrés (Eds.), Foundations and Tools for Neural Modeling. Proceedings, Vol. I, 1999. XXIII, 865 pages. 1999.

Vol. 1607: J. Mira, J.V. Sánchez-Andrés (Eds.), Engineering Applications of Bio-Inspired Artificial Neural Networks. Proceedings, Vol. II, 1999. XXIII, 907 pages. 1999.

Vol. 1608: S. Doaitse Swierstra, P.R. Henriques, J.N. Oliveira (Eds.), Advanced Functional Programming. Proceedings, 1998. XII, 289 pages. 1999.

Vol. 1609: Z. W. Raś, A. Skowron (Eds.), Foundations of Intelligent Systems. Proceedings, 1999. XII, 676 pages. 1999. (Subseries LNAI).

Vol. 1610: G. Cornuéjols, R.E. Burkard, G.J. Woeginger (Eds.), Integer Programming and Combinatorial Optimization. Proceedings, 1999. IX, 453 pages. 1999.

Vol. 1611: I. Imam, Y. Kodratoff, A. El-Dessouki, M. Ali (Eds.), Multiple Approaches to Intelligent Systems. Proceedings, 1999. XIX, 899 pages. 1999. (Subseries LNAI).

Vol. 1612: R. Bergmann, S. Breen, M. Göker, M. Manago, S. Wess, Developing Industrial Case-Based Reasoning Applications. XX, 188 pages. 1999. (Subseries LNAI).

Vol. 1613: A. Kuba, M. Šámal, A. Todd-Pokropek (Eds.), Information Processing in Medical Imaging. Proceedings, 1999. XVII, 508 pages. 1999.

Vol. 1614: D.P. Huijsmans, A.W.M. Smeulders (Eds.), Visual Information and Information Systems. Proceedings, 1999. XVII, 827 pages. 1999.

Vol. 1615: C. Polychronopoulos, K. Joe, A. Fukuda, S. Tomita (Eds.), High Performance Computing. Proceedings, 1999. XIV, 408 pages. 1999.

Vol. 1617: N.V. Murray (Ed.), Automated Reasoning with Analytic Tableaux and Related Methods. Proceedings, 1999. X, 325 pages. 1999. (Subseries LNAI).

Vol. 1619: M.T. Goodrich, C.C. McGeoch (Eds.), Algorithm Engineering and Experimentation. Proceedings, 1999. VIII, 349 pages. 1999.

Vol. 1620: W. Horn, Y. Shahar, G. Lindberg, S. Andreassen, J. Wyatt (Eds.), Artificial Intelligence in Medicine. Proceedings, 1999. XIII, 454 pages. 1999. (Subseries LNAI).

Vol. 1621: D. Fensel, R. Studer (Eds.), Knowledge Acquisition Modeling and Management. Proceedings, 1999. XI, 404 pages. 1999. (Subseries LNAI).

Vol. 1622: M. González Harbour, J.A. de la Puente (Eds.), Reliable Software Technologies – Ada-Europe'99. Proceedings, 1999. XIII, 451 pages. 1999.

Vol. 1625: B. Reusch (Ed.), Computational Intelligence. Proceedings, 1999. XIV, 710 pages. 1999.

Vol. 1626: M. Jarke, A. Oberweis (Eds.), Advanced Information Systems Engineering. Proceedings, 1999. XIV, 478 pages. 1999.

Vol. 1627: T. Asano, H. Imai, D.T. Lee, S.-i. Nakano, T. Tokuyama (Eds.), Computing and Combinatorics. Proceedings, 1999. XIV, 494 pages. 1999.

Col. 1628: R. Guerraoui (Ed.), ECOOP'99 - Object-Oriented Programming. Proceedings, 1999. XIII, 529 pages. 1999.

Vol. 1629: H. Leopold, N. García (Eds.), Multimedia Applications, Services and Techniques - ECMAST'99. Proceedings, 1999. XV, 574 pages. 1999.

Vol. 1631: P. Narendran, M. Rusinowitch (Eds.), Rewriting Techniques and Applications. Proceedings, 1999. XI, 397 pages. 1999.

Vol. 1632: H. Ganzinger (Ed.), Automated Deduction – Cade-16. Proceedings, 1999. XIV, 429 pages. 1999. (Subseries LNAI).

Vol. 1633: N. Halbwachs, D. Peled (Eds.), Computer Aided Verification. Proceedings, 1999. XII, 506 pages. 1999.

Vol. 1634: S. Džeroski, P. Flach (Eds.), Inductive Logic Programming. Proceedings, 1999. VIII, 303 pages. 1999. (Subseries LNAI).

Vol. 1636: L. Knudsen (Ed.), Fast Software Encryption. Proceedings, 1999. VIII, 317 pages. 1999.

Vol. 1638: A. Hunter, S. Parsons (Eds.), Symbolic and Quantitative Approaches to Reasoning and Uncertainty. Proceedings, 1999. IX, 397 pages. 1999. (Subseries LNAI).

Vol. 1639: S. Donatelli, J. Kleijn (Eds.), Application and Theory of Petri Nets 1999. Proceedings, 1999. VIII, 425 pages. 1999.

Vol. 1640: W. Tepfenhart, W. Cyre (Eds.), Conceptual Structures: Standards and Practices. Proceedings, 1999. XII, 515 pages. 1999. (Subseries LNAI).

Vol. 1644: J. Wiedermann, P. van Emde Boas, M. Nielsen (Eds.), Automata, Languages, and Programming. Proceedings, 1999. XIV, 720 pages. 1999.

Vol. 1649: R.Y. Pinter, S. Tsur (Eds.), Next Generation Information Technologies and Systems. Proceedings, 1999. IX, 327 pages. 1999.

Vol. 1650: K.-D. Althoff, R. Bergmann, L.K. Branting (Eds.), Case-Based Reasoning Research and Development. Proceedings, 1999. XII, 598 pages. 1999. (Subseries LNAI).

Vol. 1653: S. Covaci (Ed.), Active Networks. Proceedings, 1999. XIII, 346 pages. 1999.